Daughter
of
Mercy

Daughter of Mercy

Susie Lee

The Korean War
50 YEARS
1950 • 2000

Sweetwater Press 2000

Some names in this work have been changed to protect the privacy of the individuals involved.

All Scripture quotations used in this book are from the King James Version.

Written permission must be secured from the publisher to use or reproduce any part of this book, except for brief quotations in reviews or articles.

Author photo by Jean Chung, *The Korea Times New York*.

Library of Congress Cataloging in Publication Data
Susie Lee
Daughter of Mercy

1. Lee, Susie 2. Biography & Autobiography 3. Women 4. Korean War 5. Religion 6. Disability

ISBN 1581732007
First Printing, August 2000

Acknowledgement

My inexpressible gratitude to God for
His unfailing love, protection, and strength.

John 3:16
II Corinthians 4:7-10
Philippians 4:13

Dedication

In memory of my beloved husband,
Donald G. Beidel,
who lived I Corinthians 13:4-7.

To my children, Sophia and David,
for teaching me to live
in the liberty of the Lord.

To the Korean War veterans, whose sacrifice
allow us to live in freedom.

To all those
who have helped me
become what I am today.

Contents

Foreword

War is hell! Old men speak of it with tears and remorse. Young men lament its futility. Some of the greatest dramas of life have been written in the jaws of war – the stories of Corrie ten Boom, Hansi and now of Susie Lee Beidel.

The major wars of our generation were fought in the Orient – China, Japan, Philippines, Indonesia, Indo-China and Korea. Never before have we heard the story of war from the quiet Oriental heart. Susie lived through the ravages of the Korean War to tell the story of bombs, broken families and the bitterness that leaves its toll on men, women and especially on the hearts of the little ones.

The story of Susie is not only the story of one lonely, handicapped girl alone in a war, but as she hobbles through the devastated cities of war-torn Korea, we see the story of a once serene, secluded, almost sacred Orient exploding culturally, economically and spiritually before our eyes and emotions.

Susie's search for her family is that of millions of orphans and refugees for the past three decades. Her struggles with prejudice, pride and passion are the struggles of teenagers of a hate-scarred generation. Her loneliness, rejection and eventual bitterness are the real hell of war.

The terrifying, yet tender story strikes every emotion of the human heart. You experience her childish delight, share her feelings of rejection, loneliness, agony, hunger and fear. You even savor her Oriental cuisine from rice to kimchi. Her search for peace with men and God becomes yours. She must survive! She must find her family! She must find that serenity now broken by bombs and bloodshed! She must find love and happiness! Most of all, she must find God!

As this Oriental odyssey unfolds, you begin to look more understandingly at American involvement in sorrowful wars of Indo-China and Korea – for you see through the grateful eyes of a daughter of the Orient. It was through the hearts and hands of American armed forces personnel, especially her husband, Don Beidel, through whom Susie found love, compassion and the forgiveness of God, which her war-torn heart needed to find so desperately.

Susie's story and her present day mission of compassion to the disabled veterans in VA hospitals is really a long "Thank you" letter. Today Susie says, "Thank You, America!"

Reverend Dr. Daniel Mercaldo
Founder and Senior Pastor
Gateway Cathedral
200 Boscome Avenue
Staten Island, New York 10309

Why am I Different?

"Cripple! Look at her leg. It's like a twig!" The boy who resembled a samurai shouted, inciting other children on the playground of the Tientsin Kindergarten.

"Ha, ha! Watch how she limps," another shaven-headed boy yelled. I could find no place to hide, and I wished that the ground would swallow me. The boys swaggered toward me. Panic-stricken, I backed off. Pressing my hand over my weak knee, I hobbled to a swing and wrapped my arms around the pole.

A pretty girl stomped her foot and pushed me aside sneering, "No, you can't get on that swing!"

One rather plain girl tried to help me, but the pretty one smacked her. I stared at the heartless girl and wondered why she should pick on someone who was just trying to help me. Girls joined the boys and made a semi-circle around me.

"Why is she glaring at us? I'll fix her," one girl said and pulled my hair. "What happened to your voice? Can't you speak?"

I was too frightened to utter a word. Still sitting on the ground, I covered my head and looked down at my purplish, shriveled up leg. I hated it. My first day at kindergarten, which I had looked forward to so much, had turned into a nightmare because of this sick limb. The immaculate playground with its slides, swings, seesaws and monkey bars became a torturing forum.

Finally, to my relief, the bell rang for us to enter our classrooms. I straightened my white, starched pinafore, dusted the red dirt from my blue dress and shuffled into the classroom behind the other children. The teacher called me by my Japanese name, "Wamoto, Kiyo-ko." I almost forgot to answer. My parents had explained to me that we lived under Japanese rule and could not use the Korean language or our surname, Lee. At home, however, we used Korean, and my parents called me by my given name, Hyun Sook, which meant "wisdom," and "clear."

The teacher glanced around the room. When I finally answered, some of the children giggled. I lowered my head and did not look up or speak with anyone for the rest of that miserable morning. Instead, I worked hard at drawing and learning origami.[1]

When the dismissal bell rang, all the children filed out of the room. I trailed behind them at a safe distance. When I saw Su Ping, our maid, waiting for me at the gate with my tricycle, I momentarily forgot the morning's humiliations. "Su Ping! Su Ping!" I hobbled toward her as fast as I could. She raced toward me and stopped short.

"What happened? Did you fall?" she asked, breathing hard. Su Ping moistened her handkerchief with her tongue and wiped my eyes and cheeks. "Were they picking on you?" Her slanted eyes glistened and her young face turned grave. I nodded my head. She lifted me up onto the seat and listened to all the woes of my first day as she walked beside my tricycle.

"Oh, Su Ping, why am I different?"

---

[1] Japanese art of paper folding

She clicked her tongue and began to tell me, "I remember the night you suddenly became ill. You were almost one year old. The master and mistress woke all of the servants in the middle of the night and told us you were burning with fever. We brought in basin after basin of icy water, but your cheeks stayed red." Su Ping's eyes clouded, "The master sent for the doctor. When he arrived, the doctor said, 'Get her to the hospital immediately!' Your parents rushed you to the hospital in a jinrikisha,[2] but when you finally returned, you couldn't even crawl. You just lay still in your crib. Heartbroken, your parents carried you to doctors near and far but. . ."

We moved on silently. My thoughts turned to recent visits with various doctors. Mother told me that the doctors had given her a name for my illness – infantile poliomyelitis – but it was a rare disease. None of them had ever been able to restore the strength in my leg. A German orthopedist in Peking fitted me with a leg brace. Mother would try everything to get that brace on my leg, but I always took it off as soon as I was out of her sight. Exasperated, my parents gave up on the brace.

I recalled the time Mother took me to see an acupuncturist. She led me into a Chinese medicine shop. Dozens of herb containers were stacked on wooden shelves against the plastered walls. Nauseated, I held my breath against the bittersweet odor. A young Chinese man pinched five or six different herbs and wrapped them into packets.

I followed Mother into the back where a lone window lit the musty room. An old Chinese man sat there, his elbows leaning on a teakwood table, sipping steamy jasmine tea. A skullcap framed his balding head, and his huge ears drooped from the weight of his lobes. He looked like a Buddha, except

---

[2] two wheeled carriage pulled by a man

for his goatee. With a pudgy hand, he motioned us to sit down.

Slowly, he ambled over, took my pulse, felt my bony leg and pressed various joints and muscles. After laying me on a bench, he reached over and opened a black case. Inside silvery needles glinted. Some were short and thick. Others looked flimsy and long. With surprising swiftness, he drove the needles into my hands, between my fingers, toes and ankle joints, and around my kneecap. Oblivious to my cries, he twirled and pushed the needles into my flesh as if I were a pincushion. I felt like an electric current was surging up and down inside of me.

He told me to take a nap and left the room with my mother, with all the needles still tacked under my skin. My nose itched. I lifted my hand to scratch it but felt like Gulliver, pegged to the ground by the Lilliputians with hundreds of nails. Every time I tried to move, electricity shocked me. After that I dreaded going to the acupuncturist, but was too young to refuse. I loathed the treatment and hated Mother for forcing me to go.

Su Ping shook my shoulder gently. "We're a little early. I'll take you to one of my favorite places, you'll feel better."

I had not yet ventured much beyond my home, other than visits to the park near us, to restaurants in the French or British districts or to church. Su Ping led us away from the main street and turned onto a side road. The whole block was crammed with food stands on wheels tended by Chinese vendors. Each man shouted his specialty. Roasted chestnuts! Candied crabapples! Pork-filled buns! Yams! Boiled snails! Taffy! Bean curd whey and fried dough! Thousand-year eggs! Fried locusts!

Standing before a greasy stand, Su Ping bought a handful of the locusts, stuffed in a newspaper cone. She offered me some, but I drew back, wrinkling up my nose.

Amused by my reaction, she grinned and munched away at her treat.

Next to the locust stand, a taffy seller took a soft piece of taffy and rolled it between his stained palms. Then he stuck a straw in the center of the candy and blew air into it while his dexterous fingers pulled at the mass. Right before my eyes, the taffy was transformed into a sparrow.

At Su Ping's nudging, I reluctantly left the taffy stand. We passed long-robed Chinese pedestrians as they leisurely strolled along with fistfuls of sunflower or pumpkin seeds, spewing out hulls like pellets on the pebbled sidewalk. Chattering and giggling, Chinese women with tiny, triangularly bound feet waddled down the road while transient coolies with rolls of bedding on their muscular backs stood alongside the stands, eating their noon meal. Beggars pleaded for food from the coolies and the peddlers.

We moved on, passing alleyways. I saw several haggard men in rags curled up on the ground with painful grimaces. Others stretched out in bliss, staring vacantly into space, oblivious to the stench surrounding them. Su Ping whispered, "They are opium eaters."

At the far end of the block, my eyes caught a frightening but intriguing sight. Panting and writhing, a Chinese man guided a long green snake into his nostril. While he pounded his chest in agony, a boy in tattered clothes urged the onlookers to toss money into a coolie hat. Su Ping handed me a coin to put in the straw hat.

Abruptly she tugged at me. We had loitered longer than expected. When we got home my parents were already at the table waiting for me. "Aboji,[3] Omoni,[4] I have returned from kindergarten," I greeted my parents.

---

[3] Father

[4] Mother

"How was your first day at the kindergarten?" Father asked eagerly, pushing up his gold-rimmed glasses.

"I learned to fold a paper boat, Aboji. See this boat?"

"Did you make any new friends?" Mother asked. I shook my head silently. I could not bear to recount my painful day to them.

Soon after lunch I excused myself and anxiously waited for my elder sister, In Sook. I never addressed her by her given name. That would have been disrespectful. I called her Onni.[5] When she came home, I told her everything.

"Don't worry, Hyun Sook-ga.[6] I will take care of them!" She narrowed her huge, almond shaped eyes. Her fair oval face turned solemn as she whispered, "It's going to be all right." Onni's comforting words soothed my hurt feelings. Later, whenever children taunted me, she came to my rescue and chased them away. Still, I wondered why she always had a good excuse not to take me along when she went out visiting.

Mother bought chest after chest of silk brocade and linen to be put aside as a trousseau for Onni but none for me. She dressed her first born in the latest fashions and basked in the praises her daughter received, but she had most of my clothes made from the remnants of men's suits. Envy began to grow deep inside me.

Gradually the children lessened their taunting. Some of them even visited me at my home. Mother, like all Korean parents, upheld the Confucian ethical code of conduct. "Males and females should not sit close after the age of seven," and forbade me to play with any boys. Only girls were allowed to come. We spent afternoons making doll

---

[5] Elder sister

[6] ga – an affectionate suffix for a name (similar to adding 'y' to John – Johnny)

clothes and origami furniture, and playing with beanbags.

When I entered the Hu Yo Elementary School the teasing stopped, thanks to my first grade teacher, Miss Ikeda. She maintained strict order in her classroom. No one even dared to slump their shoulders lest she stick a ruler down our backs to keep us straight. She rapped our palms with the ruler if we scribbled on the desks. If we talked or made any noise, she stood us in a corner.

Still, though she was stern, compassion shone in her eyes, and kindness rang in her clear voice. Whenever the wail of the air raid siren intruded upon our studies, my classmates left their seats, formed a line and ran to the underground shelters. Hot panic flashed over me because I could not run. Yet without fail Miss Ikeda remained as the room emptied and came to me. Filling my nostrils with honey suckle fragrance, she squatted down so I could climb on her back. I clung tightly to her shoulders, burying my face close to her shiny black bun. Then she, too, raced toward the shelter. I revered Miss Ikeda for she never treated me differently, nor chided me for being unable to run on my own legs. She sensed my fright at the air raid siren, got me to the shelter and let me down from her back. I huddled in the dark shelter among my classmates and waited for the all-clear siren.

Whenever I felt afraid, I thought about my home. I made believe that I was walking up the marble steps to the brass-trimmed double entry doors with huge glass showcases on either side. My parents built the three story concrete building after they left Korea and moved into the city of Tientsin, China. They had started a tailoring business in 1935, shortly before I was born.

Our designers waited on customers from behind a long, highly polished walnut table. The entire right wall displayed countless bolts of fabric imported from England for men's suits. The lounge chairs to the left, upholstered in plush crimson velvet, were usually filled with Father's business associates, friends from the church or relatives. Our maids and male servants kept their quarters and their kitchen at the back of the first floor.

To get to our living quarters on the second floor, I passed around Mr. Kang, our bookkeeper. He and his wife lived with us and were considered part of our family. Mr. Kang, always smiling and sniffling, sat at his desk near the safe.

At the top of the spiral staircase, a large kitchen and dining room opened to the left. Our bedrooms were on the right. The third floor bustled with Chinese tailors and apprentices.

On weekends our living room was usually filled with thirty to fifty guests for meetings and banquets. My parents enjoyed entertaining. They especially revered ministers, missionaries and evangelists, calling them 'Servants of God.' With awe and admiration they presented a custom-made suit to each visiting Servant of God. By their example, I learned early that these people were special and were to be treated with reverence.

Still in the dark shelter, my thoughts turned to the flood of my fourth year when water from the Yellow River swelled throughout the city for weeks. Because our concrete building stood firm and was one of the higher places, many flood victims came to us for refuge. Our third flood turned into a temporary commune. To accommodate us, Chinese peddlers rowed right into the flooded first floor and up to the steps. Little boats, laden with fresh vegetables, bean curd, meat, flowers and sundries, squeaked through the entrance. Our maids haggled with them before buying anything. As I sat on the staircase, I longingly watched Onni swim with some of the other children in the first floor pool. Mother put me into our round wooden bathtub and let me float around in my own little boat.

After the flood I realized I walked differently from other children. I swayed when I wanted to walk straight and fell when I tried to skip. My right knee had no strength to support my body. Thereafter, whenever customers came into the store, my mother signaled me with her dark eyes to climb upstairs. Onni was allowed to stay. Gradually I began to sense that as much as my parents loved and cared for me, my handicap somehow embarrassed them. At that young age I did not understand the social stigma of having an imperfect child in the family.

"Why am I different, Omoni? And why am I always the butt of jokes and ridicule?"

"I have no answer, Hyun Sook-ga," Mother sighed, "but someday your leg will get better."

To make life easier, my parents bought a tricycle and patiently taught me to ride it in the park a block from our home. After I mastered the little vehicle, Su Ping and I went to the park often. Riding under the delicate cherry blossoms, sitting beneath the lavender canopy of wisteria, rolling on the emerald grass or just watching the silvery fountain spray never failed to delight me. Most of all I felt free on the tricycle. I could peddle around the park instead of limping, and no one stared.

In class they might stare, but because of Miss Ikeda's acceptance, the children dared not pick on me. Everything at school was just fine except for the trouble about the shrine. All the students were required to bow before the Shinto Shrine in the schoolyard, but my father had taught me not to worship idols, so I stood erect while everyone else made reverent obeisance.

Miss Ikeda repeatedly lectured me for not bowing like the rest. When the principal caught me, he made me stand for an entire period in the hallway outside of his office. I learned from Christian teachings that bowing to idols could not help me in any way. Instead, it eased my panic to pray silently to God, as my parents did. I decided to tell them about the shrine, even though I was afraid that they might come to the school and confront the principal and get me into more trouble.

The following week, when Pastor Tae-up Kim visited us, my father discussed the problem with him. The pastor considered it a while and said, "Hyun Sook-ga, if you cannot avoid the ritual in the future, simply lower your head and pray to our God asking Him to help the others to accept Jesus as their Savior." I thanked him. "Do you know how your father became a Christian?" Pastor Kim asked. "If he had not invited Jesus Christ into his heart, you might be worshipping that idol today."

"I have not told her yet, " my father said, clearing his throat, "but I suppose this is as good a time as any." Father pushed up his glasses, which always slid halfway down his nose. I loved my father's stories and his knack for telling them. Night after night I sat close to him, intrigued by every word and detail of the folklore and fairy tales, sometimes laughing, sometimes crying. He even made Bible stories interesting by explaining them in ways that I could enjoy and understand.

"For some reason I longed to worship a being, " Father began solemnly. "I often went deep into the mountains when I was a lad. I meditated in the woods and among the rocks, searching for something. I didn't know what. Neither Buddha nor Confucius could satisfy my deep longing." Father folded his arms and continued. "When I was about fourteen, an elderly woman in the village told me about a life-changing Western religion and invited me to a religious service. A preacher fervently talked about a man named

Jesus, the Son of God, who came to this earth as a baby and grew up to teach the people about the Kingdom of God and His love for a sinful world. He taught people to love one another by being an example. Jesus healed the sick and raised the dead. He never sinned, but some nailed Him to a cross to die. On the third day, He rose from the grave. Now He is in heaven, watching over us. God hears our prayers and will forgive all of our sins if we are truly sorry and ask Him to." Father looked up, "When the preacher finished, I knew that was the religion I wanted."

"How did the lady become a Christian?" I asked.

"Through a missionary named Reverend Thomas. This man came from England to Korea over one hundred years ago to spread the gospel to our people, but they rejected him, for our land was still a hermit kingdom. Many nations had invaded Korea, so our ancestors closed contact with other lands for ages.

"In any event, the ruler of that era did not trust the foreigner and forced him to leave. But Reverend Thomas returned to Korea on a small boat, giving Bibles to the curious people who flocked to the riverside to see the white man. Korean warriors threw torches at the boat, set it on fire and captured him. He was brought to Pyong-Yang for interrogation and the magistrate ordered his execution. Just before the sharp, blue sword struck his neck, the missionary offered a Bible to a nearby spectator. That man read it and became a devout Christian. And the Good News spread."

"But, Aboji, Missionary Thomas did not do anything wrong." I blinked back my tears.

"Well, neither did Jesus," Pastor Kim commented. "There is a legend that Reverend Thomas' blood still flows through the river. That is why there are so many believers in Korea." I could have listened to many more stories, but the maid brought in fruits and roasted barley tea. As the adults turned to the refreshments, I went to my room, considering the story. Those things happened hundreds and thousands of years ago, just like the fairy tales my Father told me. To dismiss the awful thought that my people had killed a missionary, I headed for the park with Su Ping.

One hot August morning in 1942, I woke to the robust cry of a baby. Sleepily I followed the sound into my parents' bedroom. I was confused to find Mother lying on her bed, perspiring profusely, while several women hovered about, wiping her face and feeding her seaweed soup. The servants hauled out blood stained linens and towels. Father sat apart from the women and prayed. Mother weakly motioned me to come closer. I thought that she was about to die. My throat tightened. With a faint smile she whispered, "The midwife brought you a baby sister." Under a small mosquito net, I saw a ruddy baby, squirming. I reached out and held her wispy fist in wonderment.

"Her name is Mi Sook," Father told me solemnly.

Shortly after the birth of Mi Sook, Father began to go away on business trips often, and Mother had to take on many of the tailoring responsibilities. I missed Father very much. One particular night, I was awakened by some noises from my parents' room. I slipped out of bed and peeked into their room through an opening. They were both in their nightclothes, and I saw Mother's long black hair wrapped around Father's hand. She muttered something, and Father released her hair and slapped her across the face. Still sitting, Mother backed away from him and leaned against the hand-carved bedding closet. Father had his back to the door, but I could see Mother's welted, scarlet face. Mother's black eyes flashed with hatred and bitterness. She raised her voice. "Yobo,[7] it's not my fault that we have three daughters,"

---

[7] A familiar term, such as dear, used between a couple

Mother yelled defiantly, twisting her toes, which she did whenever she go annoyed or angry.

"I want a son! Do you hear me? I need a son to carry my name!"

He raised his huge hand again to strike her, but it froze in midair as Mother hoarsely reminded him, "I gave you a son. It is not my fault that he died." She glared at him, as she rubber her swollen cheeks. "And why are you seeing another woman? You have no. . . . "

Before she could finish, Father slapped her again and again. My eyes blazed and my heart filled up with rage. I wanted to rush in and defend my mother, but my body shook and my legs felt like straw ropes and I could not move. Shaking with anger and frustration, I turned around to go to my room, but found Onni standing behind me, trembling and weeping. Together we tumbled into our room, too choked up to talk. After that night, I tried to act as if nothing had happened, and I avoided Father as much as possible.

Understandably, Mother's temperament began to change after that. Our sisterly bickering provoked her and she would walk out of the house, threatening never to return and leaving us frantic. Instead of spanking or slapping us as Father did, she would force us to watch as she inflicted pain upon herself by striking her thighs with the paddle until her flesh turned black and blue. We shrieked and pleaded with her to hit us instead.

About a year after we witnessed that awful event, Father began talking about moving to Korea and starting a poultry farm. He often described the magnificent scenery there. "I miss the refreshing waterfall cascading down the lush green mountains, the splendid sunrises and the sunsets across the calm sea. Korea has four perfect seasons. You could even have your own flower and vegetable garden." I could not imagine what that would be like because in

Tientsin the only place we saw growing plants and flowers
was at the park. Not a blade of grass grew on the streets,
except for a few acacia trees on each block along the asphalt
pavement.

"Our people are kind and helpful. At seed time and
harvest time all the farmers in the village go out and help one
another."

So, in 1944, dreaming of a poultry farm in Korea, my
father sold his business. Gradually he dismissed all twenty
tailors and servants, except a maid and an errand boy. Su
Ping got married and left us. Mr. Kang and his wife moved
away with their three daughters and we moved into the first
floor of Father's elder brother's home. While my parents
closed the business, they applied for an exit permit to move
to Korea, but the Japanese authorities delayed issuing it
because of the war.

On a sultry August day in 1945, our parents called the
three of us excitedly. "The war has ended! We just heard on
the radio that Japan has surrendered. We will be heading for
home!" We were puzzled but moved closer to hear all that
they had to tell us. "We won't be using our Japanese name,
Wamoto, anymore. We will use our own surname, Lee. You
will soon learn to read and write in your own language. We
will speak Korean in public!"

Sometime after the liberation, Father told us, "Mr.
Chiang Kai-Shek is urging all aliens to return to their
homelands. He predicts a civil war between Nationalist
China and the Chinese Communists." I thought about how
awful that would be, brother fighting against brother.

"We are allowed to take only what each of us can carry.
All of our furniture and most of the possessions we wanted
to ship to Korea will have to be left behind." Mother sighed
and twisted her toes. She had hoped that we would be able
to sell our household items, but now no one would buy

anything, since they knew our predicament.

"Let's be thankful that we have already sold our business," Father pushed up his glasses and glanced at Mother. "Those who still own property have no way to sell it now."

"Well, what good is it? Money has turned to tissue paper," Mother retorted and sighed again.

Rumors spread like fire on a windy night. We heard that the refugee ships would be sent to us by a group of Korean patriots and that Korea had been divided into North and South after the Japanese ceased to rule there. The North would be under the Communist regime of Russia, and the South would be a democratic nation assisted by the United States of America.

As the refugee ships would not be ready until the following spring, Korean children spent the winter months learning Korean history, culture and language at our church. It was fascinating to learn our own alphabet, hangul. One of the teachers explained how hangul came about.

"There once was a very wise and compassionate king, called King Yi Sejung, who saw that only the noble and the rich had mastered the difficult Chinese ideographs. The king surrounded himself with outstanding scholars and set out to do something about it. After several years, he presented his people with a new system of writing. Hangul means 'Korean writing.' Originally there were twenty-eight symbols, but four of them were discarded, and now we use ten vowels and fourteen consonants."

After the lecture, the teacher scribbled some strange characters on the board and said, "You can write almost any sound with these letters."

In the early spring, Pastor Kim told the congregation that he and his family had decided to remain in Tientsin to oversee the church. They had been deeply involved in ministering to the people in the area for so long and felt that God was calling them to continue their outreach to the Chinese people. The elders, deacons and members urged them to return with us on the ship, but Pastor Kim only grew firmer in his decision to stay in China.

At last the day arrived when we headed for the Korea-bound ship. Refugees milled about trying to locate their ships, each boarding a thousand Koreans. There was no fanfare as our ship pulled away from the pebbled pier. No matter how enthusiastic Father sounded about our real home in Korea, I could not bear to leave the place where I had always lived. I started to cry. Father pulled me onto his sturdy back and led the way to our assigned cabins, passing through the bustling crowd. Mother and my two sisters followed behind us.

Once we got settled in our cabin, Father brought out a half-finished fishnet, which he had started making in Ajoshi's[8] home in Tientsin.

"With this throw net I can catch dozens and dozens of huge fish," he beamed, but no one seemed interested in hearing about catching fish in the middle of the ocean. We stared at him vacantly. Nevertheless, he spread the net on the metal floor and seated himself comfortably on a cushion. "You'll be so busy helping me raise chickens and going fishing with me that you won't have time to miss Tientsin." Then, to lift our spirits, he began to tell us a folktale. "Gather around me, children, I will tell you the story of Shim Chung." He lured us as his hands deftly worked on the net. I had heard that story at least five times already, but Father embellished and enriched the plot each time, and I never felt bored by it.

---

[8] Uncle

Once upon a time there was a blind man named Shim Bong Sa who lived happily with his wife. She was a kind, beautiful and virtuous lady, and everybody admired her. But she died while giving birth to an infant, leaving her blind husband with a baby girl. After the mourning period, the grief-stricken man carried his daughter, whom he named Shim Chung, to fields and public wells pleading with the women to nurse his baby. He couldn't see her but everyone in the village told him Shim Chung looked just like her mother. She grew, not only in beauty, but also in character. When she was six, Shim Chung began to work for others to support her father, for he could not find a job.

One particular day when Shim Chung didn't return home at the usual time, her father began to fret. He strained his keen ears for the sound of her soft footsteps, but only the breeze rustled against the cornstalk fence. When he could wait no longer, Shim Bong Sa decided to go out and to look for her. He called her name as he walked on and on, and eventually he got lost. Unsure about his direction, he tapped his bamboo cane to feel his way around when suddenly he tripped over a willow branch and fell into a lake. Now Shim Bong Sa had never learned to swim, and he splashed about in the water, gulping and yelling, "Help, help this drowning blind man! Help me!"

It so happened that a monk was going by that road toward his temple. He stopped and cupped his ears, following the sound of Shim Bong Sa's cries. The sun had begun to set behind the mountain by the time that the monk finally spotted him. He plunged into the lake, rescued Shim Bong Sa and retrieved his bamboo cane for him.

Striking the ground with his stick, the blind man grumbled, "Oh, my cursed blindness! If only I could have seen, I would never have fallen into the lake!" When the monk helped him back on the road, Shim Bong Sa lamented, "I would do anything if only I could have my sight!"

"You could have your sight, if . . . ." The monk stared at the sightless man with deep sympathy. Shim

Bong Sa beseeched, "If what? I beg you, please tell me. What must I do to get my sight back?"

"Can you offer fifty huge straw sacks of rice to the gods of my temple?"

"Yes, oh yes! I shall offer fifty sacks of rice to your temple!"

"Think it over carefully, old man . . . ." The monk spoke solemnly, looking over the shabby attire of the blind man, "for if you break your promise to the gods and anger them, you will be cursed!"

"Yes, indeed, I understand! It shall be done!" Intoxicated by the rapturous thought of regaining his sight, Shim Bong Sa eagerly made the pledge and sang all the way home.

Now, when Shim Chung returned late that night, she found her father crouched near the wall by the door. She lit the oil lamp and said, "Father, please forgive me. Today the lady I worked for had a feast, and I could not come home earlier. Please, Father, I have brought some delicious food for you."

Shim Bong Sa only sighed and would not respond. But after much prompting, he recounted everything that had happened. Shim Chung looked around their barren, one-room shack. Their life had been the most meager in the village. They lived on leftovers from others and small amounts of barley earned by her hard day's work. Their worn clothes sported patches upon patches. The mildewed mud walls crumbled at the slightest touch. The rice paper doors were ripped. And their straw-thatched roof rotted away as the result of her father's inability to replace it. She just didn't know how she could possibly get fifty sacks of rice in her entire life. For the first time since she was born, Shim Chung was glad her beloved father was blind and couldn't see her despairing body shaking convulsively from her muffled sobs. Quickly the courageous Shim Chung composed herself and said calmly, "Father, please do not worry. I will somehow get your pledge fulfilled."

From then on, she worked from dawn until midnight. But no matter how hard or how long she worked, Shim Chung could barely earn enough to feed them both.

Then one day a woman in the village told her, "Can you imagine? I heard some sea merchants combing the village and shouting to offer a bag full of money for a maiden to be . . . ." Before the woman could finish telling her the details, Shim Chung interrupted, "Where are they now?"

"But Shim Chung, they want a maiden for . . . .oh, wait! Don't go!"

After the captain of the boat looked over Shim Chung, he agreed to deliver the promised rice to the temple. He instructed her that his men would fetch her in fifteen days. During that time Shim Chung sewed and prepared dried food for her father. She implored the neighbors to look after him.

On the day of her departure, she made her father's favorite dishes and gently guided his hands to each morsel. Halfway through the meal, the men loudly called for Shim Chung. When she explained to her father that the time had come, he was shocked and furious. He violently protested against her being sold. She tried to calm him down, but he pounded his chest and wailed, "Ai-go,[9] ai-go, I would sell my eyes to buy you, my devoted and precious daughter. What good is a pair of seeing eyes without you?"

Callously the sea merchants bellowed for her to come out. Gently but firmly she freed herself from her father and silently followed the men to the boat, leaving Shim Bong Sa flailing his cane in the air.

They sailed for days until the boat finally reached the whirlpool on the way to China. Gravely the captain explained to Shim Chung that the time had come for him to offer her to the gods of the sea so that they might have smooth sailing. Shaken, but hiding her anguish and terror, Shim Chung stepped to the helm of the boat and silently asked the gods to watch over her father and grant him his sight. Covering her head with

[9] an interjection similar to "Oh dear!" used to express surprise, lament, joy, embarrassment, disgust, etc.

her white apron, she plunged into the Yellow Sea.

When she came to, Shim Chung was shocked to find herself alive and surrounded by ladies-in-waiting in the Dragon Palace. She opened wide her brown eyes, stunned, for the walls of the palace were solid gold, studded with rubies, sapphires, jade, emerald, opals, diamonds and pearls.

"Oh, Princess Shim Chung is awake!" they cried. "We must escort her to the King." They dressed her in an exquisite royal gown with diamond beads sewn on by golden threads in the shape of dragons. Then the ethereal beauties and exotic fish formed a stately procession to the throne.

The king said, "Your love and devotion to your father has moved me deeply. Because of your ultimate sacrifice, your life has been restored to you." The king allowed her to live in the palace and showed her all the treasures of the undersea domain. He told her she could have anything she desired, but all the precious stones and merrymaking could not make her happy. When the king found out that Shim Chung was homesick for her father, he granted Shim Chung her wish to return to the earth.

By that time the sea merchants were returning from China with their boat loaded with silk, medicinal herbs and spices. One afternoon the captain spotted a gigantic lotus blossom floating upon the Yellow Sea. Excitedly he ordered his men to pick it. As soon as they landed, he carried the rare flower to the king. The king was so pleased with it that he gave the captain enough gold to retire from the sea.

It so happened that the queen had passed away, and the king found comfort in watching the lotus. One afternoon he fell asleep and dreamed that he saw a beautiful maiden rising from the center of the flower. When he opened his eyes, the woman he saw in his dream stood amidst the petals. Confused, the king asked, "Are you a ghost or a . . . . " Shim Chung stepped down, bowed before the king and told him all that had happened. He was so amazed by her that he asked her to marry him. They had a grand wedding and spent many happy days together. After the honeymoon, the king sensed that his bride was not completely happy. He told her that he would do anything to make her happy. Shim Chung asked if she could have a seven-day feast for all the blind men in the country.

From morning until dark she scrutinized each sightless man as he entered the palace gate. The seventh day had come and still she had seen no sign of her father. Greatly disappointed, Shim Chung gathered her royal blue gown and slowly headed toward her chamber, when she spotted and unkempt, skinny man who staggered through the gate. She held her breath and watched the blind man being guided into the banquet hall. Then Shim Chung raced toward him. He was unmistakably her father. She broke all tradition and threw her arms around him and cried, "Father!" An infinite amount of time passed as Shim Bong Sa stood speechless.

"Is this the voice of my daughter?" he finally asked hoarsely. "Are you truly Shim Chung, my daughter? Then let me see you!"

No one can explain what took place, but Shim Bong Sa opened his blind eyes and looked into the face of the most beautiful woman in the world.

Several days after we left China, the ship began to toss and sway. Thinking about the story of Shim Chung, I fantasized that a sacrifice might be in order. After the storm subsided, we learned that the ship had incurred extensive damage. One of the problems was that the water tank needed repair and fresh water could be used for drinking only. The cooks used seawater for everything, even for cooking rice. "Hunger is the best sauce," Mother told us, but as starved as we were, we could not manage to swallow one bite of the briny rice. We lay in our bunks, staring listlessly toward the ceiling. My teeth chattered as I broke out in a cold sweat and soaked the straw-filled mattress. We begged for food, knowing there was none. It seemed as if the time would never pass. Finally, the loudspeaker announced that Wormido, an island near Inchon, was in sight and that the Korean refugee committee had heard of our plight, and they had sent some food on board.

As we devoured the seaweed wrapped rice balls and turnip pickles, another announcement blared through the speaker. "Attention! Attention! We are sorry to inform you that a Communist has smuggled arms and ammunition onto our ship and has escaped on a peddler's boat. You are ordered to stay on board until his family has been arrested. Please be patient while the ship is being searched." Time crawled by.

At last the captain of the ship ordered everyone to assemble near the gangway. Excitedly we pushed with the multitude toward the exit. My heartbeat quickened as I saw the land and people my parents had described. We cheered to the flag-waving strangers on the dock as though we knew each other.

Father shouted, "We are home, children! We are home at last!"

Song Do

The refugee committee instructed people leaving the ship to place their luggage in a huge pile inside a barbed wire camp and stand in line to get powdered with DDT from head to toe. Everyone looked as if a giant sifter had spilled flour all over us. Then we followed the arrows to booths where each adult lined up to receive 1,000 won.[10] The officials herded us into the barracks for the night. We slept shoulder to shoulder on straw floor mats in the barren room. During the night a storm broke out and it started pouring. The next morning we found our luggage completely soaked and many pieces floating in the deep puddles. The refugees waded into the water to find their trunks, suitcases and bundles.

That afternoon, Father rented a mule-drawn wagon, piled us upon top of our wet luggage and headed for Song Do, a resort-fishing village, where one of his cousins lived. The flat houses along dirt roads looked peculiar compared to the towering buildings and asphalt streets of Tientsin. Father got off the wagon and walked alongside the driver when the path led up a steep mountain pass. My city eyes stared again and again at the emerald fields. Golden forsythia blossoms

---

[10] Korean currency worth approximately $5.00 in 1946

covered the hills and surrounded the houses below.

Mountains surrounded the village on all three sides in a gigantic semi-circle facing the Yellow Sea. Fluted tile-roofed houses and chomahk[11] dotted strips of green land. Thin streaks of smoke rose from the chimneys. I heard dogs barking and children laughing in the distance. Father pointed out an aqua-blue two-story villa nestled in the mountain near a temple and told us it was his cousin's home.

The Shin family welcomed our family, inviting us to stay with them until we found a place to live. The stucco villa housed over a dozen rooms. We addressed Father's cousin as Ajoshi, and his wife as Ajumoni.[12] They had two daughters. Ok Hee was several years my senior, but Moon Hee and I were only a few months apart. She blushed easily, and when she smiled her cheeks dimpled. Yet just as often, her large brown eyes welled up with tears. I soon leaned why. Their mother had died and Ajumoni was their stepmother. Before long I saw that Ajumoni made them work harder than any of our servants ever did in China. Since there was no water main in the village, the girls drew water from their well. They did all the cooking, cleaning, and washing. They boiled the white clothes and linens in a hug metal tub with a piece of lye and soap. Then they carried the wash to the stream, scrubbed and pounded it with a club on a slate. Every morning, before I woke up, Ok Hee and Moon Hee were already up performing their chores.

While my cousins worked, I explored the surroundings. From the veranda, I watched the Yellow Sea and the village below us. Above the villa, up on the mountain, stood a Buddhist temple and a bell that tolled in the morning and the evening. Tall pine, chestnut, oak, peach,

---

[11] a straw-thatched farm house

[12] aunt

and persimmon trees surrounded the area. Pheasants, sparrows, and swallows flew from limb to limb, twittering away. I had to admit Father was right when he said that Korea's scenery was beautiful.

One bright day Ajoshi and his family took us to the shore during low tide. My father carried me down the steep seawall on his muscular back, and then turned me loose on the beach with Moon Hee. She skirted tiny holes in the sand, and digging around each one, picked up razor and hard-shell clams. Intrigued, I followed her. Disregarding the grazes and scratches she was getting on her fingers, she twisted a clam knife between the shell and the rock. When she had pried the cluster of oysters from the underside of the slippery rocks, she scooped out the first oyster from the shell and held it out to me. I drew back, but she slipped it into her own mouth and raved about the taste. Moon Hee said raw oysters were good for the health, and I would have to get used to eating them. She smacked her lips and grinned convincingly. Daringly, I swallowed the third one. I almost threw up, but I did not want to hurt her feelings, so I gulped until finally that slimy mollusk went down. It took a good many years before I got used to eating raw oysters.

A month after we arrived at Moon Hee's house, Mother found an abandoned Japanese inn across from the resort park along the shore. My parents secured permission from the local police chief to live there and we moved in. An old pine tree stood at the entrance of the charming multi-roomed lodge. The exterior was trimmed with bamboo rods. It had large glass windows and shoji[13] with a window seat, facing a tranquil rock garden.

Even though we had plenty of land, Father had to postpone his dream of starting a poultry farm until he could

---

[13] Japanese rice-paper sliding doors or window shades

get enough funds. Instead my parents decided to open a tailor shop, using the spacious living room. They sold some of the silk and linen from Onni's trousseau to buy an old Singer sewing machine. Just like the rest of the villagers, my mother and Onni drew water from the public well, washed clothes at the stream, cleaned the house and planted seeds for vegetables.

Any flowering plant delighted me, even the most common wild flowers. I spent hours making garlands of dandelions and clover flowers. Seeing my interest, Father started a flowerbed for me, and soon gardening became my greatest hobby. I weeded and transplanted by the hour. Enchanted by nature, I visited the neighbors and asked them to trade their new plants for some of my own. Within a few weeks, I collected morning glories, balsams, peonies, tiger lilies, dahlias, snapdragons, sweet peas and Mu gung hwah[14] - our national flower. I even collected fall flowers like cosmos, chrysanthemums and Chinese lanterns to spread color. Everywhere I looked, I saw fragrant flowers of all shades and shapes. Dragonflies, bees and butterflies of all sizes, shapes and colors flitted about my sunny flower garden.

When the weather grew hotter, Moon Hee frequently came for me on her way to the beach. She taught me how to swim at a public beach pool near the seawall by making me concentrate on reaching for her red and white floating tube. Without realizing it, I began thrashing my arms and legs until I was floating in deep water. Then something pricked my legs. I looked under the water and saw tiny shrimp jabbing me. Suddenly I sensed that my feet could not touch the bottom of the pool, and I began to sink, gulping salt water. I screamed and floundered frantically, but Moon Hee

---

[14] Rose of Sharon

calmly grabbed my hair and pulled me out. She patiently instructed me until I could swim well and even jump from the high diving board into the deep water.

In the fall, my parents enrolled Onni in a high school in Inchon since there was no school in our village. I became fiercely jealous and upset that they would not send me to school, although I knew I couldn't maneuver myself over the hilly road. However, I dared not express my inner turmoil, for I dreaded punishment. As children we were trained to be submissive to our elders and to never talk back or argue with them, even if we felt we were right. There was no use in complaining, so I spent more time out in the garden and buried my frustrations in the soil.

Father must have sensed my disappointment, for he made a mini goldfish pond for me next to the flowerbed. He bought me several goldfish and a water lily plant. As I watched the goldfish swim freely in that pond, I often dreamed of going to faraway lands that I had read about or heard of in fairy tales. After gardening, I would sit on the window seat between the glass pane and the shoji and gaze at the garden. In that corner I could shut out the whole world. There I could be anything I wanted and to do whatever I wanted to do. In my dream world I saw myself walking and running, going to school, becoming famous and dancing with a handsome prince. Then my face would heat with embarrassment. If I uttered these thoughts aloud, everybody would laugh at me. Quickly I would turn back toward my favorite tree, the gnarled white pine guarding our entrance. It stood robust amidst the delicate evergreen shrubbery and stretched ever upward. Whenever I came home from an outing, I reached up and hugged its trunk or swung around and sat on a low curved branch. On the days the village children harassed me, I clung to that tree until my heart settled down. Looking at the pine tree from my nook, I felt tall inside.

Nevertheless, no matter how brave and tall I felt with my tree, I dreaded Saturdays, when I had to go to the public bathhouse with Mother and my sisters. I hated looking at my shriveled leg, let alone allowing others to see it. Ordinarily my long skirt concealed it, but in the dressing room there were no stalls. I had to disrobe in front of the other bathers. We all piled our clothes into one of the wicker baskets on the floor and climbed into the giant communal bath. I could not wait until everyone else left the hall because people were either coming in or getting dressed after their bath. I tried to cover my leg by draping the towel around me, but all the draping in the world could not erase the deformity. Still, once I got into the pool, I thoroughly enjoyed the hot bath itself. Beads of sweat rolled down my face, and my fingers wrinkled up like golden raisins from soaking so long, but I had to get out and get dressed again eventually. I hated Saturdays.

Since all Korean women sewed their own family's clothes, two months went by without a single customer darkening our door. Instead of fretting, Father scoured the sea and caught nets full of fish. Each night he hauled home a huge burlap sack full of fish. We could not eat all of them, so Mother gave baskets of fish to our neighbors and a few refugee families who joined us on Sundays for worship services in our home. The surplus she salted and dried for winter use. Then Onni learned the English word for tailor shop in her English class and put up a sign in both English and Korean on my pine tree. That very afternoon, a tall brown-haired American soldier, who had to stoop to come in through the front door, became our first customer. He gave us chocolate candies and chewing gum. He had a friendly smile and gentle gray eyes, and his big nose looked like it was chiseled out of marble.

We affectionately called Americans kojangi.[15] Using the dictionary and funny gestures, the man said his name was Hogan and that he wanted his uniforms altered. I liked him. Shortly after Hogan visited us, the US Armed Forces occupied the resort park as a Rest and Recuperation Center. Through Hogan, my parents contracted to do all the sewing and laundry for the R & R Center.

Many refugee families moved into the village seeking jobs at the R & R. When income from the shop and Sunday church attendance increased, Father decided to rent the second floor of the building next door for worship services. He invited an evangelist who had fled religious persecution in North Korea to pastor the growing congregation. Since my parents had a steady source of income, they carried the bulk of the church's financial responsibilities. They paid the evangelist's salary and gave him free room and board at our home. Families who could not tithe put aside ten percent of their grain, meted out from each meal, and brought it to the church. Evangelist Chai lodged in a room next to the one I shared with my sisters. I could hear his subdued prayers in the early hours. His greatest concerns were for his family, for those fellow believers who were persecuted by the Communists, and for revival in our church.

On Sundays he spared no words when he preached about the last judgment, but his stern, dark olive face shone with grace when he spoke about the love and forgiveness of God for us. The fervor in his long, slanted eyes seemed to penetrate into the hearts of those seated on the floor.

A noticeable change took place in my father's spiritual life after the arrival of Evangelist Chai. Father began rising before dawn to attend prayer services. He spent hours reading and studying the Bible and held family devotions

---

[15] Big nose

every evening. My parents restored their strained relationship and Father became tender and considerate toward Mother. Sometimes Father carried me to revival services in other towns where miraculous healings took place in hopes that I might also be healed. But each time we returned home disappointed. Nevertheless, Christianity had become more than religion to my father. It had stirred a new way of life.

The amount of work increased, and Father hired two more dressmakers to cope with it all. My parents had earned enough money to help our relatives escape the Communists in the North. Families flocked to our home. When his mother joined us, Father was beside himself with relief

Harmoni[16] always wore a spotlessly white jogori[17] and chimah.[18] A starched headpiece covered her silky white hair, which she braided and fastened at the nape of her neck. Her wrinkled face looked like the skin of a dried apple and her eyelids drooped slightly over light brown eyes. Though hard of hearing and bent with age, Harmoni could still see to thread a needle and insisted on helping with the sewing. I adored her, for she had a flair for telling folktales that cast a spell over all of us.

When the weather started getting chilly, Father converted our Japanese rooms into warm, traditional Korean floor, ondol. He hired workers to dig five trenches, which served as ducts leading from the furnace in the kitchen across the whole floor to the chimney erected on the opposite side of the house. They placed large slates over the trenches and sealed the top with cement. For two days the adults took

---

[16] Grandmother

[17] a short Korean jacket

[18] a long Korean skirt

turns keeping a low heat going in the furnace to dry the floor. Even as a child, the economy and cleverness of my ancestors fascinated me. They designed the ondol so that heat used to cook a meal spread through the floor and warmed our rooms. The workmen pasted sheets of thick oil paper over it and gave it many coats of a dark yellow dye, extracted from the fruit of Cape Jasmine. After the surface of the floor dried, they polished it by rubbing it with cloth until it gleamed like gold. Whenever we caught a cold and our muscles ached, Mother fed us a steamy bowl of spicy hot soybean soup and tucked us under a thick comforter over the warmest part of the heated floor. After a nap we usually felt rejuvenated.

American men and women frequented our shop. Although I could not understand their tongue-twisting language, I hung around the tailor shop whenever they came in. They acted as if my handicap made no difference to them. One of the hostesses, Charlotte Dee, had hair that looked like spun gold, and came to us often to have her dresses made or altered. She asked me my name but could not pronounce Hyun Sook, so she dubbed me "Susie." Charlotte was very outgoing and would hug and kiss my parents each time they finished her dresses. Father would inevitably turn red and blink his eyes. Her demonstrative manners were strange to my upbringing. Korean adults never showed affection in public, even if they were married. They would not even hold hands in front of their children.

At Christmas the Americans invited all the Koreans in the village to an open house at the R & R Center. In the reception hall a gigantic Christmas tree with colorful blinking lights and brilliant ornaments dominated the center of the room. Charlotte, dressed in a low-cut black sequined evening gown, stood beside the tree. As she greeted guests, an officer walked in through the door. She said something in a loud voice, rushed over to the young man, threw her arms around his neck and kissed him right in front of all the Koreans.

"Ai-go, don't look!" the women groaned. Some gasped and clicked their tongues. Many covered blushing faces with their hands. This incident impressed me more than the Christmas gifts that the Santa Claus handed out to each child or the delicious food we found on the tables.

In August, a year after Father built the ondol, Mother gave birth to another girl whom they named Wha Sook. Grandmother and Onni cooked rice and the seaweed soup, which every Korean mother ate after childbirth. Harmoni claimed that seaweed increased mother's milk and improved the circulation of her blood. Father tried to hide his disappointment, and he good-naturedly joked with those who teased him. He said that Onni would be their substitute son. I wondered if he meant it. Just the thought of a substitute son irked me. What if she married?

It was evident to all that she would marry well. Our relatives talked endlessly about what a good bride Onni would make, for they all agreed she was the perfect material to be the wife of a rich man. Still, it took us by surprise when the matchmaker came in breathlessly one day.

"Mr. Lee! I have some exciting news for you!" We all gathered to hear. Rolling her eyes, she continued, "Purely by chance I ran into a very eligible young man. He is the youngest son of a well-to-do Han family in Seoul and he already has a good start in the Department of the Interior."

We all knew that Onni would marry someone very special for she was so beautiful, brilliant, and vivacious.

"His forehead is wide, the sign of a great intelligence. His huge well-shaped ears are set below magnetic eyes." Mother leaned forward eagerly, for such signs surely predicted greatness. "He is, of course, a pure-blooded Korean, but he looks much more like an aristocratic

Spaniard. I must tell you, Mr. Lee, that he is bound for success and fame."

My parents sat captivated by the matchmaker's description of their potential son-in-law, and I sensed Mother was eager for such a match because I saw her nudging Father to set the date for a meeting between the two families. The matchmaker arranged it. Two weeks later the meeting resulted in betrothal.

Onni had two wedding ceremonies: one modern style performed by a Presbyterian minister in Seoul and one in the traditional Confucian fashion of our village. Both the bride and the groom were dressed in ceremonial costumes. Onni wore an ornate headdress above her long braided coiled hair fastened with a golden rod, and was wrapped in a long red skirt and striped multicolored bridal jacket. For the feast Mother and the relatives prepared a whole pig, a side of beef, and countless chickens and fish. Onni and Hyung-bu,[19] as we called our brother-in-law, were seated at the head table, which was piled decoratively with delicious rice cakes, apples, persimmons, Korean pears as big as grapefruits, and even a rooster and hen propped up with their heads and feathers intact.

The male guests tried everything they could to make Onni laugh or smile, but she kept her composure, for all Korean girls knew that if the bride smiled on her wedding day, she would have a daughter instead of a son. During the whole feast, she sat, neither smiling nor eating, according to the custom. She looked like a porcelain doll, sitting so still with her painted face. After the couple retired to their room, the male guests continued to harass them by poking holes in the rice-papered shoji and peeking in - an ancient, humorous gesture all newlyweds endured.

---

[19] Brother-in-law

The following day, Onni and Hyung-bu left for their honeymoon. The house felt so empty that Mother cried, and I joined her. Secretly I hoped that someday I too, would be married to a handsome and important man.

Sometime after Onni married, Hogan visited us with a black and tan puppy named Leo and told us that he was leaving for his home in America. Reluctantly he gave us the dog and left. Leo made the parting somewhat easier. We fixed a box for him to sleep in under the wooden floor of the foyer. Thereafter, Leo became the self-appointed protector of our house and grounds.

One day an unexpected letter arrived from our former pastor Reverend Tae-up Kim of Tientsin. But it had not been mailed from China. Instead the postmark read Taegu, a city near the southeastern tip of Korea. Father opened the envelope at once, and as he scanned the letter, he read portions aloud to the rest of us.

"Perhaps it was best we stayed in Tientsin as long as we could. We were able to spread the gospel to the Chinese brothers and sisters all around us. Although we were the only Koreans in our area, we didn't feel desolate, for our Chinese neighbors looked after us. But it was very difficult to leave the church I loved and shepherded for so many years."

I picked up the envelope and looked at their address: Taegu-shi Nahm-Sahn-Dong 5-ho. I hoped we would be able to see him and his wife again someday.

In the fall of 1949, Americans began to withdraw from our village and the R & R Center closed down. Most of our friends and relatives moved to Seoul, and we felt abandoned. Rumors began to spread that the Russian troops had already withdrawn from North Korea and that once the US Armed Forces personnel left the Republic of Korea (ROK),[20] the long-

---

[20] The democratic government of South Korea after WWII

awaited national unification of Korea would be consummated.

Despite all this my parents decided to stay in Song Do, for they had saved enough money to start the poultry farm of Father's dreams. So in the spring of 1950, he bought hundreds of chicks and ducklings. Every morning, after he fed the flock, he led a procession of ducklings to the shore. His ducklings never got out of line as they headed to the sea, even when the fishermen passed by with their oxen loaded with nets and fish. I loved watching Father work with his feathered friends.

During my fourteenth summer, the Republic of Korea Naval Hospital moved into the R & R buildings. An orthopedic surgeon, who attended our church, offered to perform corrective surgery on my leg to stabilize the droopy ankle. Even though I wanted to walk, I was afraid of the surgery.

As my father carried me to the hospital on his back, I asked,
"Aboji, will I be able to walk and run like others after this operation?"

Father was silent as he trudged along the sandy road, "Well, Hyun Sook-ga, the doctor could not promise, but he is going to transplant your tendons so that you might walk better."

"Will I still limp? Will the children stop making fun of me?" The silence lengthened.

As Father began to reply, his voice faltered as if he were groping for the right words. "Hyun Sook-ga, I know how much it hurts you." He sounded very tired, "I have never told you this, but it feels like a silver dagger stabbing my chest each time I see you come home with a tear-stained face." His voice trembled, and I clung tightly to his back. "I can't tell you why, but some people think that any kind of defect is undesirable, a punishment from the gods. They feel that you aren't as good as they are." Fury mounted up in my heart, but I suppressed it.

"Aboji, am I being punished by God also?"

"No, my daughter. God loves you. Tell Him all your troubles. He will comfort and strengthen you. The Lord will answer your prayers."

I could feel my father breathing heavily by the time we reached the hospital grounds. He was used to carrying me, so I knew that he panted for more than the weight on his back. I was not aware that my heartache caused as much agony to my parents as they did to me. All my sorrow rushed to my eyes, and hot tears streamed down my cheeks.

"Hmmm-how strange," Father tried to speak lightly, "Never in my life have I been sprinkled with warm rain drops on such a sunny day." He galloped with me into the hospital entrance.

While I rested on the operating table, the doctor explained to me that I would have only local anesthesia and would be conscious during the surgery. A nurse blindfolded me and I squeezed my father's hand. Soon I felt a numb sensation in my foot as the surgeon gashed my ankle, but I sensed no pain. Although I was not supposed to watch, I pushed the blindfold up a little without anyone noticing and peeked curiously. I saw the doctor lift something that dripped blood away from my foot and a pile of gauze soaked with blood on a stand. I heard screams, my own, and then passed out. Vaguely I remembered being carried on my father's back with my right leg in a full cast as the doctor sent me home to convalesce.

Mother prepared a makeshift bed for me by my window facing the garden. She thought that if I slept on the floor with my sisters, they might accidentally kick my leg and hurt me. Then, heavily sedated, I drifted into haziness.

Invaders From the North

The early morning sunlight had just filtered in through the shoji when the excruciating pain in my ankle awakened me. "Aboji," I called, but it was Mother who rushed to my side.

Quieting me, she whispered haltingly, "Father isn't here. The North Korean soldiers invaded our village during the night!" That meant war! Terror struck my heart, dulling my awareness of the pain. My small frame shook in spite of the late June heat.

After Mother left my side, I poked a hole in the rice paper shade, too frightened to slide it open and peeked outside. Our little village had turned into a battlefield overnight. Instead of fishermen leisurely herding oxen to the sea, there were unfamiliar armored trucks rumbling down the sandy road. In place of naked toddlers romping in the village park, I saw North Korean Communist soldiers in baggy ochre uniforms standing stiffly with guns drawn.

Mother came to my side again and told me that I had been sleeping for three days and that news of the invasion had been broadcasting during the night. All the able-bodied anti-Communists had fled, including our relatives, friends and Father. He had no choice but to escape without us because of his political stand and religious beliefs. Grandmother and I could not flee, so Mother remained behind with Grandmother, my two younger sisters, and me.

Harmoni brought my breakfast and reported that no one was out yet. We guessed that the remaining villagers must be hiding behind rice-paper shades and bolted gates as we did, watching the invaders. Mother tied Leo to the floor supports so he would stay inside, but he growled frequently.

After lunch, Mother sent Mi Sook out to play in the sand by the pine tree.

"Mi Sook-ga, I don't think they would harm a child," she said. "Act as if you are making a sand castle and glance at the soldiers." Mother and Harmoni waited nervously near the door. An uncomfortable hush filled the hallway.

"Oh, no," Mother gasped. "She's going toward the enemy truck!" Mother's distress shot fear through me. Within minutes Mi Sook came bouncing back through the front door, waving a dried cuttlefish in her hand. "Omoni! Look! The soldier called me and gave me this!" Mother swept Mi Sook into her arms and wept with relief, while my younger sister reported that the soldiers stood with daggers mounted on their guns and that they looked very angry.

"Keep the doors bolted," Harmoni warned us. "As soon as they win the hearts of people, they will show their true color. Red."

Just as Grandmother predicted, two days after the invasion, some of the fishermen and farmers swaggered into the foyer with a Communist soldier, and said, "We are collecting poultry to prepare a welcome feast for our friends." Before Mother could say anything, they began stuffing chickens and ducks into burlap sacks. After they lugged away all the fluttering, cackling birds, three other local Communists burst into the house. They demanded to know where Father was hiding. Mother truthfully told them that she did not know his whereabouts.

The men accused her of lying and screamed at her, "You traitors! You fattened your stomachs by working for the big-nosed devils. Share now! Give to the poor!" The men went wild, chanting Communist slogans, spitting on our floors and smashing windows, mirrors and porcelain vases as they rampaged through all the rooms. With their clubs they banged the ceilings, jabbed holes in the plastered walls and tore up boards from the floor. Wha Sook wrapped her arms around Mother's leg and wailed while Mother trailed behind the violent men.

Harmoni stooped by my bed, rubbing her gnarled hands and groaning, "Ai-go, ai-go! Heavens, why is this happening to my children?"

After ransacking every room, they began filling the front hall with bundles and huge sacks. I climbed down from the bed and dragged myself to the front of the house. Wha Sook screamed when she saw tears pouring down Mother's eyes. Harmoni grabbed the shirttail of one man, trembling and pleading with him to leave something behind. Leo growled from under the floor, too afraid to come out, but Mi Sook spread her arms across the front door, glaring at them. Oblivious to our pleas, the men shoved Mi Sook aside and began to haul out their loot. Carrying out the last bundle, one man laughed, "We will keep these things in a safe place for you, traitors! Our day has come!" Helplessly we watched them cart off our possessions.

Harmoni and Mother paced through the shambled rooms disgusted. When they returned to the front hall, Mother sighed, "They took everything except some old pots and Hyun Sook's bedding. They even grabbed our first-aid kit. I wish they had left behind the ointment for my sty." Mother twisted her toes and rubbed her inflamed puffy eyes. No one realized Mi Sook was missing, and when she pranced back in with Mother's ointment, our mouths dropped open.

"H-h-how . . . ." Mother stammered.

"I ran after them," Mi Sook arched her lips valiantly, "All the way to the station, and said you had to have it. I stood in front of the door until one man dug it out of the sack." I could just see her standing with her legs planted firmly on the ground, hands at her sides glaring at them defiantly.

"If you were grown, those enemies would have answered you with a bullet," Harmoni shuddered. Mother hugged Mi Sook and whispered a prayer of thanks for her safe return.

Later that afternoon, Mr. Pak, an acquaintance of Father, came in with an old briefcase. We heard that he had secured a responsible position in the new regime because his brother was a full-fledged member of the Communist party. I saw Mother's eyes darken at the sight of him. However, to our surprise, he looked outside furtively. He quickly whispered to Mother that he had access to confidential information and warned us not to speak out against the Communists for confiscating our belongings. Because of Father's flight we were under surveillance. Mr. Pak then blinked his eyes and explained that he had to yell at us to justify his visit, "Listen, it would be to your advantage to confess where your husband is hiding!" He smiled at us reassuringly and then stormed out of the door.

That night we peered out the window and noticed, for the first time, dark shadows lurking behind shrubs and bushes. We felt eyes watching our every move. Leo's barking kept us alert to the informers' presence, giving us a slight sense of security. The Communists, however, could not tolerate the growling dog, and they demanded that we hand him over. They said that the bombing would cause the dog to go mad and endanger human lives. Once again I climbed down from the bed and dragged myself to the front entrance. Mi Sook clung to Leo, Mother reasoned with the men, and Harmoni and I pleaded with them to let us keep the dog. Heartlessly a soldier threatened Mother with the gun aimed at Leo. Her tear-stained face nodded, and we let Leo go. He bolted and whined, but they dragged him out. Mi Sook and Wha Sook screamed as they hanged Leo on my pine tree. I covered my ears and tried to muffle his pathetic, frightened howls. Then the soldiers slit Leo's throat and skinned him.

Sometime later, on a moonless night, I heard the back door creak open. My muscles tensed, and my spine prickled. I heard fragments of whispered conversation. Mother's voice. . . Father's response. He had returned.

"Ai-go, Yobo . . . . But why did you return? The Communists are . . ."

"I guessed as much, but what good would it be to live without my . . . ."

" . . . .confiscated everything except for a few bedrolls and some kitchen . . ."

". . . . can be acquired again. The Lord will provide." I heard soothing reassurance in Father's words. The comfort of his voice choked me with emotion.

Then I heard the sound of his footsteps coming toward me. Father groped in the darkness, for we could not risk using the oil lamp after sundown. He laid his hand on my moist forehead, praying silently. Mother looked furtively outside, but she said she could not see anyone. Hastily she suggested Father should hide behind the pantry.

Weakly he replied, "I am sure one of them must have seen me coming home. How long can I avoid their scrutiny?" He sighed, "It would be a futile attempt."

For some reason nobody charged in after Father that night as we feared, but at daybreak the brutal men came. Mother and Harmoni went forward in their robes with Mi

Sook and Wha Sook crying at the commotion. Without any resistance Father stood before them. We begged them not to take him away. Mother grabbed one man's hand. He shoved her briskly, and ignoring our pleas, took my father away.

None of us left the hallway. We stared out the door long after Father disappeared around the bend of the road. Mother silently moved her lips in agonizing prayer. Wha Sook sobbed and clung to Mother. Harmoni leaned against the wall, rubbing her hands and chanting, "Ai-go, ai-go." Mi Sook stared at the spot where Leo used to sleep, her eyes blazing. I fidgeted at the edge of the floor, trying to find a comfortable position and wondering about Father.

Late that evening Father returned. His strained face looked several years older. None of us dared make any noise or press him to recount his "visit." After a quick meal he told us, "They took me to the district office. Fortunately the head of the local Communist Party happened to be Mr. Soh, one of the farmers that I helped on many occasions. After he admonished me for fleeing, someone read off my crimes: founder of a church, associated with the Americans, a member of an anti-Communist party."

"Thank God you are still alive," Mother said, "I heard that all anti-Communists are being. . . ."

"Our God is protecting us. Mr. Soh told me that they had a meeting last night upon my returned and decided to spare my life because, as he put it, 'You are know in the village as a kind and upright man who never harmed or abused anyone.'"

"So you are free. You won't be imprisoned?" Mother sounded relieved.

"Not quite free," he hesitated, pushing up his glasses. "You see, Mr. Soh pulled me aside into another room and tried to entice me to join him in the Party. He said I could have back our belongings and would be given a high position. I tried to refuse him tactfully. He said I was being foolish, and became very annoyed. He told me to reconsider. I have never prayed so hard in my life as I did in that empty room. As I prayed, I could see our Lord Jesus on the cross. When Mr. Soh returned after many hours, I firmly answered that I could not betray my principles. I saw sparks in his eyes. He informed me sharply that they would either confine me or put me to hard labor. I pleaded to do hard labor. At least I would have a chance to see all of you."

The Communists put Father to work immediately. He dug foxholes and bomb shelters day and night. He had barely enough time away from the shovel for food and catnaps. In no time at all, he looked aged and haggard. They came for Mother, too, and forced her to do the same tasks as well as cook for them. Sometimes she brought home a small ball of rice crust that she scraped off the pot. Like savages we fought over those little scraps.

My parents discovered that many of the villagers had been pro-Communists for quite some time. After the invasion, these people attained high positions in the Party. They profited from the items seized from anti-Communists. We heard that these officials even counted the fruit in orchards and estimated the grain in the fields, demanding that the farmers turn in the expected amount of their harvest to the Party. If their fields and orchards yielded less, the farmers were required to make up the difference. Even those who had been in favor of Communism, hoping for a better government, began to shake their heads in disgust. Contrary to the propaganda about equality, elevated living conditions for all people and a superior form of government, the new regime carried a high price tag. The Communists used force and threats to control every move.

Shortly after my parents began their hard labor, the allies' attacks on Communist camps increased. Fighter planes zoomed over the Communist foxholes, machine guns pelting them with bullets. Bombs burst everywhere engulfing houses in red and yellow flames like whole matchboxes catching fire at once. No place was safe. Everything exploded and burned. I wondered if this was what hell would be like.

Because of the incessant bombing, all laborers were ordered to work only after dark. During the day the ditches were covered with straw and pine branches.

The first day my parents were home, the soldiers pounded on our door. "We need this house for our troops," they demanded.

"But this is our home," Mother protested, her eyes glaring. "Where can we go with all this bombing?" Father pulled her back abruptly. His face stiffened.

'There are plenty of empty houses. Find one!" they shouted. "You have twenty-four hours to vacate."

After they collected themselves, my parents noted dryly that they should be thankful to the Communist raiders. They had no possessions left to pack except the bundle of bedding, a few kitchen utensils and some condiments. After dark, Mother asked Father to remove a ceiling panel above the kitchen furnace and bring down our worn Bibles and a picture of Jesus praying in the garden of Gethsemane which they had brought back from China. Father asked,

"How did the Bibles get up there?"

"I hid them there the night you fled." She told him. They tucked the Bibles and the picture of Jesus into the bedding bundle.

The following evening, we started up the mountain road. Father lugged me on his back, my leg dangling in its heavy cast. Harmoni held onto her son's belt with one hand and steadied her gait with a cane in the other. Like most Korean grandmothers, she was bent from years of stooping down to do housework and farm work. Mother carried the bundle of bedding and kitchen utensils on her head, and my two younger sisters tagged along, Mi Sook holding up Wha Sook as best she could.

As we made our way up the path, a dark figure materialized from the shadows, moving toward us. Terrified, I tried to keep my hands from shaking, but it was only Mr. Pak. He did not slow down at all when he met us, but whispered to Father as he passed, "Mr. Lee, you are being watched closely. Be careful with words." Without so much as a glance at us, he strode on down the road. Though the message was one of warning, his concern itself seemed like a gift from heaven, and I felt Father's steps grow firmer. Darkness thickened, and Father groped his way, almost tripping many times.

"Right ahead of us is Police Officer Young's villa," he said. "I think it might be abandoned."

Cautiously we eased through the gate and found the door. Whiffs of spoiled food pricked my nostrils. There was no sign of other people. Once inside we slumped down on the tatami[21] floor in sheer exhaustion and slept. In the morning we were surprised to find that the Young family had not had a chance to finish their supper when they fled. The house was empty except for the bowls of rotten food. Tiptoeing from room to room, my parents took stock of our situation. No one else was there. From the veranda, we saw the house we occupied protruding like a steeple, dangerously conspicuous against the side of the mountain. The garden had become a desolate mass of weeds and tree stumps. Not one tree remained to shield us from prying eyes. Worst of all we saw Communist troops encamped only about twenty yards down the road where they could have a clear

---

[21]Japanese straw-filled mat flooring

view of our comings and goings.

Below us the village and the Yellow Sea were spread out in a panorama. How breathtaking such scenery would have been in peacetime. Out of nowhere allied planes appeared screaming shrilly over our heads and zooming down on the village. Houses crumbled like sandcastles as bombs exploded everywhere. The village looked like a sea of fire.

In desperation, Father explored the area near the villa and found a vacant bomb shelter, but he could not get us all there in time. Either Harmoni or I could be taken there quickly, but not both of us. My parents tented two tatamis, buttressed them with rocks and wood blocks and draped the bedding over the top. At the sound of each new attack, we crawled into this shelter, feeling more secure than if we ducked our heads between our knees or lay flat on the floor. Even so we could not forget that mansions with thick walls were instantaneously shattered to rubble by a direct blow.

Before noon a couple and an elderly woman came to the villa and moved into the room beside ours. Father put his finger across his lips to signal that we should be discreet. Later he explained to us that they might be planted informers.

As he suspected, Father discovered that the man was a Communist Party official. Food was plentiful for them while our meager rations ran out. Each mealtime the aroma of rice, soybean curd soup, Korean pickled cucumbers, bulgogi[22] and broiled fish often wafted from our neighbors' quarters. Tantalized by the delicious smell, Wha Sook cried and begged for food.

Risky as it was my parents went into Inchon one

---

[22] charcoal-broiled sirloin strips marinated in sugar, soy sauce, garlic, scallions, sesame seeds and oil

afternoon to search for grain. They told us girls not to venture outside or even to make a noise until they returned. We waited for hours, our mouths watering whenever we remembered that they might bring food. We sat very still and strained our ears to hear their footsteps. Only the occasional subdued conversations of our neighbors broke the silence. Then the noise of the bombers began, and we dove under our shelter.

That evening Father and Mother returned without rice. No food was available. Money had become useless, they told us, and all the stores had closed down. After a long search, they managed to find a bombarded warehouse where someone had burnt barley to sell. Mother rinsed the black grain many times and cooked some into gruel while we clutched our stomachs and waited. To our dismay it tasted terrible, like watered down oatmeal mixed with charcoal powder. Wha Sook kicked her bowl and cried all the more for rice. Watching her, all strength seemed to drain out of Mother.

The next day Harmoni picked some plantain and dandelion leaves, common weeds growing on the ground. She brought them in and claimed that she ate this during famines when she was a little girl. Harmoni boiled it and seasoned it with soy sauce, vinegar and red pepper. The three of us refused to eat a salad of weeds. Our parents did not urge us. It was the best they could offer. After a few days of not eating food, I became so hungry that burnt barley and plantain salad tasted good to me. I wished I could have filled my stomach with more of it. When I gave in, Mi Sook did too. Wha Sook held out the longest, but at last even she ate it when she was hungry enough.

One morning in September, I felt a new spring in Father's steps as he returned from digging ditches all night. He motioned us to crawl toward the veranda. Pointing toward the Yellow Sea, he whispered that the vague, gray objects far away over the horizon were our allies' ships. During the night he had overheard the Communists talking about an imminent attack from the United Nations and had watched them looking out to sea with binoculars. We were thrilled to see the ships but had to lower our voices lest our Communist neighbors in the villa overhear. The presence of battleships and bombers brought us new hope for freedom but at the same time increased our present danger. Air raids and ships' cannons aimed at enemy sites sometimes hit innocent citizens as well. Many times flying fragments from explosions barely missed us.

Each night just before our parents left for their enforced labor, we held family devotions in whispers, praying for God's protection while we were apart. Father prayed as if it would be his last prayer among us. We never knew when one or all of us would fall victim to the bombs, yet our parents' faith in God seemed to grow stronger as the war raged. Just as Father finished saying, "The hand of God is resting upon us," we heard an explosion that shattered the windowpanes of our neighbor's quarters to the ground. The glass panes in our own window remained without a crack.

In the middle of September, when jet fighters buzzed around like angry hornets, Mother went out to scout for food. We all knew that she could not buy grain, but she took an empty sack over her shoulder and prepared to leave.

"Listen, I can't stay cooped up here any longer," Mother told us. "I have to find out what the situation is. And I must get some food somehow." She started down the mountain trail, and no one tried to stop her. She did not return until after dark. Harmoni and I sat close to hear her whisper what she had seen.

"I was almost at the village when Communist snipers began to shoot at me," Mother told us. "I shouted to them that my family was starving and I needed to find food for them. Then I kept on going toward our old home. When I approached I saw that the entire front section had crumbled to the ground. It made my heart sick, but I moved on. I shuffled along that stretch of sandy road toward Nam Dong Village where the Noh family from our church lives. Just as I turned up toward the hill from the shore, a Communist soldier yelled at me to stop right there. He told me to look down at my feet. I saw my shin touching an almost invisible wire stretched across the thick crabgrass. I stood paralyzed while the soldier leaped down from his post." I pictured Mother's plight. The thought of almost having lost her frightened me.

"The soldier pointed out the land mines all along the hillside and down to the shore," she continued. "He said the explosives were planted to blow up the big-nosed devils, and ordered me to go back home by way of the mountain trail. Before heading for home, I stopped at the Noh family's house. They did not welcome me. Mr. Noh told me they knew we had been branded as traitors and being seen with me could endanger them. This gave me a twinge of loneliness.

"I thought at least the Cho family would treat me differently and give me some hopeful news," Mother went on, "but when I stopped at their home, they acted just as shocked and fearful to see me as the Nohs had. Mrs. Cho cried and begged me to understand their situation and leave." Mother returned with her sack empty, but we were thankful that she had come home alive.

The following morning, the bombing worsened. It seemed death was inevitable. I told my father that if I had to die, I wanted to remove that added weight of a cast. We only had a kitchen knife and a pair of scissors. With them he chiseled and cut away carefully until at last he ripped away the cast. The leg smelled awful, and when I saw my wilted limb, I cried out in dismay. The black stitches on the ankle, which were supposed to have sealed the flesh, had given way to the untreated incision and festered horribly. Father pulled the cotton wadding from the cast and pressed my puffy ankle. Through the stitched holes, the thick green pus and dull brown blood oozed out. Father ripped off a strip of the linen apron Harmoni was wearing and wrapped it around my ankle. My leg had been itchy for so long, and I had not been able to reach it while it was inside the cast. The luxury of scratching and the lightness without the cast gave me a bit of comfort.

Then Father ordered, "Quickly, duck!" We scampered under the tatami and huddled together as the force of another explosion shook the villa. The intervals between bombs shortened and the explosions escalated. The smell of gunpowder and smoke thickened. Father prayed and called aloud, "Oh, Lord God, protect us!" Then he softly hummed the hymn, "Our Refuge is God."

Harmoni repeatedly chanted, "Ai-go, ai-go." Mi Sook and Wha Sook fussed and whined. I wept over my unhealed leg. Mother chided us to be patient. We breathed on each other's necks as the shelter became stifling. Wha Sook cried again for rice, but no one moved.

"I'll get you something to eat as soon as the bombing stops," Mother promised, but Wha Sook bellowed louder. Although Father objected, Harmoni crawled out of the shelter and started toward the backyard to cook.

Some time after she went out, we noticed that the bombing had subsided. All we could hear was the occasional crackling and buzzing of firearms or planes. It sounded as if the world had come to a standstill.

Just as we crawled out of the shelter, Harmoni hobbled in breathlessly. "Ai-go. Son, come out and see! I see strange looking… " I could not hear the rest. Father followed her to the backyard. We all started after them.

"Look at that!" Through the open door I saw her pointing to the path up the mountain.

"Mother, they are American Marines!" Father excitedly explained. She had never seen US Marines in camouflage.

"Mansei!"[23] Father shouted, waving his arms at them. "Everybody come and see the American flag! The Marines are carrying the American flag! We are free! Can you hear me? We are free! Mansei! Long live America! Long live Korea!"

Mother dragged me the rest of the way out, so I could see all that Father was seeing. Foreign soldiers stood on the mountainside above us. My proud, stoical father jumped up and down like a boy at a ball game, waving his arms wildly. Unrestrained tears streamed down his sunken cheeks. We all wept and shouted Mansei until our throats became hoarse. Our arms stiffened and ached from waving.

The passing marines smiled and waved back. Some tipped their helmets casually. Never had we seen anything more beautiful than the flag of the United States of America. The red, white and blue fluttering over the helmets of the US Marines assured us that the freedom we had once taken so much for granted was now restored. I thought my heart would burst with sheer joy. The American flag represented freedom from fear, forced labor, and hunger. We were free to go where we wished, do what we wanted, and express what we believed. But most of all, Father said, now we could worship God openly.

---

[23] Hurrah!

The Hand of God

Mr. Pak came to see us that afternoon. His slanted eyes glistened when he saw my father. Shaking Father's hand vigorously, he said, "Mr. Lee, it must be an act of your God that you are still alive! The Communists had you scheduled for execution yesterday!" His voice fell. His eyes stared at Father incredulously, "I heard about it a week ago, but I had no way of warning you."

Father's lips parted, but no words came out. Mr. Pak went on to tell us that the sudden counterattack from the UN forces had forced the Communist officers to flee. Only a handful of soldiers remained. He assumed they had no chance to carry out the execution.

After Mr. Pak left, Father led us in a thanksgiving prayer. He fervently blessed God for saving us from death. As he had so many times during the war, he asked God to watch over his firstborn and her husband. He implored the Lord that we might find them again. We had no way of knowing whether they had escaped the invasion or even if they were alive. Again Father chose the hymns, "Our Refuge Is God" and "Faith of Our Fathers." We sang until the room practically burst.

After we calmed down, my parents' eyes met and

seemed to concur. Nothing remained for us in this village but horrible memories. Father went out and returned shortly with a rented mule-drawn wagon. Harmoni and we girls sat on it while my parents walked side by side. We headed for the nearest city, Inchon.

I knew from what I had overheard that if we should encounter Communist soldiers, they might still kill us. The allied troops were also suspicious of refugees. At one point a group of American soldiers stopped us. "They probably think we are disguised Communists," Father said so quietly I barely heard him.

They searched our few belongings. Unwrapping the bedding, they came across the picture of Jesus and the Bibles. Immediately they stopped the search and waved us on with a loud, "OK!"

Once in the city, we found a mass of refugees like us, milling about the streets - buying, selling, laughing and weeping. In spite of their great losses, most faces shone. Everyone seemed happy just to roam around freely. My parents knocked on doors and made inquiries for hours before they found a tiny room to rent. It was only a six by eight foot cubbyhole, but we all crammed into it and called it home.

Our parents seemed content just to breathe free air, but we children missed food – any kind of food – to fill our empty stomachs. From that room Father went out day after day searching for a job. Each evening he came back more tired and discouraged. Mother kept reassuring him that something would come up.

One day he returned earlier than usual. "See what I have," he called to us. We all crowded to the tiny door, climbing on top of each other to get a glimpse at Father. We saw two number ten cans tied to the back seat of an old bicycle.

"Where on earth . . . ." Mother widened her eyes.

"I ran into the local garbage dealer," Father told us. "He sold me the bicycle at a very low price. And these cans are food from a US Army mess hall!" We craned our necks as Mother placed the contents into a large pan and carefully separated the conglomeration of food. Into six bowls she divided equal portions of scrambled eggs with cheese. I had never seen cheese before. Mi Sook and I grimaced, for it tasted very strange, but we consumed the mixture anyway. There were also completely untouched breaded liver slices with onions. Mother re-seasoned them with soy sauce and hot pepper. Then she trimmed away teeth marks from some half-eaten pieces of toast smothered with butter and strawberry jam. We saved those until last to enjoy at our leisure.

Another day Father brought home a can of whole milk. It tasted worse than the cheese, and I almost threw up. Father drank all our untouched milk and chuckled,

"The white people drink milk. That's why they have such fair skin."

Some days he came home empty-handed. On those occasions he placed a bowl of water on the table, and to my annoyance, quoted I Thessalonians 5:18, "In everything give thanks: for this is the will of God in Christ Jesus concerning you." I failed to appreciate the situation as he did.

One day, Father brought back something especially for me that was even better than food. "This will help you walk," he told me as he handed me an old Yankee broomstick he got from the garbage dealer. After he sawed off the broom, Father instructed me to grip the upper part of the stick with both hands, press my weak right knee against the middle, and plant the tip firmly on the ground as I walked. Supporting myself with the stick, I could move around without swaying.

Soon after this, Father rushed in with exciting news. "Seoul is free of Communists." His eyes danced, "I just heard it at the marketplace! I am going there on my bicycle in search of our In Sook!" We waited eagerly for him to return to tell us he had found Onni, but on the following day he came back disappointed.

"Her in-laws are living in the house." Father said as he trembled with exhaustion. "They said In Sook and her husband fled in June, just before the invasion, and they haven't heard from them since."

We felt less hopeful when he traveled to Seoul again, but this time he returned full of enthusiasm. "They are back! I saw them! In Sook and her husband insist that we move to Seoul immediately and live in the mansion the government is providing for them!"

As we got ready to leave, he told us what had happened. The second visit turned out to be as fruitless as the first one. Pedaling along, Father considered the possibility that they might not be alive, yet another part of him clung to hope. He scanned every passing vehicle.

"I saw a shiny black limousine speeding toward Seoul, and inside I spotted a beautiful young woman sitting beside a man. I stopped my bicycle, turned around and gazed after them. Wistfully I thought to myself, 'Oh, Lord, wouldn't it be wonderful if,'" Father's voice cracked, "'that, that girl's face I saw so fleetingly . . . .' All at once the limousine came to an abrupt stop." We held our breath. Father wiped his eyes, "I stood there spellbound. I couldn't even move a muscle. The woman jumped out of the car and raced back toward me, but my eyes turned blurry, scarcely daring to believe what I was seeing until I felt the impact of her body." By now we were all weeping. "In between her tears, In Sook told me, 'Aboji, we boarded the first ship from Pusan heading for Inchon. From the deck all we could see was miles and miles of charred buildings, rubble and ashes. As we drove through the streets of Inchon, we lost all hope of ever finding our families. We headed toward Seoul. My heart was resigned to accept the tragedy, but my eyes kept scanning every passing pedestrian along the ruins. I almost didn't recognize you, Father. You looked so old and gaunt, but somehow I felt it had to be you.'"

Father found a small wagon, piled us on it and headed for Seoul. We sang and clapped our hands and sang some more. The late autumn wind blew all our troubles behind us as we crossed the gigantic Han River Bridge into the city of Seoul.

Onni and Hyung-bu had two houses in Seoul. One belonged to them privately, and the other belonged to the government. We all went to the government mansion first. Mi Sook was assigned to the smaller house with Soon Ja, one of Onni's maids. Concrete walls with a gate of iron bars surrounded the mansion. There were so many hallways and staircases that I never managed to explore the whole place. Hyung-bu showed us all to our rooms.

In the living room Father conducted family devotions every evening. Often my thoughts would wander, taking fantasy flights, or while Father commented on a passage from the Bible, my eyes would stray toward the beautiful clock on the marble shelf. It had a gold-plated surface with Arabic numerals and a glossy walnut case. I loved the steady swing of the pendulum but even more the chimes that sounded every half hour and hour. While I gazed at the clock, I wondered when my father's prayers would end.

Onni and Mother bought a cartload of Chinese cabbage and turnips for the long winter ahead. I loved watching Mother and her helpers prepare kimjang kimchi[24]

---

[24] Korean pickled vegetables for the winter months

and I knew the process by heart. On the first day they salted the cabbage. Then, the following morning, they rinsed them. Next, they spread each cabbage leaf and stuffed it with a mixture of shredded turnips and Korean pears mixed with hot pepper powder, scallions, garlic, ginger roots, pine nuts, shrimp or oysters and salt. They placed alternate layers of the stuffed cabbages and whole turnips in five-foot earthenware jars that had been buried so that only the mouth of the crock showed. This method protected the kimchi from freezing. After a month, when it was fermented, the kimchi was sliced diagonally for serving. To Koreans no side dish was as colorful and appetizing as kimjang kimchi.

In the first part of December, I noticed a somber expression on the face of Hyung-bu and then on Onni. Hushed words passed between them and my parents. From then on, they all seemed preoccupied and would look right past me, rarely even speaking to me. Their attentions dissipated, as if a chasm suddenly appeared between us. I wondered if they blamed me for our sufferings during the war, or if I had become an eyesore to them.

One morning Onni announced that Hyung-bu had made arrangements for her to leave for Pusan, a port city in the southeastern tip of Korea. After long talks with her husband and my parents, she left in the limousine. Seoul was again in danger. I got the impression that Hyung-bu must stay in Seoul as long as he could because of his government position but that he would follow Onni to Pusan, taking with him the rest of her costly possessions. I wondered what would become of the rest of us.

About a week after Onni's departure, my parents seemed even more solemn than usual at the supper table. Once again I felt the weight of their suffering and loss from the war. When we finished eating, Mother tucked Wha Sook under the comforter. Father sat cross-legged on a royal-blue floor cushion, reading his worn Bible. Harmoni and I made ourselves scarce. In our room, she brought out her sewing basket, and slipping a light bulb underneath a hole in the sock, she began to darn.

I got out my embroidery kit, and said, "Please, Harmoni, tell me a scary story tonight." I always got scared, but found her horror stories irresistible.

"All right, I will tell you a really scary one, but don't ask me to walk you to the outhouse after dark," she chuckled, her eyelids folding over her eyes.

> Once upon a time, there was a beautiful maiden named Aeja who lived with her rich parents in a mansion, sort of like this one. She was an only child and her parents showered her with all their affection, treasures and silk. She had everything she could possibly want.

"She must have been like my Onni!" I chimed in.

"You might say that. Her parents raised their daughter properly and everyone adored her.

> Then one day, her mother became very ill. No doctor could save her, for the messenger of death had come to claim her soul.

My eyes filled up at the thought of losing my own mother.

> Well, a year after the mourning period her father remarried a much younger woman who wasn't quite as lovely as his daughter. Within a few months, Aeja disappeared and no one could find her. The stepmother told her husband that Aeja must have run off with a servant she seemed to be fond of. Aeja's father was furious, but his new wife did everything she could to comfort the enraged and heartbroken man. She happened to be very efficient in overseeing her household and began to dismiss the servants until only a

few remained. At last, she persuaded her husband that they didn't need such a huge mansion, and they sold the place and moved far away.

After many years had passed, rumors began to trickle out that the mansion was haunted. Many daring men went in, but no one ever came out alive.

One evening a warrior from a distant village heard the tale of the haunted mansion while drinking mak-kol-le[25] at an inn. Feeling full of spirit from the cheap rice wine, he decided to flaunt his courage. The innkeeper warned him not to go, but he heedlessly strode out and headed for the haunted mansion.

Swishing his sword in the air, he kicked down the gigantic gate and tore into the main room. He pulled down cobwebs, pushed aside a pile of skeletons, and sat on a thick layer of dust and drank some more mak-kol-le. At the stroke of midnight, a bluish-white hand stained with dried blood slowly slid open the rice-paper door."

I dropped my embroidery. Wrapping my arms around Grandmother, I buried my face in her white skirt. As if she were trying to cure my insistence for horror tales, Harmoni simply went on with her story.

A maiden in a death garment of hemp slithered in through the door. Her long tangled black hair, encrusted with mud and blood, was draped over her scarred, ghastly face. With a rusty dagger clenched between her darkened teeth, the maiden moved closer to the man. The warrior, who had never been afraid of anything, found himself losing courage and retreating. While he gasped for air, the girl knelt before him and slowly bowed. Without lifting her head, she began to supplicate, "Please, sir, do not be afraid of me. I am not here to harm you." She pleaded with him, as she had in the past with many others before him, to avenge her cruel death by her stepmother. She laid her dagger before

---

[25] coarse residue of rice wine

him and said, "My stepmother stabbed me with this dagger so that she could inherit the family wealth. She dumped my body at the edge of the bamboo field and covered me with coarse soil, rocks, and dead leaves. Please, all I am asking is a proper burial."

When the rooster crowed, she bowed again and left the room. The warrior picked up the rusty dagger and stepped outside to search her body at the edge of the bamboo field behind the mansion. To his amazement, he found a leaf pile at the far end of the property. Far down the road he saw a crowd milling about, craning their necks to see the live warrior. He called to the people, and together they buried the maiden under a willow tree overlooking a lake. Never again did she haunt the manor.

Just then my mother slid open the door, and I jumped. "Will you come to our room, Hyun Sook-ga?" I followed behind her. She motioned me to sit down in front of her and Father. "I wanted to wait until the baby was asleep," she said, avoiding my eyes. Nervously she picked at her teeth with a toothpick. Father kept on reading the Bible. I thought I must have done something wrong and that I was about to be scolded.

"Hyun Sook-ga, a rumor is spreading that the Communists might invade South Korea soon, but I hope it won't be so." Mother twisted her toes. I shivered. "Before your elder sister left a week ago, she told me that her husband would evacuate us from here to Pusan on a government ship should there be an imminent danger."

The thought of a ship adventure thrilled me. Mother became silent for quiet a while, and when she spoke again her lips trembled, "Hyun Sook-ga, In Sook told her maid, Soon Ja, to guard her private home until she returned."

I already knew that Soon Ja had been assigned to look after the house with Mi Sook. No one wanted to risk leaving a house vacant. Desperate refugees might help themselves to anything movable within an empty house.

"Your sister also told me that housing is impossible in the overcrowded city of Pusan. Since it's the only city in South Korea that has not been invaded by the Communists, everybody is heading for that area. Even though your sister had been evacuated as the spouse of a high official, the government could not guarantee housing for her." She sighed again, still twisting her toes. "I hope that the rumor is wrong. But then we can't take the chance. We simply can't afford to go through another war, can we?" Her eyes darkened into grimness.

"No, no Mother," I stirred from my stupor as events of the last invasion flashed before me. Mother still hesitated. Then she spoke in an imperative manner.

"I want you and Harmoni to stay in Seoul with the maid to guard your sister's possessions." She glanced furtively at me and went on. "You might be better off staying here after all. I really don't see how there would be another invasion. We'll return for you as soon as we find shelter in Pusan."

I could not believe what I had just heard. I was expected to respond, but my thoughts became confused and my words dissipated before I could form them. Silence filled the room as the clock ticked indifferently, awaiting my reply. While I wrestled with my emotions, Father sat frozen on his cushion like a cold statue, his eyes still fixed on the Bible. I wanted to cry out,

Aboji, say something! What has happened to you, the Father who used to comfort me and carry me on his back? Aboji, what has the war done to you? Don't you care what happens to me anymore? I know I have caused you much suffering, but am I not still your daughter? The words rolled around my tongue, but my voice could not break the ominous silence. Taking my muteness as a refusal to stay behind, Mother's face twisted. She turned the gold ring on her finger and stared at me vacantly.

"Well, that settles it. We will all have to stay here and go through another horrible war." Her voice sounded hollow and intimidating as if a robot had spoken. I wanted to throw my arms around her and beg her to take me along. But I surrendered to their will; it would be better if they survived.

"Y-y-yes, I-I will stay." The sickening words spilled out of my mouth as if a stranger spoke them. My head throbbed, and my stomach tightened.

"You are an obedient child." Mother let out a relieved sigh, and a broad smile spread across her face. "Don't worry. We'll return as soon as we can." She came close and stroked my trembling shoulders. I stiffened. Her touch made me shudder.

Father stirred and cleared his throat, but he avoided looking at me directly as he pushed up his glasses. He pulled out a small roll of paper money. "A little spending money for you until we return," Father muttered as he handed it to me.

"W-when will you be leaving Seoul?" I asked, still stupefied.

"Er, tomorrow, at noon."

If I had a magic potion I would have stopped the clock of life. But the dreaded noon of December 15, 1950, came all too soon for me. As if in sympathy, the sky spread a dismal gray blanket over the city. Minutes before the truck sputtered away, Mi Sook bounced in for the food supplies and my parents lifted her onto the back. *Why not me?* I shouted in my heart.

Swirling a flurry of snow behind it, the dark green truck carrying my parents, Mi Sook and Wha Sook pulled out of the driveway. The clock struck twelve, and the last gong echoed in my ears as I crumbled like a heap of ashes.

The tears I could no longer restrain poured down.

We can't afford to go through another war, can we? Can we? Can we? My mother's words echoed in my head. Harmoni, helpless to comfort me, left me alone. Not until night's darkness had invaded the empty rooms and hallways of the mansion, did my flood of bitter tears finally dried up.

With nobody else around except Grandmother, the mansion loomed eerily each morning when I woke up and every night as I fell asleep. Even Hyung-bu fled to lodge in other government quarters closer to his office. After my parents left, he seldom came to the mansion.

At the end of each day I tore off the number on the calendar, hoping that the next day my parents would finally come for us, but the days dragged on and on. One evening I noticed the date on the calendar was December 24, Christmas Eve. The most anticipated holiday had come this year without my counting the days. I tried to sing a few Christmas carols, but the words would not come out. I could only hum. Harmoni had already spread our bedding, and I had no one to rejoice with me.

"I shouldn't be sad on Christmas Eve," I told myself, but I could not shake my gloom. In all my fifteen years, I had never been away from my family at Christmas time. Deliberately, I forced my mind to recite the lyrics of "Silent Night."

> Koyo-hahn-bahm, koluk-hahn-bahm,
> oh-du-meh moo-chin-bahm,
> Ju-eh Bu-mo ahn-jo-so, kahm-sah ki-do tu-lil-te,
> A-ki jahr-do jahn-dah-ah, ah-ah-ki jahr-do jahn-dah.

I crawled into my bed and pulled the covers over my head so that Harmoni would not hear me crying. Slowly my thoughts turned to Christmas the year before.

All the families celebrated Christmas at church with a candlelight service, magnificent organ music, a choral presentation, and a Christmas pageant. Afterwards, the mothers spread a feast in the sanctuary. They served tray after tray of home-cooked festival dishes. At the end of the program, Santa Claus handed out trinkets to each child. We accepted our gifts with such wonder.

Then the young people, accompanied by the choir director and chaperones, walked all over the snow-covered village, stopping at each house where a lantern with the sign of the Cross was lit. Usually the hosts handed them gifts or invited them inside for refreshments. Our home was their last stop. My parents served steamy tok-kook,[26] dried persimmons, roasted chestnuts, fruits, and rice cakes. They played Chinese checkers, charades, Bible quizzes or yut.[27]

Reliving those memories, I drifted off to sleep. When I awoke, I felt sure I heard my mother's voice echoing from the kitchen. I hurriedly limped toward the kitchen calling, "Omoni? Is that you? Omoni, where are you?" Only my grandmother sat in front of the furnace, staring at me uncomfortably. I shrieked, "Omoni!" and dropped to the cold cement floor.

A few days later, while Harmoni and I were in the kitchen I saw a man glaring in through the glass in the rear door. His fierce black eyes terrified me and I screamed. Grandmother jerked and shattered a blue jar. But when she looked up, the awful face had disappeared. She stared at me as if to accuse me of imagining things again.

If that man returned, there was no one here to protect

---

[26] rice cake soup topped with savory beef strips, shredded egg, and vegetables

[27] a Korean game traditionally played on New Year's Day

us. I harbored my fear alone. When my brother-in-law stopped by one evening, I told him about the stranger. He looked gloomier than before and told me curtly, "I plan to get you out of here and move you into my own house. The smaller place will be safer." That comforted me a little.

On the last day of December, Hyung-bu came with a truck, a driver and Soon Ja to move the furniture and the rest of his possessions. Harmoni went through the cupboard and packed small sacks of rice and barley, several jars of condiments and a huge crock of kimchi. Soon Ja seemed about my height, four feet, but despite her frail body, she carried huge bundles on her head without any effort. Brother-in-law walked around the mansion one last time, piled the three of us in the back of the truck, and got into the front seat.

I had not been outside since I came to Seoul a few months earlier, and the fresh air lifted my spirits. Once we turned into the main street, I noticed a great crowd of people – men with enormous bundles on their ji-geh[28] and women balancing equally large loads on their stout heads, all hurrying in the same direction we were. I wanted to ask my brother-in-law about them, but I restrained myself.

The house stood at the dead end of a quiet street. Hyung-bu unlocked the huge padlock and opened the gate to let the truck into the courtyard. The first room we entered faced the gate and the living room and bedrooms faced the inner court. I hadn't been here other than a weekend visit during the first year of my sister's marriage. I recalled the fun I had had with the newly married couple.

The driver helped Hyung Bu carry in the last piece of furniture and left the yard. Brother-in-law bolted the gate from inside and came in through the inner room. Without

---

[28] A-frame backpack

saying a word to any of us, he strode toward the foyer to leave. Frantically I limped behind him,

"Hyung-bu, how long will we have to wait here? When will my parents come for us? And all those people I saw on the street today - were they refugees heading for the Han River? Please, tell me, when will you come back again?" His jaw tightened and without even blinking an eyelid in my direction, he reached down to open the front door. "You are coming back for us before the Communists flood into Seoul, aren't you?"

He did not answer or turn toward me. I could only see his handsome profile, now twisted with grimness and distress. A gust of icy wind swept into the house, as he left without looking back.

What has happened to him? Had the prestige of his public status caused him to become arrogant or was he as frightened as the rest of us?

Now what would become of us? Father had always said that the outstretched hand of God protected us. Would He watch over us?

Listlessly, I returned to the inner room and untied my bundle. I had a comb, toothbrush, soap, one towel, a Korean flag, and the small Bible, which my father had given to me before he left. I peered into a crate near the kitchen and looked over the food we had brought with us. The provisions would last a month at the very most.

Interrogation

Soon Ja and I wandered out to the main street near the house. Black smoke columns hovered about the city. Citizens who had remained in the city to guard property now dashed about, as if doing a macabre dance to the accompaniment of distant explosions. In the midst of this chaos, Soon Ja exclaimed, "Look! That woman has a huge sack of flour on her head, and there's another!"

"Where did they get it?" I wondered. I hobbled forward and extended my hand toward the next woman I saw with a sack of flour. Without noticing us, she hurried on. Still we kept seeing people carrying more sacks.

"Please, someone tell me where you got the flour." But no one would bother to answer. "This is so unlike my people," I muttered. Discouraged, I stood there with Soon Ja and watched the parade of grim faces pass. Then a woman with two sacks on her head slowed her pace long enough to shout,

"Why are you just standing there? Go get some flour! The government has opened the flour warehouse to the public. If we don't take it, the enemies will!"

"Where is the warehouse?" She pointed the way and hurried on. Soon Ja and I started immediately in the direction she had come from. In the distance we spotted a crowd of people carrying sacks on their heads, shoulders or on ji-geh. As we neared the warehouse my heart sank. People stood packed, shoulder-to-shoulder, two blocks from the entrance. The mass hardly moved. It would be hours before we could get near the doorway.

"It would be foolish to go home empty-handed when we have come this far," Soon Ja said. We squeezed ourselves into the jostling, noisy mob, and in the confusion, I got separated from Soon Ja. I began shouting just like the rest of them. I was hopelessly sandwiched between frantic flour-seekers, and there was no way to pull myself out. Clutching my stick tightly with both hands, I tried to hop on my strong leg each time someone pushed me. Once I did not hop fast enough and fell down. I cried for help, but the noise scattered my voice. The mass trampled me, kicking dust and flour into my nose and mouth. Their feet rubbed my hands into the ground and my fingers became raw and bloody. Again, a heavy foot stepped on me, but this time it was a man who forcibly pushed the others away and pulled me to my feet. Gruffly he told those around us to make room for me. His stocky body and muscular arms wedged me right in front of him until we arrived safely at the entrance. I thanked him for saving me.

Once inside he disappeared behind the stacks of flour. I had never seen such a gigantic warehouse. Even though hundreds of flour sacks had already been lugged away, piles still towered up to the high ceiling. Greedily I headed for the largest sack I saw, a fifty pound one. As hard as I tried, it would not budge. Finally I found a twenty-five pound sack. I was determined to take at least one sack with me even if I died in the attempt. I could not lift it, either. A pockmarked man helped haul it onto my shoulder, and somehow I crawled out of the warehouse. Once on the street I could only stagger a few steps at a time.

By now the explosions had grown louder and were spewing fragments of shrapnel through the air. I saw a girl running along and crying, her hands on her head in an attempt to stop the gushing blood pouring down her face onto her pink blouse. In panic I tried to move faster but only fell more often.

Dusk enveloped me. Snow covered the desolate road, and gusts of wind pushed drifts like hundreds of slithering snakes. I looked around for someone to help me, but no one was in sight. In desperation, I spilled half of the precious flour onto the ground and staggered on. Then I saw Soon Ja racing toward me. She had already carried her own load of flour safely home and was searching for me.

After we returned, Grandmother tenderly washed the cuts and grazes on my hands and feet. Soon Ja prepared supper and brought it in. Between mouthfuls I told Harmoni what we had seen that day. Even though signs of another invasion were inevitable, the flour secured us against immediate hunger at least.

It continued to snow, but the three of us warmed ourselves on the ondol floor, comforted by each other's presence. Before I crawled into my bed, I looked around for some place to hide the Korean flag, the Bible and my ID card, which was issued to me after the first invasion. I inserted the ID card between pages of the Bible and pushed it under the bedding closet along with the flag.

The following evening, just as we sat down to our meager supper, we heard an urgent rapping on the wooden gate. I thought it was my father or Hyung-bu banging anxiously at the entrance. Soon Ja dropped her spoon and eagerly dashed out to open the gate, but rushed back immediately, her face pale with terror and her coal black hair covered with fresh snowflakes.

"T-two men in rags. . . Coming!" Her eyes bulged, and she stammered breathlessly through chattering teeth. My heart skipped a beat as two complete strangers in tattered farmers' clothes barged into the inner room and stood before us. My courage vanished and my body became limp.

"Who are you? What do you want?" Harmoni found her voice first.

"We saw smoke from your chimney. We want food." We pushed our supper table toward them and retreated in a huddle to the far corner of the room.

After they devoured our supper, they began to smoke and to whisper to each other in Japanese. Neither Harmoni, nor Soon Ja, understood the language, but I listened carefully to what they said. From their conversation, I gathered that the Communists had re-invaded Seoul that afternoon and these two men were soldiers from the Republic of Korea (ROK) Army. They had been separated from their company and were wondering how to relocate their unit.

"Let's ask them to let us stay here overnight," one said. "We can't go anywhere now. We'll figure out the way back in the morning."

"Won't they be scared out of their hides if we ask them?"

The other man chuckled and said, "We can't help it. Ask them."

"We are not Communists," I told them. Their faces lit up, and they told us more about the fighting in the city.

"Just hold out until spring. This is a temporary military retreat. One of the reasons for our defeat now is that we were not equipped to fight the nimble-footed North Korean infantry during the winter months. They were trained for years in combat on foot during blizzards and on rugged mountains where the tanks and army vehicles couldn't maneuver.

"But come spring, we'll return and counterattack the enemies with UN Armed Forces, not only to Seoul, but right beyond the 38th parallel. We'll push up as far as the Manchurian border! Our forces will tear down the wall separating the North and the South. We will fight until our land is free and unified!"

We sat, captivated. In gratitude for the ray of hope, we offered to let them stay overnight. At that moment we would have risked the danger and kept them as long as they needed a place to hide.

However, after we retired into our separate rooms, the two men began to sing at the top of their voices. Still confused and worried, I worked out the words. They were bellowing ROK Army marching songs. Perhaps their own brave talk had encouraged them, but I was afraid that the Communists would hear or that these men were enemy informers in disguise or that if they were really what they claimed, the Communists would captured them. All night long hundreds of fears pounded through my brain. Exhausted, I fell into a troubled sleep.

We fed the men breakfast but waited to eat our own later. When they had finished, I worked up my courage and asked them to leave. I held out a third of the money my father had left me.

"Please take this money and leave us now. I fear what the enemies will do to us should they find you here."

Reluctantly they agreed to leave and stepped out onto the fresh snow. Relieved, I went with Soon Ja to the woodshed in the back yard to chop wood for the kitchen fire, but the piercing north wind chased us back indoors. Soon Ja made some roasted barley tea and we sat and sipped our bo ri cha leisurely in the inner room. Suddenly, we heard knocking at the gate again. My face stiffened, and my throat refused to swallow. We sat motionless, not knowing what to do. The pounding became insistent. Someone had to open the gate or it would be broken down. Soon Ja went. The caller wore a uniform with breeches and high black boots – the uniform of a Communist officer. Casually he questioned us about our living situation. How long had we lived there? Why didn't we leave with the other refugees? I answered as lightly as possible, trying not to reveal any information that might be damaging. Our parents' political affiliation and Hyung-bu's high official role in the ROK government raced through my mind as the officer pressed for more direct answers.

"And have you seen any strangers wandering about?" he asked. The officer must have sensed the tension in my stiff denial.

"You could not have missed them," he insisted. "Did they threaten you not to reveal their identities? Were the men old or young?" The questioning persisted. "What were the men wearing? Were they spies?"

I tried to sort all the questions and answers in my mind to make sure I had not let anything slip out. The more I tried to be careful, the more I seemed to contradict myself. My head throbbed as he pressed for information. His voice grew louder and sharper. All at once he grabbed my wrist and shouted, "What about the huge footprints in the snow outside your gate? Now, stop your senseless babbling and tell me. Who were they and where did they go?"

I was broken. "I-I-I don't know. All I know is that last night two men in rags burst in here, demanded food and left this morning." My mouth quivered, but I bit my lower lip until I tasted blood. Hysterically, I challenged my interrogator, "Go ahead and kill me! Kill us!"

Obviously startled by my outburst, the officer released his iron grasp on my wrist, leaving white finger marks on my skin. Clenching his teeth, he said hoarsely,

"That's all for today. But tomorrow you will report to our office for further questioning." Stepping into the foyer, he turned and glared at us, "Don't do anything foolish-like trying to run away. We know everything you do at all time. Report to me at once if any strangers come near here. You are living in a glass bowl. Remember that!" Terror and exhaustion overtook me as he stormed out.

As if reading my thoughts, Soon Ja promised, "I'll stay with you no matter what happens. Remember what the men said last night. We must hold out until spring."

"What good will that do," I snapped at her, "It's too late. We're hopelessly caught right now!"

Without answering me, she went quietly into the kitchen to prepare our supper. Only then did I realize that the interrogation had lasted right through lunchtime and into the late afternoon. While Soon Ja was cooking supper, we heard more rattling and banging at the front door. We held our breath, hoping it would stop.

"Open up or else," a deep voice roared. We had vowed never to open the door for anyone again, but he left us no choice. Reluctantly Soon Ja unlocked the door. A Communist soldier filled the doorway. Brushing Soon Ja aside, he swaggered in through the foyer and came to the inner room. He scanned the room with a dark piercing stare and growled, "Why didn't you open the door immediately? I saw the smoke in your chimney and knew somebody lived here. How many of you are here?"

"Three of us," I whispered. My mouth felt dry.

"How much grain do you have?"

We dared not answer. Harmoni strained to listen, and when she caught on that the soldier asked about grain, her wrinkled gentle face began to tremble and twist. She grabbed her rusty scissors and stood as straight as her frail bent body would allow. Breathing heavily she advanced unsteadily toward him. Holding out her scissors, Harmoni rasped, "Why don't you kill us with the scissors? Then you'll be free to take whatever you want."

The soldier seemed momentarily taken aback, but somewhat amused at the rash behavior of this daring old lady. Soon Ja and I tried to signal her to stop, but she went on. "Three years ago I escaped from North Korea barehanded," Harmoni shook her gnarled finger accusingly at the soldier. "You enemies stripped my son of everything he . . . ."

Horrified, I pulled her away from the man. Her statement had revealed our identity. I tried to cover it up.

"Please, don't pay any attention to my Harmoni. She is senile. She meant no harm," I hastily explained, but the soldier knew. In desperation I blurted out, "Sir, we were already questioned today. I was told to report any strangers who came to this house." The man narrowed his eyes. He seemed about to say something but apparently changed his mind and hastened out the door.

We were shaken to the very core. That night I tossed about restlessly. I could hear Harmoni moaning and Soon Ja clearing her throat repeatedly. In my fear and confusion I tried to pray, but "God in Heaven . . . ." was all I could say. I knew the Lord's Prayer and the Apostle's Creed by heart, but I found I could not find even these words.

I tried to take comfort in thoughts about the times my family had spent in evening devotions before the war. My mind pictured the whole family gathered submissively around Father. Weary from the day's chores, Mother sat with her eyelids drooping, my two younger sisters falling asleep in her Mother's lap. I liked to listen to the stories he read from the Old Testament about heroic men and women: Esther's passionate devotion to her people, Daniel being thrown into the lion's den. He made Bible stories interesting, but I raised my eyebrows when he insisted the miracles of

God had actually taken place. I silently mocked the thought of the Lord commanding Moses to stretch his staff over the Red Sea to part it and to allow the persecuted Israelites to walk through on dry ground. The seriousness of his countenance as he read would set me giggling audibly. He would glance at me sternly over his glasses and continue reading. God was way up in the clouds with a long white beard. It was impossible for Him to hear our prayers. Sheer nonsense.

Now in the dreadful solitude of this ominous night, Father's booming voice kept hammering in my ears, *God hears our prayers! By faith Moses crossed the Red Sea. God answers prayers!*

I kicked off my warm covers and threw myself onto the chilly ondol floor.

"Oh, God please help me!" All night long I drifted between empty prayers and nightmares.

The sound of pots and pans clanging in the kitchen awakened me. I found myself still on the icy floor next to my bedding. I shivered a little but waited for the floor to warm as Soon Ja cooked the breakfast.

I ran my fingers over the shiny floor and felt a pang of longing as I recalled the loving care and warmth of the secure days. I missed my parents terribly.

Soon Ja brought in a basin of warm water for me to wash up. Then she folded my bedding and put it back into the closet. After the breakfast I prepared to leave for my appointment with the interrogator. I wished I did not have to, but there would no way I could get out of it.

"Ai-go, Hyun Sook-ga," Harmoni clicked her tongue, "I wish I could go in your place. If only I could walk that far." She dabbed her moist eyes with the sash of her jo-gori and followed me to the front door. "Why did your father . . . .? It hurts me to see you suffer. Be careful, my child." Her tenderness weakened my already intimidated spirit.

I managed to stagger up the steps and into the gray concrete building that housed the Communist District Office. The guards stood rigidly on either side of the entrance. Another guard inside pointed me to a door at the end of a gloomy brown corridor. Passing closed doors on both sides of the hallway, I finally reached the office. My hand shook as I reached up to knock. Timidly I walked in.

The barren office was filled with smoke and a musty odor. An unlit pot-bellied stove stood to the left. The officer who had summoned me sat behind a wooden desk piled with stacks of documents. A skinny man in an old gray suit leaned on his desk littered with papers and two ashtrays filled with cigarette butts and ashes. With a lit cigarette between his smoke-stained fingers, he scanned some papers. The officer pulled out a stool and motioned me to sit in front of the man at the desk.

His bloodshot eyes examined me while he stroked a receding hairline. He looked as if he had been hiding underground for years. His sunken eyes under short coarse brows and his waxen face sent chills down my spine. After a spell of deep coughing, he cleared his throat loudly and lit another cigarette.

"Ahem! What is your name?"

"My name is Lee, Hyun Sook."

"Your age?"

"I am fifteen years old."

"Your address?" My body shuddered as he raised his voice. He yelled again.

"I said, your address!"

"I don't know, sir."

"Your parents?"

"I don't know where they are." His eyelids twitched and his jaw muscles rippled.

"What was your father's political party?" He pursed his thin grayish-brown lips, impatiently. Avoiding his eyes, I tried to think of safe answers. The man glared at me.

"Did you hear me? I asked you about your father's political affiliation!"

In panic I decided to lie, "My father was an ardent Communist. He told me to follow in his footsteps before he disappeared." My heart started pounding, and my ears felt like hot embers. His black piercing eyes seemed to look right into my thoughts. Clenching his fists the man bit his lower lip menacingly. Still glaring at me, he opened his mouth to speak, but instead his jaws hardened. He picked up a pen and tapped his lips with it. His silence threatened me like a knife held to my throat.

"How about the two men you entertained the night before last?"

"I didn't entertain them!" Unconsciously I became defensive. "They demanded food and left yesterday morning."

"Why did you let them stay overnight? Were they your friends?" Sarcasm twisted his words.

"No, sir, I had never seen them before in my life." The interrogation went on and on. While the thin man probed and pressed for more information, the Communist officer continued writing.

The man fished for another cigarette in his vest pocket. Crumpling an empty pack, he pulled out a worn leather pouch and removed some tobacco and a small white tissue. He put a few pinches of tobacco on the paper, rolled it into a cylinder, and moistened the edge with his tongue. As he lit the cigarette, his terrifying eyes glared at me. He stood up and paced about the room. The officer stopped writing and silently pored over a document. The man returned to his seat, took another long puff and blew circles of smoke into the stale chilly air. Curtly he turned and motioned the officer to follow him into an adjoining room. I waited. It seemed hours before they returned. The skinny man said, "Since you obviously can't go very far, we'll not confine you at this time. But, for your own good, I hope you have told us the truth. We shall find out who the two men were, who your parents are, their present location, and their political involvement!" His voice grew louder, "We will find out everything!"

I clutched my hands together to conceal the trembling of my fingers. All the blood in my body seemed to rush to my face, making my head throb. I ran my parched tongue over cracked lips.

If they did find out about my family, it would be the end. Suddenly I remembered Harmoni confronting the Communist soldier and blurting out more than she should have about my father. I felt as if someone had thrown a bucket of iced water at me. I would eventually die at the hands of these men unless I could figure out a way to hide.

Late in the afternoon they released me. Out on the street, a gust of freezing wind ripped through my thin jacket, yet I did not feel the cold. My eyes were so bleary from the whipping wind that I missed a patch of ice in front of me on the snowy sidewalk. My stick slipped from my hands and landed several yards away and sent me sprawling. The noise of the stick clattered in the dead silence of the deserted street. I crawled toward my stick, leaving patches of blood from my scraped hands on the ice.

I fell repeatedly on the frozen road. Finally at dusk, I made it home. Harmoni fussed over me while she dressed my hands. Soon Ja hurried in with my supper. Although I had not eaten since breakfast, nothing would slide past my throat. She poked her head in from the kitchen.

"Ai-go, the soup is cold," Soon Ja clicked her tongue. "Shall I reheat it for you?"

"No, don't bother. I don't feel like eating."

She nodded, picked up my table and left me alone. I was sorry that I had spoken curtly, but too proud to apologize to a maid, I sat brooding. Then without waiting for her to spread my mattress and comforter on the floor, I pulled down the bedding myself. It felt good to crawl under the thick pad of my comforter. My fingers ran over the brilliant red silk brocade trimmed with blue. Deeply immersed in my fears, I fell asleep.

The Frozen River

"Fire! Fire! Everybody outside!" A voice intruded on my sleep. Suddenly I found myself outside at an unknown location. People, young and old, darted about in every direction. Confused, I stood rooted to the ground. Red flames engulfed me.

"Help! Somebody save me," I screamed. I saw my father across the licking flames, but strangely he did not respond. He just flickered behind the fire.

"Aboji, how did you get here?" I shouted, "I heard the trains had stopped running, and bombs are exploding everywhere! I'm scared. Please help me," I implored. This time Father raised his hands beckoning me to him. The flames grew higher and hotter, but I dared to go through. Then, in an instant, the figure of my father disappeared.

"Don't go away! Aboji! Please don't!"

Startled by my own scream, I jerked myself out of bed. Awakened by my shriek, Soon Ja rushed in. Even Harmoni awoke and shuffled in behind her.

"I just had a nightmare," I explained, feeling embarrassed and foolish. "I'm sorry for the commotion."

"What did you see in your dream?" Harmoni asked, sleepily stroking my hair.

"Fire! The flames licked me. And I saw Aboji."

"Ai-go, you had a good dream. Fire in a dream is a good omen. My mother used to tell me that." Her age-dulled eyes glistened as she drew closer. I glanced at her with a tinge of annoyance.

"Harmoni, that is a superstition."

"You sound just like your father." She shook her head. "But it is supposed to be true. Well, I am going back to sleep." Harmoni yawned and shuffled out of my room. Her black ribbon tied to her silky white hair trailed behind her. Even though I had tossed it aside, Grandmother's interpretation of the dream comforted me. I buried my head under the comforter and brushed away my tears.

Nearby explosions shook the house and echoed throughout the deserted city at frequent intervals. Gradually the whistle of flying shrapnel grew louder and the shrill noise made me shudder each time. In the midst of the din, Harmoni's soft snoring slid through the sliding door. How could she sleep through this terrifying mayhem? I wondered. Any minute a bomb could land right on us, and the fear of death hung over me like a shroud. The thick comforter suffocated me, but I dared not poke my head out for a breath of fresh air.

Gloomy questions circled in my head. Would I die the death of an animal, or is there a way out of this? If this is all there is to life, why was I born? Where would I be after I died? Above these despairing thoughts, I heard my father's words echoing in my mind: *God hears our prayers. He answers prayers.* Abruptly I kicked off the cover and knelt on the floor, pleading to God.

"Jesus, if you can use me someday save me from the hands of my enemies. If not, please take back this useless life!" The rest of the night I prayed whenever I woke from intermittent nightmares. For the next three days and nights, I continued this routine. I wished I could just walk out of

Seoul. But that was not even a remote possibility with a leg like mine.

On the third night, however, I awoke to an extraordinary realization: I could walk out of Seoul. Carefully I pulled aside the blackout curtain and looked out. Not a star hung loose in the darkest sky. The only sound I could hear was shrapnel whizzing over the rooftops. I crawled quietly to Soon Ja in the room next to the foyer. I hated to wake her, but I could not wait until morning to tell her about the feeling that had just come to me. She yawned and rubbed her eyes, but when she grasped what I had to tell, she chattered excitedly.

"Really? You can come to my home and stay," her slanted eyes shone. "The trains have stopped running, but I know the way to my home by heart. We'll cross the Han River Bridge and take our time walking."

"How long will it take?"

"For you -- about three days." She sat up, her eyes wild.

"Three days!" I gasped, "I'll be worn out before we even reach the Han River!"

"But we have no choice. The longer we stay here, the more dangerous it'll be."

"We'd better go in and tell Harmoni of our plan," I said crisply. "I hope she will agree and come along with us."

Harmoni squinted her eyes at me for being awakened. "What has come over you in the middle of the night?" she demanded. Her droopy eyelids looked comical when she got cross. I tried to explain my midnight experience.

"Harmoni, I have been praying to God to save us. And just a little while ago I suddenly felt that I could walk out of Seoul!"

"My poor Hyun Sook-ga, a feeling is one thing, but reality is another matter," she snorted, still half asleep.

"But, Harmoni, this time it's different. I have never felt like this before! I somehow know that God will help us!" Vehemently I continued, "Besides, we really have no choice! The Communists know, I'm sure, that I lied to them about Aboji the other day. They only let me come home because they think I can't go very far."

"Please excuse me, Harmonim," Soon Ja interrupted, addressing my grandmother respectfully. "She is right. We must flee before they come again." She lowered her eyes, "They have a way of digging up anyone's past and . . . ."

"You children listen to me," Harmoni bolted upright, bitterness twisting her gentle face, "I have survived three invasions. I'll survive this one, too!" Her determined lips met in a firm, straight line. "I'd rather die in a house than die like a dog on the road. I've lived eighty long years. And I am ready to go any time. Just don't force me to die the miserable death of gak-sa."[29] She shook her frail, gnarled hands in protest. She, like all Koreans, dreaded the thought of dying while on a journey. Her voice faltered and her eyes glistened as she continued, "You are young and have a great future ahead of you. I'll be here waiting when your father comes for me. Now, go on!" She lay back down and pulled up her cover. Soon Ja and I stared at each other, not knowing what to do.

Back in my room, Soon Ja watched me carefully. She broke the uneasy silence by asking, "I know your feelings, but we are both asking the same questions. Do we leave Harmonim or do all of us stay?" She did not even blink her soft brown eyes. Her little round lips twitched as she groped for the right words. "They will do something horrible to you because you lied to them. But what could they do to your grandmother? They are Communists, but they are of the same blood -- Koreans. And they have grandmothers, too.

---

[29] to die while on a journey

I'm sure they won't harm her." Her common sense and composure impressed me, but as she talked guilty feelings spread through my heart like poison. A scene from my early life in Tientsin flashed before me.

I saw myself playing with a classmate near our maids' quarters. A beggar woman had come pleading for food under the window. My friend and I glanced at each other, and then at the clay dough in our hands.

"There's some leftover rice. Let's make a rice ball stuffed with clay. She'll munch away and . . . ."

Now in the darkness, I felt my face flush with shame and remorse. "O God, I am so sinful! I am awfully sorry for all the wrong things I have done. Could I be forgiven, too? O Jesus, I am about to be destitute. Maybe, maybe I ought to be dead."

"Miss Hyun Sook, please listen!" Soon Ja shook me violently. "We have no time. We must leave here before the sun rises. Don't you realize what the enemies will do to us if we stay?" Without waiting for my consent, she dashed into the kitchen and brought out a dusty old knapsack and a few leftover steamed buns that she had made for supper the night before.

"I found this knapsack hanging on a peg in the woodshed," she said. "I used it last summer when I visited my family during the invasion. I thought I would never need it again." She looked around the dimly lit room. The bedding would be too bulky to carry. She had a few changes of clothing, but I had only the thin jacket and the long baggy pants I wore. I brought out my Bible from under the bedding closet and flipped through the pages for my ID card. The pocket of my jacket would be too risky a place to hide my ID card should we be frisked on the road. I slid it between the two layers of socks worn over my weak foot. Then, I held my Bible and wondered whether to take it with me or to leave it behind. Soon Ja took it from my hands and placed it in the knapsack. She added her clothing, our combs, the buns and a box of matches. Haphazardly I looked around, trying to figure out what else to take along. I pulled out the flag from its hiding place and started wrapping it around my waist, next to my skin. Soon Jan strapped the knapsack, but when she saw the flag, she gasped.

"Oh, no, Miss Hyun Sook! That's too risky! If they should search us on the road and see that, they'll kill you right on the spot!" She swiftly unwrapped it from me and pushed it back under the bedding closet.

Gently but firmly she grasped my wrist and led me out into the dark, moonless night. My heart ached with guilt and sorrow as we left Harmoni behind and set out. The crackling sound of our footsteps on the deep snow frightened us. We hunched our shoulders like two spies being pursued by enemies. I kept looking back. We walked and walked. It felt as if my feet were chained to the ground. Even in the below-freezing temperature my jacket became drenched with cold sweat.

I breathed a prayer of thanks for the snow on the sidewalk. Bare ice meant slipping and falling. Nevertheless as exhaustion crept through me, I sighed for my father's strong back.

When the black sky began to lighten over the mountain peaks, Soon Ja said we were not far from the Han River Bridge. I continued to pray and struggle on, and as I prayed something strange happened. Instead of limping and dragging on with the stick, I began dashing forward using the stick like a pole vault. We became exuberant and giggly as I vaulted along.

Nearly forgetting our peril, I bumped into something solid and stumbled. A straw rice sack had been thrown over a corpse, which sprawled against a crumbled red brick wall.

Gray matter tinged with blood, oozed out of his shattered head. Goose flesh crept over my whole body. Muffling our screams, we scurried away.

My heart throbbed violently as dawn slowly unveiled the new morning. Seoul, the capital city of once free South Korea, home of ancient palaces existing in exotic harmony with towering modern buildings, was now a holocaust of destruction and desolation.

In the early light, we saw other southbound refugees emerging from all directions. Every one of us headed for the Han River like an army of ants toward an open sugar jar. Old folks hobbled with canes trying to keep up with the young. Some squatted down on the snowy sidewalk in despair, unable to continue. Farmwomen carried crying babies tied to their backs and balanced gigantic loads on their stout heads. We passed a screaming infant still fastened to her dead mother, lying facedown in a pool of blood. Over the noise of the explosions, frantic parents shouted for their missing children. A waif, wrapped in a quilt, sat on the snow gnawing at a crusty rice ball, oblivious to the commotion about her.

My expectant heart sank when we saw the Han River Bridge. The bridge, our sole hope for survival, lay before us completely demolished. I felt sick. My legs weakened and I dropped down on the icy riverbank. I stared at the frozen river and listlessly followed flaming columns of smoke up to the sky where they spread like storm clouds.

"O God, You let me believe I could get out of here." I cried resentfully. "I can't walk on ice. What am I to do? Why don't you just let me die now!" Soon Ja crouched in front of me, trying to console me.

"Go on! You're free to go to your home. Just leave me alone," I yelled at her, but she would not budge. My head felt like a cotton ball.

Then something unexplainable happened. I became aware of a pushing sensation on my back, as if someone impelled me forward. I turned to look. No one was behind me. Soon Ja still sat in front of me. Obeying the impulse, I picked up my stick and stood up. Soon Ja's face lit up as I moved again. Together we walked toward the river, now a sheet of glazed ice. Before I knew it, we were among the other refugees trudging across the frozen Han River. Even as we walked, I could not understand how I, with my withered leg, was able to remain upright on that sheet of ice, let alone move across it. Such a thing had never happened to me before. But, as if I were in a dream, I kept moving.

Soon Ja's shouts jerked me back into awareness. "Miss Hyun Sook," she clapped her hands, "We crossed the frozen river, and you didn't fall, not even once!"

I looked around in amazement. The rhythm of war continued. Shrapnel shrilled inches over our heads, and the nearby explosions almost swept me off the ground, but I stood still without shrieking or flinching. My desolate and hopeless heart began to fill with peace and hope I had never experienced before in my life. I turned my head toward heaven and thanked the Lord.

"Aboji, you were right!" I whispered. "God did perform those miracles in Moses' time. The same God performed one for me just now."

God's Protection

Confidence replaced the defeated spirit within me. I no longer feared death. Soon Ja and I walked confidently through the streets of Yong-Dong-Po. All the stores along the sidewalk looked abandoned. Shattered doors and windows exposed their shambled interiors. Direct hits had reduced most of the buildings to heaps of rubble. The bombing increased as the sun climbed higher. We decided not to risk the streets in daylight and hunted around for a suitable refuge.

At last we found a shabby store. Parts of the front wall and the sides were wrecked. Nothing remained but a broken stool, a rusty brazier, and rubbish. We stepped inside and went through a passage into a murky back room. A small window diffused a glimmer of light on a barren room. The floor was cold, yet it felt good just to sit down somewhere with a roof over our heads.

After a while Soon Ja unwrapped the steamed loaves. We could not bite into them for they had frozen dry, so we scraped the edges with our front teeth. Dejectedly, we tossed them back into the knapsack.

"Maybe we can find something to eat in the kitchen," Soon Ja suggested. We rummaged through the debris but found only a small packet of cornstarch. "What could we do with that?" she muttered as she put it into the knapsack. Hungry as we were, we dared not risk a fire in the kitchen stove for fear of being discovered. Instead, we curled up on the dusty floor and slept, occasionally awakened by the frightening noises.

"Miss Hyun Sook, it's getting dark," Soon Ja gently shook me as she spoke.

Rubbing my eyes, I sat up and mumbled, "All right, let's start again."

We staggered out into the darkness. While we rested in that cold shelter, night had spread itself across the sky like black paint spilled over blue satin. Not even the faintest glimpse of a star lit the sky. We groped our way through narrow back alley roads. The infrequent explosions gave just enough light to guide our way. Whenever we passed a Communist patrol, I breathed a silent prayer, and we tried not to look like runaways.

As we came near the foot of a hill, something suddenly exploded in the void before us like fireworks, illuminating the whole area. We looked at the desolate land around us. At that moment our world looked like an uninhabitable planet. Then, without warning, bombs began dropping everywhere. It was impossible to guess where the next one might explode, so we moved on blindly, hoping the next bomb would not crush us into the ground like a couple of ants. As frightened as we were of the bombing, we were able to take advantage of the imposing glow it cast across the sky, lighting our path. Goaded solely by our will to live, we pushed on. At last the bombing subsided and the brilliant light faded away.

Towards dawn, we stopped to rest in a deserted farmhouse. I fell asleep, but the shack shook as if hit by an earthquake. We dashed out and kept going. We found ourselves on a smooth thoroughfare lined with leafless poplar trees. I felt uneasy about the area, for there was neither a house nor a human to be seen. "After we reach the last tree on the pavement, we'll rest," I told Soon Ja, but the road led us on endlessly. The tree trunks merged into a line, and the last tree refused to appear. It was an effective ploy. We persisted and I marched on.

My leg numbed and ached, but after walking so long, sharp pains drove into my ankle at the site of the sutures and deep into the bone. Yet motivated by the comforting expectation of sitting in Soon Ja's home, I ignored the aches and blisters.

Around mid-afternoon, we met an old lady with a large bundle on her head. She called out in an authoritative voice, "Children, let me join you. I am glad to see people other than enemies!"

"Oh, please do," we replied, just as delighted as she seemed. We called her Harmoni, a title of respect for elderly ladies as well as the word for grandmother. As we trudge on, she told us she had lost her family and now traveled alone. We walked on, each deep in own thoughts. I missed my own grandmother terribly and wondered what would happen to her. I wished this companion were my own Harmoni.

As evening drew near, I noticed the older lady was breathing heavily. "Wait, children," she said, "I can go no further. Let us take refuge in that deserted house off the road."

Although the left wing of the house was destroyed, we could still see traces of wealth etched into the deserted mansion. Impressive brass dragons, now tarnished, adorned the gate of the tile-roofed entrance. The center of the court presented remains of an artistically landscaped rock garden. To the left, a goldfish pond in the shape of the Korean map lay frozen and lifeless. The shards of frosted glass panels from windows and sliding doors littered the ground. As we stepped into the kitchen, our eyes widened. The whole kitchen wall, cracked deeply from bomb vibrations, was made of milky porcelain tiles. Soon Ja opened the kitchen stove and found some half-burned wood buried under the ashes.

"I think it's safe here," she said, carefully striking one of our precious matches from the knapsack. "No one will see the smoke coming from the chimney."

Soon she had water boiling. We looked through the cupboard, hoping to find at least some tea leaves but discovered nothing. Soon Ja remembered the small packet of cornstarch we had found in Yong-Dong-Po.

"Well, shall we see what cornstarch gruel tastes like?" she asked, waving the packet in the air. "I'll try adding a pinch of salt!" She picked up a pale green salt jar, covered with dust. "Please go into the inner room. I'll be right in with my new dish." Her eyes twinkled impishly.

The adjoining room was absolutely bare of furniture. A thick blanket of dust covered the floor. Cobwebs hung lazily from the corners of the high ceiling. Every one of the windowpanes facing the court was shattered. We squatted on the cold floor blowing lukewarm breath onto our purplish hands. In a few minutes, Soon Ja entered with bowls filled to the brim with the cornstarch gruel. "Please drink it while it is hot. This will warm our chilly bones."

We were giggling and sipping the steamy gruel, when the sound of heavy footsteps approached the room. Brandishing a bayonet, a greasy-faced North Korean soldier kicked the door down and barged in. His darting eyes glanced first at the old lady, then at Soon Ja and finally rested lustfully on me. The hefty boots clunked slowly toward me. I shuddered and dropped the bowl, spilling it. Feeling like a trapped animal, I scooted backwards until I pushed myself against the icy unyielding wall. His coarse, stubby fingers reached out to caress my numb cheeks. My throat refused to choke out even a whispered protest.

"Comrade, don't be afraid," the soldier spoke thickly. "Let's enjoy life while we can." He crouched down in front of me as he wrapped his arms around my shoulders. My body convulsed, and my stomach turned almost losing the gruel.

"Wait a second, good soldier," the old lady spoke calmly, yet with the same authoritative voice we had heard earlier that afternoon. "We haven't had a grain of rice to eat for two days. See what we are drinking?" She raised her steamy bowl, "Watered down cornstarch." The soldier turned his head to look at her, somewhat mollified by her tone. "You'd be wise to feed this maiden first . . . ."

Her words evoked a mysterious power. The flimsy cobwebs on the ceiling ceased shimmering while we held our breath. The colossal soldier lazily stood to his feet. Deliberately he dug for a cigarette and pulled one out. Placing it between his teeth, he lit it, all the while gazing at me with smoldering eyes. Then, with a contorted smirk, he swung around and left.

Terribly shaken, I wept. The old lady hugged me tightly. Then abruptly she ordered, "Children, we can't dawdle. Let's be gone before the evil one returns!" She grabbed our wrists and briskly led us out into the dusk, leaving her bundle behind. We headed toward a track leading up to a hill behind the mansion. Even though refugees had chopped down most of the trees, this path still had some. The branches would give us some protection against discovery by the soldier. I stumbled repeatedly on rocks and tree trunks. Soon Ja practically dragged me up the slippery trail.

"No need to fear, children," our protector said. "We'll be many hills away when the enemy returns!"

Halfway up the hill, we glanced back through the pine trees. Below us, the deserted mansion appeared helplessly small and naked. The smoke still billowed from its chimney, as though the house pleaded to be shielded from the rampaging hands of the intruder. As if reciting a poem, the old lady said, "Preserve yourself for the man you shall marry some day. A molested maiden is like a broken bowl."

She urged us to continue our flight. We could barely keep up with her adaptable feet on that rugged trail. All night long we hiked. The crunching of our footsteps on the snow broke the dreadful silence. Not until dawn did our protector lead us down to the main road. They both sat down with me on a rock to rest since I could not take another step. The sun broke through the trees as we stood up to resume the journey. Our companion told us that the road would lead us to our destination. As the surroundings began to look familiar, Soon Ja grew excited.

That morning passed more quickly than any other day, and we chattered happily the entire time. I cannot recall at what point, when or where, but our precious protector disappeared from us just as mysteriously as she had joined us the day before. We wept and called for her, but only the mountains mimicked our voices in derision. She was nowhere to be found, and we felt deep loss and grief.

"Do you suppose she could have been an angel in disguise?" I asked Soon Ja. "Could God have sent her to deliver us from that evil soldier?"

She pulled my arm, silently leading me forward. Toward evening she spotted a lone straw-thatched farmhouse huddled at the base of the mountains.

"Somebody is living in that chomahk," Soon Ja pointed. "See the dim light and the smoke curling up from the chimney!" I stood frozen when I caught sight of it. I had heard too many spooky stories from my grandmother about a lone straw-thatched shack deep in the mountains. I recalled a tale about a fox disguised as a beautiful woman who transformed the chomahk into a palace to lure the woodcutters and how they became the prey of the sly fox. Oblivious to my fear, she pulled me forcibly to the shack. I almost tripped. She rapped urgently on the dilapidated wooden gate. We stood there until a woman came and peered out through the crack in the gate. Seeing only two girls, she undid the bolt and let us in.

"What on earth are you doing, two maidens out alone?" she asked in whispers. I felt relieved that she was not a beautiful woman.

"We are heading for my home on the other side of the mountain," Soon Ja answered, "But it's getting dark, and we are afraid. May we come in and rest?"

"I must ask my parents-in-law," the woman said, disappearing into the house. She returned shortly to tell us that we could come in, and led us into the main room where her in-laws sat side by side on coarse cotton cushions.

An old man picked up his two-foot long bamboo pipe and stuffed it with tobacco. He put the pipe to a red piece of charcoal in the brazier and took short puffs. Looking at us over his bifocals, he asked, "Whose children are you?"

"I am from the village on the other side of the mountain, sir," Soon Ja answered politely and identified her clan.

"Well, that's my wife's clan, too. Welcome! What brings you here?" His eyes lit up. We glanced at each other and then told them of our predicament and of the South Korean soldiers' prediction of the UN counterattack in the spring.

"Our son joined the ROK Army before the war," he said, letting out a long smoke-mingled sigh. "He is somewhere in hiding from those red devils right now. My mind is relieved to hear this good news." His eyes held a faraway look. Then suddenly, he shouted to his daughter-in-law to come in from the kitchen. "Listen, your husband will be returning in the spring!" He cleared his throat. "This child is one of our clan. Bring in the supper table for these children, also." The hopes of seeing their son and husband again left the two women speechless. Tears ran down their cheeks.

It is customary for Koreans to refuse politely when something is offered, except at the consent of one's parents and only after it has been offered several times. But now, neither Soon Ja nor I could take the chance of passing up a good meal after starving for three days. We just bowed our heads in gratitude and picked up the chopsticks.

The barley, eaten only by the poor, never tasted so good. The bean paste soup with dried turnip greens and the briny coarse green kimchi so filled our shrunken stomachs that when we finished, we felt as if we had dined at a king's table.

Early the next morning, we thanked the kind family and left with renewed strength. We almost felt carefree with the world at our feet as we started off toward Soon Ja's home. "See the mountain ahead of us," she exclaimed as she pointed with her little hand. "After we go around it, we'll come upon a hill. My home is at the foot of that hill. It's not too far now!"

Eager to reach her home, we quickened our steps. We passed the mountain by midday and reached a sleepy village. Farmhouses were strung along both sides of a broad dirt road. Snow covered the rice paddies and mountains, but the road was clear. The whole village looked completely deserted with not a sign of life. Not even a dog barked. Too anxious to reach our destination to anticipate any danger, we sang merrily as we strolled along the road.

Suddenly a roaring sound came out of nowhere and a fighter plane zoomed over the mountains. Shattering the still air with its shrill noise, the plane swooped down to just a few yards above the rooftops. It flew so low I could see the pilot looking down. The plane circled once and then flew away, only to return seconds later. The nose of the plane aimed near where I stood in shock. Soon Ja scampered out of sight. In panic, I stuck my head into the cornstalk fence. The pilot shot at the farmhouse, seemingly at me. Six-inch long shells pelted the yard, kicking up smoke and dust. Then just as fast as it had appeared, the bomber disappeared behind the mountains.

I struggled to pull my head out of the fence after the plane had vanished, but my eyes caught sight of a Communist soldier staggering out of the chomahk, groaning. Fresh blood dripped from his hand, and blood from a head wound gushed down his face and onto his padded ochre uniform. Still in a daze, I pulled my head out of the fence and crawled across the road. Hoping to be shielded from further danger, I crept behind a wooden gate.

Then I heard a shrill voice call out for all to assemble. Hurrying footsteps followed. "The enemy fighter plane spotted us. We must relocate immediately." The voice struck fresh terror into my heart as it continued, "If you find two girls, capture them. They might be enemy contacts!"

"O God, please don't let them find us." Cold sweat poured down my back. I stayed there without moving and barely breathing until long after the footsteps died away behind the village. Cautiously, at last, I peeked out through the gate. I saw Soon Ja, creeping along the mud walls, searching for me. When she saw me waving my arm, she ran over to me. We hugged, cried, and then laughed at each other. She had been hiding under a haystack and was covered with straw. Giggling at me, she said I looked like a chimneysweep as my face was streaked with mud and soot. With the edge of her sleeve, she wiped my face.

"I think we ought to go on," she said solemnly.

"What if they spot us?" I balked.

"I don't think they are still here. Besides," she bit her lip. "I don't want to cross that last hill after dark." Her eyes clouded, "There are beasts . . . and graves. . . and ghosts."

Wild animals and ghosts! My heart drummed. Impulsively I cried out, "Let's go then!" Tired as I was, I managed to continue without too much trouble. The anticipation of meeting her mother and her two brothers carried us on, but most of all the thought of eating supper on a warm ondol lent us the motivation we needed. When we passed by the cemetery, instead of being scared, I envied those resting under the ground totally immune from war, hunger and fear.

At the crest of the hill, Soon Ja cried out, "Look! Can you see that house to the left of the hill?" She waved her hands and pointed at the smallest chomahk at the edge of the village. "That one with the chimney smoking. We're home at last!" She gasped with excitement. She picked up two broken branches from the ground, and said, "Squat down and hold onto me like this." She sat down in front of me and began to pull us forward, using the two sticks to propel us down the hill. Several times the bumpy spots on the icy trail bounced us off our course. I panted from the speed.

"Don't be scared," she shouted. "I used to do this all the time with my younger brother!" Forgetting our recent scrapes with bombs and planes, we squealed and giggled all the way down to the foot of the hill. The sun sank reluctantly behind the mountains, leaving a magnificent array of red, orange, and purple.

"That's my home!" She raced toward it. To her the sight of her home must have been as welcoming as a mansion, though I saw only a farm hut with mud-plastered walls and a faded straw roof. "Omoni! Omoni!" She called to her mother as we rounded the cornstalk fence. I felt a rush of unfathomable sorrow and loneliness. If only I could call my own parents.

A middle-aged woman came out of the low door, her face registering joy and surprise to see her daughter again. Soon Ja's two brothers also came out and hovered about her, but I stood off to the side, longing for my own family.

Unwanted

"Who is this girl?" Soon Ja's mother asked, finally noticing me in all the commotion.

"Omoni, she is Hyun Sook, the sister of my mistress."

"What is she doing here?" Her eyes glowered at Soon Ja, demanding an answer.

"Omoni, we barely escaped the Communists. She has no place to go now. Please, Omoni, let her stay here with me until the war stops."

"Get inside! We'll have to talk this over with your elder brother."

While they conferred, the beautiful sunset burned itself out into an oppressive, dark, void. I stood outside feeling unwanted.

At last Soon Ja came back out. "I got a very bad scolding," she muttered sullenly, "but you can come in now. Just don't say anything, no matter what they say to you."

Though unwelcome I limped into the small gloomy hut. The partition between the kitchen and their only room was patched with old newspapers upon newspapers. The walls had been roughly plastered with mud and straw. Coarse brown paper covered the ondol floor. There was nothing in the room except two sets of comforters, three pillows, a plain wooden chest and an oil lamp stand that looked like a cat's scratching post.

I sat down, feeling like a sandbag, in the farthest corner where the ondol heat did not reach. Their contempt felt worse than the daily harassment I got from children before the war. Soon Ja headed for the kitchen to bring me some food, but her mother grabbed her arm, and hissed, "She can go out and get it herself! You're no longer a maid!"

Choking down my humiliation, I slithered out to the tiny cubbyhole kitchen for something to eat. The fire was dead, and the soybean paste soup was already cold. All the cooked barley had been eaten except for what stuck in the bottom of the pan. Tears welled up as I squatted down to scrape off the crust. The chipped earthenware soup bowl felt as cold as ice. I spooned in what I had salvaged and lifted the bowl up to eat. I sighed shivering in the cold wind. Just then, a huge mouse poked its ugly head from a corner of the crumbling wall. I screamed and dropped the bowl.

"What's that noise all about," Soon Ja's mother yelled.

"A-a mouse," I stammered.

"Better get used to it," she retorted curtly. "There are plenty of them around here."

In the murky kitchen, I hurried to finish and get back into the room. The mother and her two sons stared at me in disgust as they picked lice from their clothing.

"Soon Ja's mother," I said respectfully in the proper way, "Thank you for taking me in."

She made no reply. "I hope I won't be too much trouble to you. Right now I have nothing, except a little money." I pulled the small roll of money from my pocket and offered it to her with both hands. Without hesitation she took my money, and her face softened somewhat.

Soon Ja rolled out the bedding, which was stacked neatly in the far corner of the room. The brothers shared one set, and she and her mother the other. As soon as her mother blew out the lamp, she let me lie by her side. The darkness silently enfolded me. In my heart, I vowed that I would tolerate any humiliation or suffering as long as I could find my family again.

As the days went by, Soon Ja's attitude toward me began to change. She no longer seemed to be the same loyal, daring girl who looked after me. During our escape she marshaled our morale, made the decisions and consoled me when I became discouraged. She had become whiney, often pouting and arguing with her younger brother. She would ask me to go to the outhouse with her after dark, and no longer showed any concern about my welfare. It bothered me at first, but soon I adjusted to my new role. I had become just another unwanted mouth to feed.

About two weeks after we arrived, I noticed some pieces of meat floating in the soup bowls. It smelled rather odd, but anything tasted good to an empty stomach. Just as I swallowed my first mouthful, Soon Ja complained, "Eew! Dog meat! They don't eat dog meat in the city. I don't like it anymore." She grimaced and put her spoon down.

Soon Ja's mother snatched the bowl, saying, "Then I'll eat it. Too much fat lines your stomach!" She poured the food into her own almost empty bowl. I tried to pretend that I liked the dog soup but began to feel nauseated. The nickel spoon became coated like wax with the floating fat from the cooling soup. I simply could not put the spoon into my mouth again.

"I am not very hungry," I whispered sheepishly.

"All right. Nothing for either of you!" Soon Ja's mother glared at me.

After doing the dishes, I crawled into the room where she sat erect like a statue. "Come here. I must talk to you," she commanded slapping down the money I had given her on the night of our arrival. "Here, take back your money," she snapped.

"I know it isn't much, but it's all I have." I pushed the thin roll of paper currency back toward her.

"No, you keep it!" Stiffening her twisted face she shouted, "I have no use for this paper! You can't even buy a grain of barley with this stuff!" She flung the money at me. "You will leave my home tomorrow morning." Her statement stunned me.

"Oh, please forgive me for upsetting you at the supper table. I have never eaten dog meat in my life before. I just couldn't bear to swallow it." Soon Ja and her brothers sat watching the scene indifferently.

"I promise I'll eat anything you give me from now on. And if you'll let me stay until I find my family again, they'll repay you tenfold."

"Now, you listen," she yelled. "Any minute a bomb could fall on my head. I can't be bothered about tomorrow. I must feed my own right now!" A sneer crept into her voice as she went on, "If you weren't a cripple, my son could marry you, and you could be of some use to us."

My eyes blazed, but I suppressed my indignation and tried to reason with her. "Please, where could I go?" I reached out to touch her knobby, coarse hands.

"Don't touch me," she yanked away.

"If I must leave, could I please take Soon Ja with me? I don't know the way." As soon as these words spilled out of my mouth, I realized I had spoken foolishly.

"Has your soul left you?" she rasped in astonishment. "She stays here!" Her tone indicated finality.

All night long I lay awake wondering what I would do. Up to now Soon Ja had guided the way. The ghost of Aeja, who was mistreated and murdered by her stepmother, intruded my troubled thoughts. Soon Ja's mother seemed just as cruel. To be chased out of her home now seemed a worse alternative than being stabbed to death.

The next morning after a scanty breakfast, the woman spoke to me in a softer tone. "Don't hold a grudge against me. You'll understand after you have your own children."

"I won't hold a grudge," I replied. "I—I just feel lost. Thank you for keeping me even for these two weeks."

"My children will walk up to the hill with you. Tell them which way you want to go and they will show you the path." With that she disappeared into the chomahk and sent her children out.

Solemnly we walked. Strangely, with each step now, I felt little bits of courage well up inside me. Survival no longer even mattered, and I felt unafraid. The parting with Soon Ja was not as agonizing as I had anticipated the night before. It seemed almost adventuresome to be on my own for the first time in my life.

At the parting point on the crest of the hill, I hesitated. Though the desire to return to my grandmother overwhelmed me, I could not risk going back to Seoul. As badly as I wanted to go to Pusan in the South, I knew all the roads leading there were either blocked or converted into battlefields. I had no other place to go except Inchon. At least I might find someone there I had known before the war.

Few people traveled the path that Soon Ja's brother directed me to take. To keep myself from getting scared or lonely, I sang hymns like "What a Friend We Have in Jesus" and "I Can Hear My Savior Calling." From time to time I scooped up a handful of snow and tried to fill my stomach. Despite the sounds of airplanes overhead or of explosions, I just kept on singing and marching. Once in a great while an old man or a woman with a child on her back would pass me. Seeing another person gave me momentary comfort. I continued walking all day, stopping only long enough to rest and eat some snow.

Toward dusk on the second night, I reached the outskirts of Inchon. More people appeared as I approached the city. My tired body dragged my worn spirit down. I didn't know anyone in the city, and I felt lost and discouraged. Hoping against hope I would meet someone I had known, I searched for familiar faces in the crowd. Then walking in my direction behind a woman came a pretty girl with fair skin and rosy cheeks. As they came close I recognized the girl as Moon Hee. Limping toward my cousin, I remembered the pleasant days when she taught me to swim.

"Ai-go, Moon Hee-ya, it's like a dream to see you!" I called as our eyes met.

"Who are you?" she asked, stepping back. Her shocked question startled me.

"I am Hyun Sook. Don't you remember me?"

"Oh, no, Hyun Sook-ga, what on earth are you doing here alone?" she gasped.

"I'm searching for my family." For an instant I lost control and tears rolled down my cheeks, unchecked. "I don't know where to go." Fumbling for words, I reached for the comfort of her hand and asked, "Could I come with you?"

"Oh, no. I-I-I can't take you." She stepped back as if I had the plague. "I'm separated from mine, too. I mustn't lose my aunt. She's all I've got. Sorry. Stay well!" With that she raced after her aunt who had not so much as slowed down.

My last spark of hope snuffed out. Darkness wrapped itself around me like a shroud. I threw myself on a muddy snow pile along the road and hoped a bomb would fall on me.

Through the Hands of Enemies

An explosion wrenched me out of my stupor. A bomb burst on a house nearby. Carrying what looked like a baby in her arms, a woman dashed out of the burning building. She stared at the object in her arms and then at the flame-engulfed house. She started wailing as though someone had died.

"Ai-go, ai-go, I thought I grabbed my baby, but it's my pillow!" She threw it away and ran as she screamed, "Somebody help me! Help save my baby!" I stared after her, too numb to feel anything. The pitiful sound of her voice faded away as she trotted aimlessly up and down the streets.

Darkness had deepened so that I could see only the outlines of people hurrying by. I folded my arms around my legs and wondered how much longer it would take for me to freeze to death. Would the Communists leave my poor grandmother alone? My thoughts had returned to that horrible interrogation when someone shook my shoulder. I turned my head and gasped when I saw it was a Communist officer.

"Don't be afraid. I will not hurt you," he assured me. I stared at the dark outline from his black boots up to the visor of his cap.

"Why are you here alone?" Even though he spoke quietly, I could hear the commanding tone in his deep voice.

"I, I am waiting to die," I replied defiantly.

"Where is your family?"

"I don't know."

"Let me take you to my station."

"No! No! Please, I beg you, I have nothing more to tell." I backed up against the muddy snow pile.

"We are in desperate need of a kitchen helper. Come with me."

"No, please leave me to die."

"You will not be asked any questions." He sensed my terror. "And for your work, you will eat and have a place to sleep." Firmly he pulled me up and set me on the back seat of his bicycle. He sped through the streets, stopping at last in front of a tile-roofed house in a secluded area.

"Now, don't say anything. My name is Kim. If the others ask, you are an orphan. Understand?" he cautioned. In bewilderment, I nodded my head. I followed him through the wooden gate, across the courtyard to the huge kitchen where a plump woman stood busily scrubbing a pile of bowls.

"I finally found a girl to help you," he told her. I limped behind him.

The woman smoothed her coal black hair away from a round plate face with very small eyes, a tiny flat nose and flushed cheeks. The cold wind had chapped her small lips. She glanced at me and asked in disappointment, "Ai-go, what can she do?"

"You show her what you want her to do," he told her sternly. Whenever he stopped speaking his thin lips closed firmly below a sharp nose. "Do you have any leftover rice for her?"

The cook's face softened and her eyelids almost closed

as she feigned a smile. "Come, sit here." She motioned me to the low platform of the built-in cast iron pots, which spread across almost three feet in diameter. Noisily she lifted the heavy lids and rested them on the side. She filled two huge bowls, one piled high with rice and the other with meaty soup. Her plump hands scooped out a dish of kimchi. "There's more. Eat plenty."

I bowed. Had I been alone, I would have devoured the food like a savage. Officer Kim instructed me to come into the living quarters after supper and left the kitchen.

The cook began to chat about the bombing and complained how dangerous it was. I barely managed to agree between mouthfuls.

"I come to cook before sunrise and leave after sunset. Tomorrow morning you start the cooking fire before I get here," she ordered. I did not know how to start a fire but was afraid to tell her, so I told myself that I must try and replied that I would.

After the kitchen chores, I went obediently into the officer's quarters. I saw seven men in one spacious ondol room. A bedding closet stood opposite the door, several brass ashtrays were cast here and there and an oil lamp sat on a low wooden stand. A young officer with a disdainful expression sat behind a low desk, reading. My heart pounded.

"This comrade is our new kitchen helper," said Officer Kim. I bowed and went to sit in the corner of the room close to the door. The floor was warm and my legs and hands itched from the heat. The heavy atmosphere and my full stomach made my eyelids droop, and I yawned repeatedly. Officer Kim suggested that I go to sleep.

"There are three bedrooms, but the other two are being used as a storage area. We all sleep in this room." My face dropped. "Relax, we are all comrades." Since I had no choice, I curled up at the end of the room and slept undisturbed even by the explosions.

When I awoke the following morning it was still dark. I slipped into the kitchen and tackled the task of starting the fire. At first it seemed simple; the dry grass used as a starter burned fiercely, but quickly turned to ashes. Pretty soon I used up all the grass. I blew at the faint spark on the twigs. Only raw smoke belched back at me. To my relief, the cook walked in just then, waving her hands to scatter the smoke.

"Move over! You don't even know how to start a fire!" She clicked her tongue in disgust. Remembering Soon Ja's mother, I shuddered.

"Now go to the woodshed and bring some more dried grass and pine twigs," she yelled. Once out of the kitchen I got on my hands and knees to get to the shed faster. With an armful of grass and twigs, I hopped back inside. Squatted down beside her, I watched carefully without a word.

"I can see you are going to be a big help," she snorted. "First lay the grass on the bottom like this. Next, split the twigs into thin sticks and put them on the grass. Then pile up the split logs crisscross." I did not want to be kicked out of this place, too, so I made every effort to learn and work well. I tried not to get in her way, and any food she gave me, I ate.

Several nights later, I felt more tired than usual. I finished the chores of washing the bowls and sweeping the dirt floor as quickly as I could. In the quarters I excused myself earlier than usual and curled up in my bedding in the corner. It must have been the middle of the night when something awakened me. One of the officers put a folded towel over my mouth and hoarsely whispered into my ear, "Don't make a sound. Unless you do what I tell you, you'll be in trouble." He lay down next to me, exposing himself. I thrashed fiercely to free myself from his grip, but he only pressed the towel harder. "It's no use struggling. Everyone is fast asleep," he breathed on my neck. Still, I managed to swing one arm and hit his nose.

"Ai-go!" he groaned. While he rubbed his nose, I crawled toward the door, but he jerked me back to him. "You'll either get caught or bombed outside!"

"I'd rather die than do what you demand," I hissed back. By this time the others stirred and grumbled at him to be quiet. Reluctantly, my attacker released me.

Later, when the steady sound of snoring filled the room, I quietly slipped out into the kitchen. My teeth chattered as I leaned on the flat surface beside the pots, unable even to pray. My shoulders began to tremble, and I sobbed uncontrollably. I fumbled for a match and lit the oil lamp.

My head reeled, watching the thin streak of smoke curling up to the ceiling. Listlessly, my eyes caught sight of the beam across the top. Tales of horror that I had heard as a girl came back to haunt me. In one, a hopeless daughter had hung herself on the kitchen beam.

"Maybe the easiest way out of my misery would be to hang myself," I said half aloud. Nobody cared whether I lived or died anyway. The shadow of my body gave me an eerie feeling. I looked around the kitchen for a rope, quaking as though Harmoni was telling me the horror story for the first time. A huge rice sack with straw ropes beside it caught my attention, and I struggled to untie the coarse knots. My fingers became raw, but I wrestled on.

I noticed the chipped earthenware bowl that we used for measuring rice, and the bowl reminded me of the old lady who had rescued me from the hands of the lustful soldier. Her wise words of advice rang in my ears. *A molested maiden is like a broken bowl.*

A shudder ran through me, and I dismissed the thought of hanging myself. I had managed to remain undefiled after all, I reasoned. I need not kill myself. My hands dropped to my sides leaving the rope to dangle.

"What are you doing?" the cook yelled as she entered the kitchen. "You should have started the breakfast fire!" Her voice made me jump.

"I'm sorry. I didn't know it was already that time." I covered my face and began to cry. That made the cook very angry.

"Can't I scold you for delaying breakfast?" Her small eyes glared at me.

"No, I am not crying because you scolded me."

"Then, what is it?" Prying hands away from my face, she demanded to know. "You have been crying for a while. Your eyes are red and swollen."

"Oh, no!" I shook my head emphatically. I had no idea how to begin.

"Trouble or no trouble, I must know!" She grabbed my arms, her fingers digging into them. "What are you, an informer or a Communist? I've been wondering about you for quite a while. If you tell me truthfully who you are, I'll tell you who I am."

I looked at her round face. She was such a simple woman. Telling her would make no difference now. The worst thing anyone could do would be to kill me.

Slowly and fearlessly I explained to her about the separation from my family and Soon Ja's family and about how I had been brought into that kitchen. I ended with the incident that night.

"Ai-go, I'm relieved." She dabbed at her misty eyes with the tip of her white apron. "My husband and I had been married for several years," she began, but all at once she jumped up. "My spirit must have left me! We haven't even washed the rice yet!"

I scurried over to the rice sack, and with the chipped bowl, meted out the rice. Holding the bowl with both hands,

I looked at it for a second. I handled it gently as though it were a precious friend. The cook's experienced hands swiftly washed the rice and measured the water. In seconds she had the soybean-curd soup ready to boil. I watched her work in a daze as I fed the fire. Hurriedly I set the tables. While we waited for the rice to cook, she continued her story.

"Anyway, we owned a small farm and were very happy at first. But two years went by, and still I hadn't borne him any children." She blew her nose on the back of her apron and went on. "His family accused me of being barren. My husband became unhappy – no son to bear his name. One day he came home from the marketplace and told me that he had joined the ROK Army." Her narrow eyes blinked as she tried to stop the tears. "He left home last year about this time, visiting me once before the war. Now I don't know where . . . ." She just shook her head. I did not know what to say, so I just pressed her hand in sympathy. "I told these officers that I am the widow of a Communist. I had to lie to them because I had no food and was about to . . . ."

"Is breakfast ready yet?" an officer called from the next room.

We sat up like two frightened rabbits and answered simultaneously, "Yes, we will bring the tables instantly." Automatically we filled all the bowls, and as she carried out the first table, she whispered, "Don't reveal my secret, and I won't tell yours."

From that morning on, the kitchen became a place of comfort where I had someone in whom to confide and with whom to share my troubles.

That night after finishing the supper dishes, the cook went home, and I went into the living quarters. It startled me to see only the youngest officer in there. I felt uneasy around him, for he very seldom talked and carried an air of arrogance. I looked around questioningly.

"They are all out on an assignment. They will be back very late." He looked me over and beckoned to me. "Don't be afraid, Comrade. Come down here. It's warmer." I shook my head and remained in the far corner of the empty room.

"I am the senior officer." He cleared his throat. "Tell me about yourself." Was this going to be another interrogation? I wished the cook were still here. Futilely, I tried to make my way to the door, but he strode over and blocked my passage. Grabbing my wrists he pulled me to the opposite side of the room and embraced me. "Don't waste your energy. Nobody can hear you!"

"Oh, God, help me!" I cried.

"Ha, ha," he mocked. "There is no God! Stop that stupid talk!" His face was moist and his eyes turned dark as he shed his uniform.

"O Lord Jesus, help me. Help me, please!" I screamed, crossing my arms around me and grabbing onto my sleeves.

"Stop that nonsense!" he yelled, shaking my shoulders violently, "There is no God!"

Presently I lost all sense of fear. With my head I butted his chin. I bit his arm, wrist, leg, any place my teeth could reach. Filled with a strength I had never known before, I braced myself against the wall and kicked him with my healthy leg. We thrashed about the floor like two animals. I was determined to die rather than to be conquered by an enemy. I don't know how long we struggled, but finally he let go of me. I sat up, smoothed back my hair and straightened my jacket. He put on his uniform and lit a cigarette with trembling hands.

"You are very strong and quite a determined girl. I've never come across a girl like you." His wild, bloodshot eyes glared at me. "Stay pure. Some day when the war is over and this divided country of ours is unified, I'm going to come back and look for you."

I shuddered. I wanted to scream at him, but swallowed my words. He blew a long streak of smoke into the grim silence.

"Tomorrow, after supper you'd better go with the cook." He took another puff, and squinting his eyes, said, "It's not safe for you to spend the nights here."

The following morning I told the cook briefly what had happened the night before. She listened sympathetically and readily agreed to take me to her home. I found it to be a long trek, but those two close calls made the walk seem worthwhile.

The cook's house had only one bedroom. Her possessions consisted of a bedding closet, a brazier, two cushions covered with green cotton and an oil lamp.

Sometime after I began staying at the cook's home, Officer Kim came into the kitchen. He looked around and then pulled out two bars of soap with 'Lux' written on the wrapper. They smelled very fragrant. He whispered, "Hide them for me. I'll come here to get them one day." He had a strange expression on his face and almost opened his mouth to say something more, but the cook came in with the table just then. He put his finger to his lips behind her back and left.

I told the cook about the soap. "Do as he says. We'll hide them under my bedding closet."

As the weeks passed, the food supply dwindled drastically. Each day there was less left over for us to eat. The weather got warmer as the days passed, but the bombing knew no seasonal change. The idea that the war would end in the spring now seemed like an empty dream.

One night after an especially exhausting day, we fell into a deep sleep. After midnight a loud banging on the gate woke both of us. I kept my head under the cover waiting for it to stop, but the banging persisted. Finally the cook went out to check. To our relief it was Officer Kim. He hurried into the bedroom and said breathlessly, "I came for my soap."

I pulled the bars of Lux from the bottom of the bedding closet. Swiftly he stuffed them inside his undershirt and warned us, "Don't come to work tomorrow. You might as well know. We're pulling out now." He started for the gate but turned abruptly and said, "Don't step outside your gate tomorrow." With that word of caution, he faded into the dark night.

We sat shocked for a moment before we realized that the war had ended. We clasped each other's hands and shouted. The rest of the night we sat up talking about how would it be when we saw our families again. We reminisced about the happy days, but more than anything else, our words and thoughts kept turning back to the kinds of food we liked and wanted to eat.

The following day we stayed indoors. It would have been restful if only we had food. The cook went into her kitchen and brought in a packet of powdered milk, the only thing she had in the cupboard. We had no use for it. Koreans did not drink milk once we were weaned from our mother's breast.

"I toasted the last packet of milk powder to make it fit to eat," the cook chuckled. She placed a pan on the brazier, as she stirred the powder, it turned golden brown and filled the tiny room with a nutty aroma. It became tiny grains of airy morsels that tasted like saltless cracker crumbs.

"Tastes better than drinking that stuff," I muttered as it dissolved in my mouth.

The following morning, we noticed the world outside sounded unusually quiet. There was not even the sound of buzzing firearms. The cook got cleaned up and headed for the gate.

"I'm going to walk down to the camp. You stay here until I return." Alone in the room, I could hear my stomach churn. I squeezed my stomach, trying to diminish the hunger. The tin pan in which we had toasted the milk powder was still in the chilly room. I picked it up, hoping to find some left over. I found a few grains and placed them on my tongue, but they only intensified my desire for food.

As the bleak morning wore on and I sat alone looking forward to nothing except more hunger and uncertainty, I began to feel things crawling on my back, chest and under my arms. It felt as if an army of red ants had invaded my body and were attacking me. I scratched fiercely and peeled off my threadbare jacket and underwear. To my horror, I discovered multiple colonies of lice along the seams of my underwear and jacket with sizes ranging from clusters of transparent nits to full-grown lice as big as half a grain of barley. Large ones, fattened on my blood, swaggered about the seams, while the newly hatched lice swiftly scrambled into hideaways under the folds. Goose bumps broke out like a rash over my flesh. Shivering and sighing, I spent the rest the morning attending to the disgusting task of crushing the hideous vermin between my thumbnails as I had seen Soon Ja's family doing.

Toward noon I heard the gate burst open and the rushing footsteps of the cook. Hurriedly I draped the badly soiled clothes over my body. As much as I wanted to throw them away, or even better to burn them, I had no other garments to change into or soap with which to wash them. Just as I buttoned my jacket, the cook bounced into the room. Her cheeks were red from the cold wind and excitement.

"They fled," she shouted. "The Communists are gone! The villagers are swarming into the camp and looting anything they can lay their hands on!"

"Have they really gone?" I asked, not quite able to believe it. "Are we really free now?" My mind could not grasp it. I, too, had to go out and see how it felt to savor the freedom for myself. I stood up as if under a spell, and thanked the cook

for her kindness and care. She eyed me quizzically,
    "Where are you going?"
    I had no answer.
    "Hyun Sook, the outside isn't very safe yet." She broke
the chain of questions in my head by asking again, "Where
will you go? Where is your family?"
    "I don't know." I stood still, lost. Feeling awkward, I
smoothed my sleeves but only found another bare spot on the
elbow. "I'll just have to start looking for them." I started to
open the sliding door. She came after me and took my arm.
    "Please, Hyun Sook, do stay another day," she insisted.
"I heard that some Communist soldiers are sniping. What
if . . . ."
    Strange as it seemed, I felt that overwhelming need to
step out into the new air. "I'm not afraid. Really, I'll be all
right. Thank you for all you have done for me."
    "Well, I can't insist that you stay, I have nothing to feed
us," she sighed, reluctantly letting go of my arm. "Farewell
my little friend. Do be careful!" She walked me to her
weather-beaten gate and stood waving her arm until a turn in
the dirt road separated her from my sight.

Sitting Duck

Aimlessly I limped toward Inchon. In spite of the wreckage everywhere, I sensed an air of vitality among the people. Down the street at an open market, I saw hollowed-eyed old men and women on either side of the road. Squatting in front of crates and baskets laden with vegetables, dried fruits, fish, grains and food, they hawked their wares. One woman, nursing an infant tied around the front of her, shouted, "Kong-nah-mur![30] I had not seen kong-nah-mur since the previous fall. My mouth watered as I recalled the savory bean sprout salad my mother used to make with transparent mung bean noodles, and seasoned with red hot pepper, green onions, garlic, vinegar, soy sauce, sesame seeds and oil. My shrunken stomach growled and ached again.

Next to her sat an old woman with several kinds of rice cakes. I stood in front of the tray of chap-sar-tuk,[31] my favorite kind. My mouth drooled as I remembered how my parents pounded steamed glutinous rice in a huge stone mortar until the hot grain became a large sticky lump. After

---

[30] bean sprouts

[31] sticky rice cake

dividing it into balls the size of bread loaves, my mother dredged each in roasted soybean powder or in red beans sweetened with sugar. My favorite kind had the sweet red bean filling. Overtaken by a desire to bite into one, I swallowed hard and asked the old woman how much she wanted for it. My eyes widened. The rice cake would take almost half of the little cash I had in my pocket. Nevertheless, I fumbled for the money. The woman must have sensed how badly I wanted that rice cake. She lifted the tempting tray right under my nose, urging me to pick one. My finger almost touched the largest piece, but just in time I realized that I could not part with the money. I did not know what lay ahead of me, I might need every cent later on. Briskly, I moved away.

"Come here, maiden," she shouted angrily. "How much do you want to pay for this chewy chap-sar-tuk?"

I was not in a position to haggle with her, lest I be tempted, so I walked on without turning around.

"Look at that! Acting like a ridiculous cripple," she derided me. Ripples of laughter followed me from the marketplace. My face felt hot with humiliation. The war had not only ravaged the land but also the hearts of some people.

"I wish they would be more considerate even if they are bitter over great loss," I thought to myself. "It's not my fault that I limp. Oh, Aboji, I wish you were here to carry me on your back."

As I thought about my father, I recalled one of the times he had carried me to a revival service. In my mind's eye I saw the huge hall where people of all ages with various ailments and afflictions. They fasted and prayed all day and night. The minister, endowed with the gift of healing, preached and repeatedly told the people, "If you have faith the size of a mustard seed you will be healed!"

I did not know what size a mustard seed was or how

people got faith like a mustard seed, but my father and I prayed earnestly.

At dawn while the minister prayed, many people got up to claim that they had been healed. One woman stood up to say that her tuberculosis had left her after she felt an intense burning sensation upon her entire chest. She claimed that she had x-rays to prove it. Another person blissfully reported that his eyesight had returned after ten years. One elderly man lifted his arm and shouted, "Hallelujah, I can raise my paralyzed arm!"

My desperate father peeked at me during the ardent prayers to see if his daughter would leap to her feet and start walking and jumping. Nothing happened to me. I only sat feeling condemned and unworthy. I felt sorry for my father who longed more than I to see me healed. At the end of the third day, I burst into tears and blurted,

"Aboji, I just don't have it. I don't have faith as big as a mustard seed!" The salty tears trickled down my cheeks and onto my dried lips. "Father, maybe it's true. Some people have told me that I was cursed by the devil. Others say I am paying for my sins or the sins of my ancestry!"

My father gripped my shoulders and tried to calm me down, but I refused to be consoled. People in the hall began to pray louder, "Lord, have mercy upon this child!" Their loud droning drowned out my cries.

"Hyun Sook-ga, that is not true," Father whispered into my ear. "You are not being punished for your sins or the sins of your ancestors. Our Lord Jesus took care of all our sins when He died on the cross." He stroked my tousled hair.

"Aboji, I want to know then, why doesn't God heal me? Please tell me, what must I do to be healed?"

"I am sorry, Hyun Sook-ga, I cannot answer that. Who can fathom the mind of God?" He avoided my eyes. "Who can understand the will of God? Let's pray some more.

Maybe . . . ."

Engrossed in my memories, I forgot to watch the road. My walking stick flew out of my grasp as I tripped over a loose cobblestone. I skinned my knees and scraped my callused palms.

"O God, why am I not healed? Lord God, You have the power to perform miracles. You helped me cross the frozen Han River. Why can't you heal my leg? Answer me, Jesus!" I cried into the empty road. My own voice bounced back at me, frightening me. There was nobody else around. The dull sound of distant bombing deepened my agony.

I pulled myself up to my feet and continued wandering through the streets. Driven by an instinct or by coincidence, I drew near to the neighborhood where we had lodged after the first Communist retreat. As I recognized the road, I felt an urge to see that tiny rented room where my family and I had lived in such cramped conditions.

The wooden gate stood ajar. For a moment my heart leapt in hopes of seeing someone I knew. Pushing the rusty iron handle, I walked hesitantly into the yard. There I found an old woman stooped over, sweeping the dirt ground. Timidly I walked closer. To my surprise, it was the landlady. Her once healthy plump face now looked like crumpled parchment tacked on a skull. Her neat shiny hair had dulled to gray and fell disheveled around a blank stare.

"Who are you? And what are you doing here?" She asked irritably, sweeping continually with her short handled broom.

"Ahn-nyung hah shim ni kah?"[32] I greeted her, trying to hide my shocked reaction. "Don't you remember me? I am Hyun Sook, the second daughter of your tenant last fall." After a pause I went on, "I lost my family . . . I just came to

---

[32] How are you?

see familiar faces and our room. . . ." My voice faltered.

"Well, you won't see any familiar faces here. I am the sole survivor." Her body twitched like a bent willow branch on a windy night. "My son and his wife died instantly in the bombing." Her face grimaced in anguish, "My son, my only son . . . ." I shuddered and retreated toward the gate as she continued to sweep the already clean yard without looking up. A chill filled my heart. Perhaps I was no better myself.

Wisps of early spring wind circled and kicked dust at my face. Even the sun hid behind passing clouds. I trudged up one deserted road and down another. The skeletons of red brick buildings and shattered houses looked as revolting as deer carcasses left by a pack of wolves. Unburied corpses sprawled here and there throughout the city, filling the air with a vile stench.

I had no idea how long I had walked when I spotted an ROK Army truck. Several South Korean soldiers busily unloaded freight. I stood as in a trance, staring at them from across the street.

"Such a wonderful sight!" I spoke aloud to myself, "Now I know that the Communists have fled!" I stood there watching for quite some time, letting the feeling of well-being flood through me. One of the soldiers walked over and tapped my shoulder.

"Why are you standing here for so long? Is something wrong?"

"I-I was just watching."

"Are you alone?" he asked sympathetically. That was all I needed. My eyes brimmed at his kind inquiry.

"I have lost my family and my grandmother is still in Seoul." I wiped my eyes with the back of my dirty, chapped hands.

He stood there looking perturbed. Pressing his lower lip with his thumb, he said, "I'll be right back." In a few minutes he returned. "I didn't get to tell you my name yet. I am Sergeant Song. I think there is an officer in our company who might be able to help you. But for now you had better come in and have some rice."

"Rice!" My stomach growled loudly.

"Yes, rice." He held my arm and gently led me over the pebbled road.

Trembling with hunger and weakness, I entered the house where the ROK Army liaison team were temporarily lodged. Every bone in my body ached. Sergeant Song left the room and soon and elderly lady brought in a table and put it before me. I dared not move a muscle or touch the food, lest the feast spread before me should disappear like a soap bubble.

"Don't be bashful. Eat before your rice gets cold!" Sergeant Song spoke as he entered with three other soldiers. "Our tables will be brought in shortly." He sat next to me and handed me a pair of chopsticks and laid a spoon on the soup bowl. I blinked my eyes, and then I ate and ate as though I had a bottomless pit in my stomach. At last I reached the point where even I could not take another bite. I tried to sit up, but my eyes kept closing, and I yawned in spite of myself. I bit my tongue to stay awake, but I simply could not resist the overwhelming sleepiness.

"Do you feel rested?" The cheerful voice of Sergeant Song awakened me.

"I am very sorry." Feeling embarrassed, I rubbed my sticky eyes.

"No need to be." He looked at me with misty eyes.

"Thank you for being so kind to me."

"Don't mention it. I would be grateful if someone took care of my mother and younger sister."

"You don't know where your family is?"

He shook his head gravely. I wanted to say something

to comfort him, but I could not think what to say. He changed his tone of voice, "We'll have to leave in a short while. It's getting dark enough to travel."

After he left the room, I scratched my body fiercely, wishing I could somehow wash my tattered jacket and pants. By now I scratched myself whenever I was alone. I hoped I would soon get some clean clothing to wear before the lice drained all the blood out of me. The sound of footsteps warned me to stop and straighten out my clothes.

"We are ready to leave, Hyun Sook. Let's go." I followed Sergeant Song outside. Three other soldiers were already waiting in the jeep. Sergeant Song placed me in the back between his friend and himself. They latched the side flaps and the jeep started to move. They remained quiet as we moved through the streets of Inchon, but once we passed the city limits they began to talk, sing and smoke. I felt happy for the first time since the war started. I even felt like singing along with them but was too shy to join in.

"We are heading for Yong-Dong-Po," Sergeant Song told me between bumps on the road.

"Yong-Dong-Po!" I exclaimed. "Then I could go over to my Harmoni in Seoul!"

"No, Hyun Sook, Seoul is still not safe."

"How long will I have to wait?"

"Nobody knows." As he exhaled deeply, the faint glow from the cigarette showed the same expression I had seen when he told me briefly about his missing family. "But don't worry. The officer whom you'll meet tonight can arrange a ride for you down to Pusan."

"If you'll just help me get to Pusan, I'll find my family somehow." I felt my heart flutter as I voiced the empty words of courage. He turned toward me in the dark. In the cigarette glow, I saw his concern once again.

"What do you mean, you'll find them somehow? I

thought you knew their whereabouts." He sounded exasperated. "How would you find your parents in Pusan?" he demanded to know, crushing his fresh cigarette on the floor. "Do you realize what condition Pusan is in right now?"

"No, sir, but I somehow feel I'll find them. The Lord . . . ."

"Listen, let me tell you some cruel facts," Sergeant Song interrupted. "All the government officials, UN troops, and refugees from both North and South Korea have poured into the little port city of Pusan like bean sprouts growing in a crock." His voice sounded older and harder. "I was in Pusan not long ago, and I saw how the refugees live."

Everyone in the jeep was quiet, listening to our conversation. The jeep bumped over the highway. The headlights picked out wreckage all along the road. Sergeant Song calmed down and pulled out a fresh pack of cigarettes. He smoked silently.

"Please let me tell you why I feel I'll find my family." I told them about my prayers, the escape from the Communists and the miracles I had experienced. I spoke intensely of God's protection over me.

"Well, I'll buy that simply because you have no reason to tell me about your conviction unless it actually happened to you. But what I'm trying to tell you is that Pusan isn't going to be what you visualize." He let out a smoky sigh. My head had begun to ache from the smoke and the gas fumes, but I didn't complain. This was paradise compared to walking.

"Every space is taken up by matchbox houses. The mountains at night look like tall buildings all lit up. But the sunrise reveals five by five foot shacks that the refugees have built with rubbish discarded by American troops." He paused to tap the long ash from his cigarette and took another puff. The pain and frustration of what he had witnessed reflected in his eyes.

"Unemployment, shortages of food, and shelter are accepted facts. Every day we read in the newspapers of tragic events. Children and adults alike swarm at every public faucet. They wait in line for several hours for just one bucket of water." He wrung his hands. "Are you ready for this? Some girls secretly become call girls to support their families. Some fathers, after their families have been starving for days, actually go out and steal. They get caught and are put into jail. Others get a bullet through their heads. The saddest news is when a whole family who won't bend their moral standards chooses to give up and die together. The parents mix rat poison in their final meal. Maybe they are better off that way than to be callous and become disgraced."

"Do you think my family is all right?" I asked shaken.

"I can't tell you. I really don't know. But let me tell you I don't think you'll be safe in Pusan, especially since you don't know where to find your family."

"I could go to a Presbyterian church and ask. My father is a deacon." I spoke confidently. Gnashing his teeth, Sergeant Song crushed another cigarette on the floor of the bouncing jeep. He yelled, "Don't be stupid!" but instantly he shook his head. The soldier at my other side interrupted.

"Look, Song, you're overreacting. What does this girl know? She is a naive, shielded child."

"I'm sorry," he apologized. "Listen, the reason I tell you these things is so that you'll not be disillusioned when you get to Pusan."

"I don't think that I am either naive or shielded," I spoke defiantly.

Disregarding my statement, he continued. "There are countless numbers of children, both from high and lower class families, who are either abandoned or have lost their parents in the mad confusion. Some fortunate ones are put in crowded orphanages. The American soldiers give food and shelters to some of these boys. But many homeless children wander through the streets as beggars or pickpockets. At night they sleep under the bridges, by the railroad tracks or in back alleys, only to be driven away by the authorities. The daring ones rummage through the garbage cans near the US Army camps. Sometimes they run into sympathetic guards who just walk away, but at night they shoot all moving objects near the barbed wire fence."

"We are almost there," the driver announced. He had turned off the headlights and slowly wove through a narrow dirt road with rows of farmhouses on both sides.

"This is our temporary post," Sergeant Song whispered. "We are waiting for Seoul to be cleared of the Communists."

I tried to get out of the jeep, but my legs had the cramps. Sergeant Song pulled me out and carried me over his shoulder into a dark, barren, musty room. Apprehensively I glanced at him.

"I have duties to attend to. I must leave you here alone, but don't worry. The officer will come shortly to talk to you."

After he left I looked about the gloomy, unheated cubicle and hunched forward to keep myself warm. At that moment the door flew open. A slender girl and a soldier stood there silhouetted against the half moon. They stepped in.

"Hmmm, I just heard that a girl had been picked up for the Lieutenant," she snorted, turning the blinding beam of her flashlight on my face. "Aha, another sitting duck!"

"I don't understand what you mean. I'm waiting for a ride to Pusan."

"Huh, I was promised a lot of things too. But there's no way out. You just wait and see." She turned and left the room with her companion. After the girl had slammed the door behind her, I tried to figure out what she meant. I began to feel uneasy when the door opened again and a man entered.

"I am Lieutenant Chai, the officer you have been waiting to see," he said as he stooped down to take a close look at me by the flame of his cigarette lighter. "I heard about your predicament. Let me see what I can do for you."

He pulled out a pack of cigarettes and offered me one. I shook my head both surprised and offended that he should offer a cigarette to a girl. Mustering my courage, I asked, "Please excuse me, but a girl came in here a while ago and told me I was another sitting duck, and there was no way out. What did she mean, and who is she?"

"Oh? She was here?" He hesitated a second, his voice registering shock. "Well, then, I must tell you what she is. When I first met her, shortly after she escaped from North Korea last fall, I intended to marry her. But I found her to be too independent and strong-willed." He tossed out his cigarette butt and stretched his arms. In an almost confiding manner he went on, "And she made herself available to the men around the company, including me. I refused her for I don't care for indecent girls. Once I realized what she was like, of course I dropped her. Ever since then she's been jealous of any girl brought into this camp."

I nodded understandingly. He edged a little closer and leaned against the wall. "Don't let her bother you."

It seemed he enjoyed talking for he began to unfold to me the story of his life. Having nothing else to do, I simply sat and listened. His parents had died while he was a toddler, and he had been bounced around from one relative to another. His childhood had been a deprived one – no time for play, second-hand clothes, and leftover rice. I listened sympathetically, for I had come to understand deprivation only too well myself. He went on to say how determined he had been to study and become somebody. He had attended night school and achieved good grades. As a result, his uncle decided to put him into an elite university where he graduated with honors. He took a long time to tell his story, and I marveled at the obstacles he had overcome to reach the goals he set for himself.

"Now I speak several languages fluently, especially English. I plan to go to America some day to further my studies." He talked on and on in the darkness. I found myself nodding off to sleep. All at once my eyes flew open. I felt his breath hot on my neck. He had moved closer, muttering about the futility of achieving so much and yet having no one.

"I've been searching for someone to share my life. At last I have . . . ." He put his arms around me.

"Oh, no!" Startled, I pulled away.

"It's obvious that you don't believe me." His voice sounded more hurt than angry.

"No, sir," I said. "It isn't that I don't believe you. It's just that I-I am a handicapped girl. Why would anyone want me?"

"Don't belittle yourself. Sergeant Song said you need my help. Let me take care of you for the rest of your life." He slipped off his watch and put it over my wrist, whispering into my ears, "I can't get you a ring, but take this gold watch as my token for you. I have chosen you above all other girls."

My heartbeat quickened. I had dreamed about marrying a handsome and successful man, but no matchmaker would arrange a marriage for a handicapped girl. It sounded unbelievable, but he removed his gold watch.

Sensing my emotions, he kept on talking and wooing, "I am sorry I can't get a ring for you. And I know all girls dream of a big wedding, but I am living day to day for my country. I don't know when or where my life might be snuffed out on the battlefield." Taking my hands, he urged that I, too, give my token.

My head spun as I tried to think sensibly. He said he wanted to marry me and that he might die any day. He sounded kind and impressive, but what if he meant this in jest?

Instinct somewhere deep inside me reacted violently. I shouted, "No!" My refusal infuriated him. Without warning he covered my mouth with a handkerchief.

"Don't scream!" he said trying to intimidate me. "You have no ground to stand on." He pushed me down banging my head on the hard floor. Breathing heavily he declared, "Nobody has ever refused me!" My head whirled as I struggled against the man nobody had ever refused before blacking out.

I could not recall how much time had passed before I was able to sit up. Lieutenant Chai reclined in the darkness beside me smoking. A vague sense of vileness hovered beneath my numbness. If it were filth on my hands and feet, I could have washed it away, but sin itself had penetrated my body and soul, where soap and water could not reach or clean. I had no power to undo this evil.

After a long silence, Lieutenant Chai informed me aloofly that I could not stay in the camp. Furthermore, it was impossible for him to help me get a ride to Pusan, for no civilians were permitted to ride in army vehicles.

I sobbed, as I wished I just had another nightmare. "Why did you lead me to believe you could help me?"

"Stop crying," he snapped at me irritably, "Listen, I'll take you to the mother of my best friend who lives some way from here. I'm sure she will let you stay at her home until you can get a ride to Pusan." With that statement he exited the shack as if nothing had happened.

My teeth chattered from cold and rage. I felt as if I was plummeting down into the pit of hell. I covered my mouth to keep from screaming. *I'm a broken bowl!* My thoughts blared. *I wish I had never been born!*

Before long Lieutenant Chai returned with a jeep. He told me to get in and duck my head behind the front seat while he drove out of the camp. As I climbed into the seat, I wondered if Sgt. Song knew what had happened to me.

Lieutenant Chai drove along farm roads and then wove through pine trees and up a winding mountain path. Lighting one cigarette after another, he told me about his friend's mother, Mrs. Ming. "Her husband disappeared during the first Communist invasion. She lost one of her two daughters during the bombing. Not too long ago her husband's body was discovered and given a proper burial. Their only son and I were as close as two brothers. He is supposed to be alive, but nobody knows where he is . . . ." I listened silently, temporarily distracted from my anger. He sighed and drove on for a long time over the desolate trail. The dawn broke and a hazy beam filtered through the trees. As if he could not tolerate silence, Lieutenant Chai babbled on.

"They were very, very wealthy, but lost their possessions during the war. Their mansion is partially damaged from the bombing." He careened around a sharp bend on the steep hill, unnerving me a little. "She lives with her daughter. The mother is a noble lady. You'll like her."

After a long drive, the jeep halted in front of a huge gate with brass panels, which were impressively engraved with the words 'longevity' and 'happiness.' "Longevity and happiness snuffed out in a bloody war!" I muttered.

Lieutenant Chai got out of the jeep and knocked on the gate for a long time. At last the lady of the house responded. Recognizing him, she opened the gate. "Come in! Come in! I am glad to see you again!" After an exchange of greetings and much bowing, she asked, "But what in the world are you doing at this early hour?"

"This maiden was sent to me to help locate her family, but it is not possible for me to do so at this time. I hope that you will look after her until I send word to you." Lieutenant Chai spoke as we strolled through the courtyard toward the mansion. "Of course, I will provide the food." Mrs. Ming nodded. Lieutenant Chai walked us to the foyer, then bowed and wished the lady well.

"Why don't you wait a while and have your morning meal with us," she invited.

"Thank you, but I must report to my company immediately. Excuse me, please." He bowed again and started back to his jeep. Just as we stepped onto the highly polished oak floor, I heard his footsteps again.

"Er, Hyun Sook," he called, "I almost forgot my watch. Thank you for holding it for me." His tone of voice was patronizing. I stared at him, shocked. Mrs. Ming glanced at him and then at me. Without a word she slipped into the kitchen. Uneasily he held out his hand for his gold watch, avoiding my resentful glare. Bitterness filled my heart, and my fingers stiffened as I restrained an intense urge to reach up and claw the eyes out of his brutish face. I never wanted the watch! He had deliberately violated me and betrayed my trust. It was too much for me to bear. Humiliated and hurt, I handed him the watch.

Long after he left, I stood still, rooted to the floor. It seemed that there was no meaning to my existence. The whole world seemed to condemn me. Now, I would be doubly despised--not only for having a disability, but also for being unable to preserve myself.

Hostility surged through my veins and guilt filled my

heart. I felt as if my shame showed on my face, like cracks on a broken bowl.

After a while Mrs. Ming called me to the kitchen. "It is nice to have someone living with us," she said as she fed the kitchen fire.

"Thank you for taking me in," I said. To my relief she made no attempt to probe into my personal life.

"I hope you'll find your family soon. My daughter will soon be up. She didn't sleep well last night." She checked the steamy rice. "We are often awakened in the night by foreign soldiers wanting young girls. Of course, my daughter is safe in the secret attic of her room behind the scroll, but still it is rough. Yes, yes, it is a terrible war." Her comment shook me. She glanced up.

"Don't look so frightened. I have a hiding nook for you, too! Later on I will show it to you." She piled rice in three bowls and ladled soup while I placed silver spoons and chopsticks on the table.

Comfortably seated on a warm ondol once again, I bowed my head and asked God's protection for this family and for me. I felt a deep sense of serenity and composure about this woman in spite of all her loss and suffering. The graying hair framing her oval face was neatly parted in the center, pulled back in a bun and fastened with a gold hairpiece at the nape. I admired her for not having allowed the war to harden or embitter her spirit.

Her daughter came in quietly and joined us. She resembled her mother in appearance and in manner. However, except for our greetings, she remained silent throughout the mealtime and solemnly excused herself as soon as breakfast was over.

"Please do not mind her," Mrs. Ming sighed. "She has been that way ever since her father's funeral."

After we cleared the dishes Mrs. Ming took me to an

exotic bedding closet in her room, adorned with mother-of-pearl on an exquisite black lacquer finish. Pulling out all three drawers of the lower section, she removed a thin plywood panel. Behind the drawer prop, between the panel and the back of the chest, was a small cubicle. She said this would be my hiding nook and told me to squeeze into it. It was so narrow that I lay on my side with my knees crushed against my chest. My head was tilted, caving into my shoulders. Mrs. Ming replaced the plywood panel and closed all the drawers. Satisfied, she let me out.

The following night we heard the gate rattle. Mrs. Ming winced and signaled us to put away our bedding. Her daughter slipped into the opening of the secret attic behind a scroll on one side of the wall and I crawled into my coffin. After she replaced the last drawer of the closet, she went out to open the gate. Heavy footsteps and rough noises approached and soon the sliding door to the room where I was hiding slammed open. My heart pounded in my mouth as I strained to listen.

"These soldiers want to see some young maidens," a Korean interpreted.

"As you can see, sir, I am the only one here."

"That's what they all say," he retorted. "Well, we want to search the rooms." Jabbering in their strange language, the foreigners came near the bedding closet where I hid trembling. The upper panel doors banged open, and the noise from their rummaging hammered in my ears. Abruptly they left the room rampaging through the rest of the house. Unlike the drill I had the day before, their search went on for hours. Laughing and shouting like drunken pirates, they refused to leave. My bones ached, and my taut neck muscles felt as if they would snap at any second. Crushed against the drawers, I gasped for air. To make matters worse, I urgently needed to use the outhouse. Desperately I prayed. At long last I heard Mrs. Ming's footsteps and her voice.

"You may come out now."

After that harrowing experience, I began to dread the approach of night. Several days went by with no word from Lieutenant Chai about my ride to Pusan. Mrs. Ming did not utter a word of complaint, but the strain from protecting and hiding two girls began to show in the dark circles under her eyes and in her hollow cheeks. One morning I explained my plans to be on my way to find my family.

"You are welcome to stay here as long as you need," she assured me, but I politely declined her offer and prepared to leave. Mrs. Ming's kindness left a hollow inside me once I stepped out of her gate. Desolation swept over me, but I walked away toward the road she had pointed out for me.

The Smuggled Ride

As I pushed toward the main road to Pusan, I noticed patches of green grass and azalea branches bearing buds. Spring had always been my favorite season, and I usually waited eagerly for the first hint of it. It delighted me to watch the forsythia blossoms transform the bleak, dead fields of winter into a laughing world of gold. Yet this year, spring arrived without its customary fanfare, and my heart remained cold and harsh in its own winter. I trudged somberly down the road. A few old men passed me with their heads down.

Around noon I spotted a local policeman in dark blue uniform. Without hesitation I rushed over and told him of my need for a ride to Pusan. He took me to a road patrol. The police flagged down an approaching ROK Army truck, and the Korean soldiers readily consented to give me a lift. Placing me on the back of the open truck, one soldier took off his army field jacket and draped it over me. Another removed his helmet and pulled it down and on my head in an attempt to cloak me from the scrutiny of sentries along the highway. As a final touch, another soldier planted a rifle over my shoulder. The truck moved off, bouncing along the bumpy road.

At last I was on my way to Pusan. I became so engrossed in daydreaming about a reunion with my family that I did not even notice the changing scenery. The truck stopped for clearance and was rumbling on again when, unexpectedly, a lanky US MP shouted and jogged toward us. A Korean interpreter raced behind him barely keeping up. The MP blew his whistle and rolled out words I could not understand. My own English vocabulary was limited. The MP peered through his gold-framed glasses and pointed a long index finger at me. He waved his arm vigorously, motioning for me to get down.

"No Communist! Hello, no Communist!" I shouted, slapping my chest and waving my hand. The MP's face turned scarlet, and the interpreter told me I had better get down. Hurriedly I removed my stinking socks and pulled out the identification card, which I had hidden there the night I fled from Seoul. I waved my stained, worn ID card, and shouted frantically again, "Hello, no Communist! No Communist!"

The MP snatched away my card and strolled back to his post. The interpreter told me to follow. After I climbed down, the truck sped away, leaving me choking on the dust. I limped behind the MP, who glared at me and spewed out a string of angry words. The Korean explained that I had no business traveling by army vehicle, and if I were caught again I would be in big trouble. I was strictly banned from the highway.

After this fierce warning, he handed back my ID card. By this time a big crowd had gathered about me. Shoving and pushing one another, they craned their necks to get a glimpse of me as if I was a circus freak. My face grew hot. Just to get away from the mob, I desperately hunted for a refuge. I spotted a shabby restaurant and rushed in.

In an attempt to regain my composure, I studied the

small blackboard menu hanging on the wall. My thin roll of money would just cover the cheapest dish offered. My distress was so dire that I decided to part with the money in exchange for a corner to sit in for a while.

Halfway through the meal I noticed a plump woman at another table staring at me. Without asking she swaggered over to my table and sat down across from me. She looked wealthy.

"What are you doing, eating that bi-bim-bahb?[33] That's just leftovers thrown together. Let me order some decent food for you. You look as if you need it." She clapped her hands for the maid. To my amazement she ordered bulgogi, accompanied by bahn chahn,[34] bean curd soup, and rice. Then she watched me devour the food hungrily. When I had almost finished the feast, she began talking and asking me questions.

"I saw you being dragged down from that truck." She narrowed her eyes, "Why were you caught? Are you in trouble with the law? Where were you headed?"

I told her of my attempts to reach Pusan. As she listened, her eyes widened with concern. When she found out that I had no place to go in Pyong-taek, she invited me to stay with her for as long as I needed. The woman paid for my dinner and led me out of the restaurant. Silently I followed this woman who seemed so kind and sympathetic.

The sun was setting when we reached her home. She offered me the warmest spot on her ondol floor and covered me with a pink silk comforter.

"Are you comfortable? Good." She seemed pleased as she mothered me. I felt overwhelmed by her unexpected

---

[33] Rice topped with savory beef strips, shredded vegetables, a fried egg, and hot pepper paste

[34] assorted side dishes, usually cold seasoned vegetables

hospitality. "Now, tell me again. How did you lose your family?" She seemed interested and curious to know about my family and me. She listened to all my woes patiently. Then quite suddenly she changed, like a tempest raging unexpectedly over a calm sea. She shouted, "Don't tell me you don't know why your parents left you behind. They didn't want you. They wanted you dead!"

"That's not true," I protested defensively.

"Now, listen to me. If I were you, I would take revenge!" Her face grew red and her cheeks jiggled. "Do you know the best weapon for revenge?" She pulled out a thick stack of Korean paper currency from her pouch and waved it wildly in my face. "Money! Money! The greatest power in the world! Don't be a fool. Listen to me, and I'll show you how to make plenty of money, until you can blow your nose with it!" Her eyes darkened and gleamed greedily. I shook my head confused. "There is a village near here with lots of soldiers. I'll teach you how to make money there."

The meaning of her words became clear, and I threw the cover off and sat up.

"No, I don't want money! I just want to find my family again. I won't listen to you!"

The enraged woman yanked me off the warm place and pushed me up to the cold section of her room. "I have helped many girls become rich," she said. "You are a cursed and ungrateful fool for not heeding my advice!" My ears rang with the shrill sound of her voice. "I would throw you out right now if it weren't for the curfew. You get out as soon as it lifts!" she screamed.

At the first hint of dawn, I crawled out of the room and sat against the fence waiting for daylight. At last a thin lavender streak pushed back the blue-black sky. Soon it was followed by a bursting array of gold, red and orange spreading over the mountain peaks and hill crests. The brilliant ball of fire caressed my cheeks and gently invoked me to start on my way. Enchanted by the ageless pageantry, I momentarily forgot my troubles.

Slowly I got up and walked down the dirt road, which presently became a narrow rice paddy path. "How am I to reach Pusan walking on rice paddy roads and mountain trails? O Jesus, please help me somehow," I implored as I limped along the bumpy track sobbing in despair. All at once I bumped into something tall and solid. I looked up and found a police officer holding me steady to keep me from falling. He asked me why I was weeping.

I told him of my plight, about the Madam, and of my fear that I would never find my family again. He spoke to me kindly, "Don't worry. We'll figure out something. Now dry your tears." He led the way to the home of the village elder and asked him and his wife to care for me overnight.

"Tomorrow morning I will take you to a police check point along the highway. There, we'll find a ride for you to Pusan."

"But, sir, I am banned from the highway."

"I know. But I also know that you are not a Communist spy." He patted my head. "Let me take care of it. I take exceptional cases under consideration. Even police officers are capable of sympathizing and helping, you know." He flashed a teasing smile and left.

Too restless to wait inside, I sat out in the yard and glanced repeatedly toward the sun, which faded slowly and deliberately. "Somewhere beyond the twilight lies my family," I whispered wistfully. The need to tell my parents how much I missed them grew so strong that I felt my heart would burst.

"Come in child. Supper is ready," the lady of the house called. Anticipation had driven my appetite, but at the urging of the couple, I ate.

All night long I tossed about in my bed. With the sound of the first rooster, I slipped out of the room and washed my face at the well in the yard. I had to keep myself busy to push the clock forward, so I started the kitchen fire. When the lady came into the kitchen, she seemed pleased at what I had done. Just as breakfast was ready, the police officer came for me. I jumped up and started for the door, but he blocked me.

"We are not going anywhere until you finish your morning meal," he said. Reluctantly I sat and forced the food down. I bowed many times as I left the kind couple.

The police officer led the way, and I pole-vaulted behind him with my walking stick. I dared not lose sight of him. At last he pointed toward the police box. The road patrolman, sitting on the stool inside the booth, jumped to attention when he saw us. The officer briefly explained my predicament to his junior.

"Yes, sir. I will take good care of her and get her on the first vehicle to Pusan." They saluted each other and parted. I bowed and waved at him. To help pass the time, the patrolman told me a familiar folktale, a Korean version of Cinderella, which I had heard many times before. Then he taught me a song based on the story of a girl lamenting the cruelty of the stepmother, who had ordered her to till twelve strips of rugged field with a wooden hoe. I sang the song over and over until I memorized the words. As sad as the song sounded, it gave me great comfort to know that her troubles had a happy ending.

Is It Really You?

Half a dozen ROK vehicles stopped, but none of them were heading for Pusan. Between the intervals, we kept on singing. In the afternoon, just when I began to get restless, a US Army jeep pulled up. The policeman jabbered tongue-twisting sounds.

"Taegu," I heard the American driver reply.

"Taegu?" I exclaimed, my heart suddenly fluttering at the word, Taegu. As though in a trance, I jumped up, for an address had flashed into my mind in clear bold letters. Still in a daze, I implored, "Please ask them to take me to Taegu!" But the policeman stared at me puzzled. Urgently I tugged at his jacket, saying, "I can't explain it, but the address of my former pastor in China, who now lives in Taegu, just came to my mind!"

"Are you sure? Will he still be at the same address?" He frowned doubtfully. For a distressing second, I faltered. The address which I saw so clearly now seemed hazy, and I felt unsure, but then, I reasoned, going to Taegu could not be any more risky than going to Pusan.

"Yes, I am positive," I insisted, hoping that he would not sense the trembling I felt inside.

"OK . . .Taegu . . .Go," was all that I could pick out of

their conversation. As the policeman lifted me into the jeep, he interpreted that I would have to be smuggled into Taegu in the sleeping bag. After I crept inside the musty bag, the soldier seated in the back seat zipped me up, leaving just my face showing. I looked back at the kind policeman through the dusty plastic rear window. As the jeep sped away, I felt again the excitement of crossing the frozen Han River.

Lifting their helmets, the GIs introduced themselves to me: Joe, the driver, John, seated next to Joe, and Paul, in the back seat with me. Paul, who reminded me of Hogan, pulled out a pack of spearmint gum, which I had not tasted since the US Army R & R Center withdrew from our village in 1949. He unwrapped a stick and showed me how to chew it. His gestures amused me, but I refrained from giggling.

"Thank you," I said smiling as I let him put the stick into my mouth. I blushed feeling stupid, but he just nodded his head and started to hum a tune softly. The other two joined in the chorus. They sang so lightheartedly that I wanted to be joyous with them.

After bouncing along the highway for quite some time, the jeep stopped on the side of a secluded hilly area where a dilapidated cabin stood. They all got out, stretching their long arms and legs, and scouted around the place. John and Joe gathered some firewood and rocks to build a fire, while Paul unloaded a box of cans. Then he came over and gestured that it was safe for me to come out. He unzipped the sleeping bag, helped me down and led me over to the fire. They gave me the first can of food, hot and bubbling. It had minced potatoes mixed with salty red meat. I like the taste. Each time they handed me food, they told me, "Chop, chop." I supposed 'chop' must be the word for 'eat' in English. Paul handed me a large tin cup of steamy cocoa to drink. They hovered around me and treated me as if I were someone special – just the way a man is treated in Korea. At home we could not even lifted our chopsticks until Father had begun to eat.

After our leisurely roadside meal, they smothered the fire, and we climbed back into the jeep. I crawled into the sleeping bag and promptly fell asleep. When I awoke the jeep was still moving. It embarrassed me to discover that my head had been resting on Paul's arm, but he said, "OK, OK," and patted my shoulder.

The jeep careened around a curve and onto a crowded street. The sky was very dark, but the bright storefronts and street lamps lighted the streets. I had not seen electric lights since last winter in Seoul. Slowing down, the jeep wove through the bustling streets. We passed food stands, grills and restaurants from which tantalizing aromas enticed me. Several bars blasted loud music as red, green and blue neon signs flashed by. I looked out dazed, feeling as if I had entered a strange land. Paul, sensing my thoughts, said, "Taegu, Taegu."

As the driver skillfully navigated through the milling crowds, the soldiers began to sing the songs they had sung in the afternoon. I treasured snatches of the words, not knowing then what they meant: "You are my sunshine . . .Working on the railroad . . .Good Night, Irene . . ." My eyes began to mist over. I would hate to leave these three friendly Americans.

Joe stopped before a tall, imposing, iron gate where MPs and Korean policemen stood at attention. After an exchange of words, a white-gloved MP waved us in. Passing through a park-like garden, we stopped in front of a huge concrete building. I glanced apprehensively at Paul, but his handsome face flashed a reassuring smile and again said, "OK, OK." He unzipped the sleeping bag and helped me down. The three men escorted me through impressive double doors where white-gloved guards stood at attention.

The GIs sat me down on a wooden chair in a spacious

hall and hovered around me protectively while MPs and Korean policemen flocked from every direction, stretching their necks and talking. Their faces melted into a blur, and their words buzzed in my ears. One policeman yelled for all to hear, "What is she? A Communist informer or a shabby prostitute?"

I saw Paul's hands tightening into fists and his eyes flickering angrily, obviously understanding the accusation. Gradually I collected myself, removed my tattered shoe, pulled out the stained ID, and told the policeman, "I am neither an informer, nor a prostitute." Keeping my voice calm, I continued, "Would someone take me to the residence of Pastor Kim, Tae-Up at Taegu-shi Nahm-Sahn-Dong, 5-ho, please?"

"All right, no more questions!" one of the policemen, who appeared to be the senior officer, commanded. "She 's harmless."

After the curious onlookers scattered, the senior officer said something to my three friends. They each came and shook my hand before they left. Paul stroked my head gently, his blue eyes glistening. I could not understand the words he spoke, but I sensed that he might be telling me that I was in good hands. The three GIs went toward the door, waved again and stepped out into the night.

The officer said it was too late to take me to Pastor Kim's home right then, but that he would send me there first thing the following morning. He had an army cot and blankets set up for me behind a folding screen. With mixed feelings of excitement and anxiety, I tried to sleep.

When I awoke, something smelled delicious, but it was not the cooking aromas to which I was accustomed. The men bustled about, and when one of them noticed me stirring, he told the officer, who promptly sent in a GI mess plate loaded with foods for which I knew no names. I had never had an American breakfast and had no idea what to eat first.

By the time I finished eating and cleaned up, the officer told me that an MP and a Korean policeman would escort me to the address of Pastor Kim. As the jeep wove around narrow dirt roads, troubling thoughts bombarded me. What if the address was wrong? What if Pastor Kim had moved? Would I ever find my family?

The Korean police gestured for the MP to stop in the middle of the road and helped me out of the jeep. Shakily I followed him up the slope, painfully aware that each step brought me closer to the end of my journey or to the beginning of another endless search. As he knocked on the modest wooden gate, I clenched my fists, my nails digging into the flesh. My heart stopped at the sound of the gate creaking open. I bit my lips to keep them from trembling as I hid behind the man.

"Ah, excuse me, please," he sounded uneasy and hesitant. "Do you, ah, happen to know a maiden by the name of . . ." he glanced down at his papers, "Lee, Hyun Sook?"

Hours seemed to pass as I waited for the answer.

"Hyun Sook? Did you say, Hyun Sook? Why, yes! Yes, I know her. Where is she? What happened to her?" The unmistakable, angelic voice of the pastor's wife rang in my ears. The policeman let out a long sigh and stepped aside. We stood there, face-to-face, unable to speak or move as if we were fused to the ground. We both reached out, but the distance between us felt miles long, each of us trying to touch the other and yet unable to move.

"Hyun Sook-ga, can it really be you, or am I seeing things? We heard that you were left behind in Seoul, but never imagined that you could actually . . . ." She choked up. My voice failed me as well, but I rushed into her outstretched arms, burying my head and all my hurts into her bosom as I wept convulsively. Everything else faded away. I even forgot to thank the men who had brought me.

After a long while, the pastor's wife loosened my arms. "Hyun Sook-ga, let me take a look at you!" Then she gasped, "Oh, no! Look at your nose! You're bleeding!" Blood streamed from my nose, saturating her white jogori and chimah. "Ai-go, my poor child, let's go inside."

When I finally opened my eyes, I found myself in an immaculate room. A beam of sunlight streamed in through the window. I looked about me and saw that I was dressed in fresh nightclothes and was lying on a thick bed with starched linen. I felt so clean. "Where am I? How did I get here?" As I strained to recall, I saw Sah-mo nim[35] tiptoeing toward me. Still in a daze, I thought I was having another dream. Bewildered, I whispered, "Sah-mo nim?"

Kneeling beside my pillow, the pastor's wife nodded her head. Without a word her gentle brown eyes welled up and tears coursed down her delicate cheeks. She stroked my head, squeezed my hands and left the room. Minutes later she returned with a tray. As she fed me bean curd soup and rice, Sah-mo nim explained that I had not moved a muscle for three days since collapsing in her arms at the gate. Every now and then she had come to take my pulse and check my breathing. When she sensed my ability to absorb more, Sah-mo nim told me,

"Hyun Sook-ga, I have good news for you. Mr. Kang, the bookkeeper who worked for your parents in China, is now living in Taegu. He knows where your parents are. Mr. Kang told us that your parents are doing very well in Pusan." She flashed a smile, showing her straight, pearly teeth. "We sent word to him, and he is coming for you today to escort you to your parents. Isn't it marvelous?"

---

[35] Pastor's Wife

"Truly?" I asked breathlessly. It sounded too good to be true. As hard as I tried, I could not allow myself the luxury of believing it.

The pastor's wife removed the breakfast tray and came back with a clean set of clothes, which, she said, one of her daughters had outgrown. Graciously she spared me the embarrassment of telling me about the lice-infested rags I had been wearing all these months. I hoped she had burned them.

In the late afternoon, Mr. Kang came for me. I wished that I could have seen Pastor Kim before I left, but Sah-mo nim told me that his responsibilities as Director of the Taegu Bible Institute and would not prevent him from returning home until late that evening. She explained that he had looked in on me and prayed for me while I slept those three days. The pastor's wife clasped my hands and prayed for God's protection and blessing on me. Thanking her profusely, I bowed and left.

I found Mrs. Kang and her five daughters crowded into one small bedroom. She hugged me and looked me over and then hugged me again while the children stared at us bewildered. My surviving the war and finding them gripped her so that she could hardly speak. She wept and laughed and wept some more. At last she found her words. "You are really here! I would never have believed such a miracle . . . ." After the excitement of greetings died down, Mr. Kang rubbed his hands and told me, "Hyun Sook-ga, you'll have to spend a night with us here. I'll take you to Pusan tomorrow."

I stared at him deeply disappointed. Having come this close to my destination, it would seem that one more day should not make any difference, but it bothered me terribly. I was so impatient and upset that I tossed about all night long.

At dawn Mr. Kang and I mounted a Pusan-bound commercial truck. The passing landscape blurred as my mind drifted away. I had suffered, prayed, and waited for this day. Now finally I would see my family, I should have been ecstatic, but I felt frantic. How should I act when I faced my family, especially my brother-in-law? I began to feel mounting anger turning into bitterness. How would my parents react toward me when they see me? Would I be welcomed or become a burdensome bundle to them? What would they think of me if I told them I had left Grandmother behind? How would I tell them about those beastly men and what they had done to me? How could I reveal my shame to my parents who had never so much as held hands in the presence of their children? I could never tell them. They would surely die of disgrace.

Desperately I tried to restrain terrible thoughts and guilt from overwhelming me, but rage reared its venomous head from the pit of my stomach. Hate permeated my heart, and I vowed again that I would never trust anyone. Somewhere inside me an iron gate slammed shut.

Reunion

"Hyun Sook-ga, are you still with me? You haven't said a word since we got on," Mr. Kang remarked as he grinned and sniffled.

"I'm sorry. I was just thinking." My voice trembled with the jolting of the truck.

"We aren't too far from Pusan now." Rubbing his hands apologetically, he commented,

"I think I had better tell you before we reach the city that I don't know your parents' address. I'll have to take you to your brother-in-law and elder sister's place, and they'll get in touch with them. Just don't be upset with me if you are not able to see them tonight."

I stared at Mr. Kang, stunned. I could not handle one more day of delay in seeing my parents. I felt the last bit of energy draining from me. I was losing what little control I had over my emotions.

Mr. Kang located my sister, and she took me to a one-room shack, which my parents had rented for Mi Sook and Wha Sook to live in. He told me that the only way to contact my parents was to go to the United Nations Civil Assistance Command (UNCAC) post by the shuttle truck provided for Korean employees in the mornings and evenings.

The following night, to my chagrin, only my mother came to see me. I was extremely disappointed that Father did not come, but dared not express it. Neither one of us could speak. I felt like a stranger. Awkwardly we fell into each other's arms and wept. Somehow the inexpressible thrill, the pounding of my heart, and the soaring of my spirit that I had experienced when I saw the pastor's wife wasn't there for my mother.

"Hyun Sook-ga, we prayed for your safety. But now you are actually here, I can hardly believe that it's really you!" Mother shook her incredulously.

Instead of filling with balmy comfort, my heart contracted, turbulent and unsure. I studied her face. Did I see relief? Contrition? Shame? Or was it simply feigned gladness that her crippled daughter had returned? I could not tell. Unexpectedly, from the dark corners of my memory, the vengeful words of the madam in Pyong-taek echoed in my head: *Why are you trying to find your family? Don't tell me that you don't know why they left you. They didn't want you. They wanted you dead!* I had gone through hell and struggled each step of my way to this moment, but the joy I anticipated was not present, and I could not conjure it up. Abruptly I shook my head, trying to blot out the horror of the war and that woman's menacing words from my muddled head. I wanted to ask Mother if what the woman had said held any truth, but fear of further rejection kept the question buried deep, very deep down. Instead, bitter tears began streaming down my flushed cheeks.

Mother stoked my back, saying, "Don't cry, Hyun Sook-ga. It's all over now." My flesh tightened at her touch. I sobbed all the more, feeling both unwanted and betrayed.

The following night, my father came out sporting a new suit and a gray felt hat pulled down to his brows. By now any anticipation and excitement I had about seeing him had soured. He seemed like a remote relative, visiting me out of duty or courtesy. We went through the formality of greeting each other, but whatever he said to me that night sounded meaningless and fabricated. My heart accused him. *If you really were glad to have me back, you would have dropped everything and rushed out to see me the minute you learned of my return!*

Because of their workload, my parents could only come out to see us on Sundays. I desperately needed their presence to relieve me of my recurring nightmares from the war. I would often jump up from the bed in the middle of the night screaming and find my fists tight and clammy with cold sweat. But, whether out of my strong need to be accepted or fear of being alienated, I masked my inner conflict with compliance and a placid expression when my parents and relatives were around. Without a word of complaint, I took up living in the gloomy shack with Mi Sook and Wha Sook.

Mi Sook, eight years old, was doing practically everything: shopping, cooking, cleaning, and taking care of three-year-old Wha Sook. After dark she went to one of the few public water faucets and stood in line with hundreds of others deep into the night. Sometimes she had to wait as late as two or three in the morning before her turn came for one precious bucket of water. We used our drinking water sparingly and washed all three of our faces from the same water in the basin.

The hardship of being a refugee would have been bearable if the residents had treated us kindly. But, annoyed by the masses pouring into their city from other battle zones, they isolated themselves within the comforts of their fluted shingle-roof houses. Most of them refused to rent their spare rooms to the refugees. My parents, at least, were able to rent a room in a dilapidated neighborhood. The shortage of housing, however, drove most of the destitute masses up to the barren mountains, just as Sgt. Song had told me. The men began copying one another by nailing together apple crates, cardboard, flattened out tin cans, straw sacks, and scraps of torn tents in hopes of keeping out the miserable wind and rain. Located on the southern tip of the peninsula, Pusan was immune from the harsh winters of the north, but oppressive musty chills penetrated doors and windows.

A few weeks after I located my family, Mother came to see us. "Hyun Sook-ga," she asked, "How would you like to come into the UNCAC and learn to sew at our tailor shop?"

"Oh, I would!" I exclaimed. Anything to get away from the shack! I started working at the command post the next day in a Quonset hut.[36] Most of their customers were young American enlisted men. They brought in baggy fatigue uniforms and asked to have them altered to fit skin-tight so that every rippling muscle would protrude. The pile of uniforms for alterations mounted up so high that the three of us could hardly keep up with the demand. My parents bought two additional sewing machines and hired several seamstresses and a maid to handle the workload, but still, as hard and as fast as we worked, we seldom finished sewing before midnight.

Although I spent all my waking hours working, it made me happy to be around the American soldiers. They smiled and whistled happy tunes a lot. I found their good nature contagious. The GIs always carried chocolate candy bars and chewing gum in their roomy packs and shared these freely with others. I could not understand what made them so generous.

My parents maintained a high standard of integrity

---

[36] military prefabricated semicircle shelter

and strove to produce outstanding work. Their good reputation reached the commanding officer. When he learned that my two younger sisters still lived off post, he requisitioned additional army cots for us so that my parents could have all three of their daughters living with them.

The best part of the Quonset hut was its location, right by the shore of the East Sea. Tranquil fishing villages stretched out on either side of us, and we enjoyed a breathtaking view of lush blue-green mountains and hills surrounding the villages like fortresses. A white sandy beach stretched around us in an enormous horseshoe. As we moved in, I thought ahead to summer. At high tide we would be able to swim in the surf, and at low tied we would go clam digging. After dark, I strolled out to the beach and saw the moon etching thousands of silvery strokes on the face of the sea. Perhaps, one day, I might be able to let the tide carry away all the ugly memories and rage, and be at peace with myself like the calm sea.

In the spring, we heard that Seoul was opened to civilians. Father immediately left to fetch Grandmother. Father found her living at the same house. Her arrival thrilled us all, especially me. Although she had lost a lot of weight and her dentures, she was still alert.

When at last I could be alone with her, I clasped her hands and asked, "Harmoni, please tell me, what happened to you after we left you? Did the Communists come around to harass you?"

"Ai-go, Hyun Sook-ga, after you left I even said a prayer to your father's God." Her toothless mouth quivered as she continued, "I said, 'Omnipotent One, it does not matter what happens to me, but please put hedges of Thy protection around my crippled granddaughter.' Your father's God is truly good!" She wiped her tear-brimmed eyes and said, "Hyun Sook-ga, you are really alive!" She stroked my head, my back and squeezed my hands and acted as if I had returned from the dead.

"Yes, I know, Harmoni, I found out God really hears and answers our prayers." I eagerly told her how I was able to walk the frozen Han River. Tearfully I asked, "Harmoni, please tell me what happened to you after we left? How did you survive?"

She looked far away, beyond the four walls, as an expression of pain twisted her wrinkled face. "A few days after you left, the Communist officer who had interrogated you started coming often and ordered me to produce you. He demanded to know where I had hidden you and Soon Ja and said that if I didn't tell him, he would lock me up."

Her words spread a chill over my body. I shook my head feeling terribly guilty for her suffering. "Were you locked up?" I asked.

"No, of course not. I told that Red Devil I did not know where you were. How could I know? Somehow I was not afraid of him, so I dared to tell him, 'Do whatever you want to do! I would only be a rice worm to you. I would really like to be in a jail for food and protection from the bombs!'"

All at once Grandmother and I burst out laughing and crying simultaneously.

"He sensed that I wasn't afraid." Her hazy eyes twinkled. "What could he possibly do to an eighty-year-old woman?"

"What did you do about food?" I asked hesitantly, almost afraid to know.

"I don't remember when, but one afternoon several of them came and tore up the whole house. They ransacked the rooms, removed the tatami in the living room and pried up the boards underneath. They found the rice and flour I had hidden under the floor. They took it all." Recalling those events, she shivered.

"Oh Harmoni, how did you sustain yourself?"

"I went around the neighborhood. There were only two families left in the whole area. They gave me a little food, but mostly I rummaged through all the empty houses. I faced a few famines in my youth, so I learned how to survive. One day I found dried turnip greens strung on a straw rope, some salted fish and dried persimmons in buried earthenware jars in one house. In another house several crocks were buried under the eaves on the side of the kitchen wall, concealed under a straw pile. Inside there was kimchi, bean paste and red pepper paste. I found some barley and soy beans, too." She wore a look of triumph.

"Harmoni, please forgive me. I feel terribly guilty that I left you behind . . . ."

"Ai-go, Hyun Sook-ga, heaven destined for you to leave Seoul when you did. They might have killed you. I don't remember how soon it was after they took my food, but the Communists came in and demanded to know where your brother-in-law was. They had found out who the house belonged to and knew he was one of the top officials of the South Korean government. They put a gun to my head, so I roared at them, 'You insolent sons! Don't you have grandmothers! You ought to be ashamed of yourselves. Think about it before you pull the trigger!'"

"Harmoni, they could have shot you instantly," I gasped.

"So? I wasn't a bit afraid of death. It would have hastened my day of eternal rest." Tears welled up in her eyes again.

"Harmoni, would you please forgive me?" My heart felt as if it was about to break.

"What is there to forgive? And why are you taking the blame?" she asked. "I am alive!"

Sergeant Fleming

One evening a tall brown-haired Army sergeant came into our shop to have some tailoring done. We could tell he liked children, for he spoke tenderly to Wha Sook, who was still a toddler. He started coming in more often and made a point of bringing along food for her. Sometimes he brought a piece of meat between two slices of white bread or a piece of cake or cookies neatly wrapped in napkins. One particular evening my brother-in-law was still in the shop when Sergeant Fleming came in with a turkey sandwich and a slice of pumpkin pie. Through our brother-in-law, he told us that it was Thanksgiving Day. After he gave Wha Sook the food, he asked if we could teach him Korean. We agreed and asked if Sergeant Fleming in turn would teach us English.

Thus we began an English and Korean class each evening at the shop. Come rain or shine, Sergeant Fleming arrived with food and Dixon's Conversational English. The only time he missed the class was when he had night duty. I paid close attention to his teaching, drilling myself in pronunciation, memorizing each new word and practicing writing the alphabet. Sergeant Fleming seemed to have infinite patience. He would go over one sentence as many times as we needed.

He must have sensed how badly I wanted to learn, for inconspicuously he began to spend more and more of our class time teaching us English, leaving little time for his Korean lessons. When we noticed, he excused it by saying he would not be able to use our language in America.

More than anything else that Sergeant Fleming taught us, the lesson that made the most lasting impression on me, was about the Empire State Building. When I read:

> The Empire State Building is in New York City . . . It has one hundred and two stories . . . It is the tallest building in the world.

I was flabbergasted. Could one see the top of the building from the street? Could one touch the clouds from the 102nd story? Would I see the Empire State Building someday? The last question startled me. How could I even dare to dream such an unlikely thing?

Whenever any one came into the shop, I remained seated in my chair until they had gone to keep my handicap hidden. Every evening I hid my legs under the desk before Sergeant Fleming arrived, but he must have noticed anyway, for one afternoon he came with a Korean medical doctor. After introductions, the doctor said, "This American soldier is very concerned about your well-being. He asked me to tell you that there is no reason for you to be ashamed of your handicap."

I could feel my face flush, and my heart sank as I thought, "Now Sergeant Fleming will despise me as so many others do."

"With your permission," the polite doctor continued, "Sergeant Fleming would like to arrange an appointment for you to see a specialist." This exposure embarrassed me so that I could hardly manage to nod my head in consent.

At the appointed time, Sergeant Fleming and the doctor came to take me to the clinic. The examining doctor felt that he could not do anything to help me. Although nothing came of the appointment, something began to change in my own heart. Sergeant Fleming's concern and friendly attitude did not change even after he discovered my concealed disability. He only tried harder to teach me. This instilled a new hope and confidence in me.

One gloomy day in June, Sergeant Fleming neglected his usual Korean greeting, "An-nyung ha-sim ni-ka?" His large, brown eyes looked very solemn. By this time I had learned enough English to carry on a simple conversation, but he asked brother-in-law to interpret what he wanted to say.

"Hyun Sook, my term in Korea has ended. The time has come for me to go home to Mikuk."

Mikuk, the Korean word for America, 'the beautiful land.' Many GIs came from Mikuk and left for Mikuk, and I was accustomed to transient servicemen, but this time I felt a deep sense of impending loss. Huge tears dropped on my skirt, and his fatherly image blurred before my eyes.

"Hyun Sook, keep on learning." Sergeant Fleming came closer and gripped my shoulder. "But please be careful what you learn because there are some soldiers whose speech is not respectable." His moistened his lips and continued, "Please be sure to ask, 'Is this correct English?'" Although he spoke solemnly, when Brother-in-law interpreted what Sergeant Fleming said, we all burst out laughing. He smiled uncomfortably and turned serious again.

"My wife and I have been married for many years, but have not been blessed with children. Had we had a child, she would be about your age, Hyun Sook. I think of you as my daughter." He paused for a moment, "Now, I must go. But I will not say goodbye. I will say, 'We shall meet again!'"

Heaviness filled the room. My father thanked him and suggested that we sing the hymn, "God Be with You Till We Meet Again." Sergeant Fleming sang it in English while we sang it in Korean. I could only hum the tune, for a big rock had lodged in my throat. Father prayed for the Lord's blessings upon the sergeant and his family. Slowly Sergeant Fleming turned to leave. With one foot out the door he turned again and said, "Tah-shi mahn-nahr-te kah-ji – till we meet again."

After Sergeant Fleming left Korea, my parents had some advice for me. "Hyun Sook-ga, use more of your time in the tailoring trade rather than studying. There is nothing like a skilled worker. Learn all phases of it diligently," Mother urged me.

"Furthermore," Father groped for words, "You must accept the fact that you have a bad leg and, uh, you won't be able to, well, what I am trying to tell you is that it won't be easy for you to find work. And you won't be able to marry. Live with us and take care of us in our old age."

I knew my parents were trying to prepare me for a limited future, since Korean society had little or no room for people with disabilities. I even felt sorry for them. They had to choose me to take care of them in their declining years instead of a son. I understood their reasoning. I knew that they meant well for my future as well as theirs, but my heart revolted against their statements. I wanted them to be proud of me. It enraged me that they considered it a waste for their handicapped daughter to get an education.

In rebellion, I made up my mind to learn in spite of all opposition and obstacles, even if it took my whole life. I started with the only available source of learning, the English language. After my sisters and parents went to sleep, I turned the light back on and went over the lessons in my

English textbook. But Father always awoke and scolded me, ordering me to turn off the light and sleep. He even slapped me several times. His objections, which I resented, only made me more determined to study. I could not smother my burning need to learn. One night I thought of a plan. The light in my sleeping section in the Quonset hut hung down from the ceiling on a long cord that would reach within a foot of my cot. It could be adjusted by moving the electric cord around. When Father's snores vibrated from the adjoining section, I crept out of bed, untied the knot in the cord and let the light hang loose over my pillow. I focused it over my book by wrapping a piece of black cloth around the light shade. Then I could study as late as I sometimes wanted, until two or three in the morning.

That August, we received several post cards from Sergeant Fleming. He wrote to tell us that he arrived home safely and resumed his life as a civilian. Nothing pleased me more than to receive mail from America. I was so happy that sometimes I forgot to eat and lagged at my work.

It was one thing to receive mail from America, but quite another matter to reply. After work I labored over a letter, stringing together all the words I had learned. I pored over my Korean-English dictionary for new words, working at it for several nights. After my frustrating attempts, my letter still did not sound at all as I wanted it to. Finally I decided to show the whole embarrassing jumble to a private who came into the shop early the following morning.

As his hazel eyes went over the maze of words, the blond, boyish soldier tried to conceal his grin by pressing his lips together. He took a pencil and marked the paper and then handed me the corrected draft. I saw connecting lines up and down, arrows here and slashes there, crossed out phrases and corrected spellings, omitted commas, periods, and misplaced exclamation marks. When he finished it looked like a tourist's map. My face heated with embarrassment, but I was grateful for his help. Eagerly I mailed my first letter to America.

Long after Sergeant Fleming left Korea, our family continued to think fondly of him. In our family devotions, we prayed for him that God would bless him and his wife with a family.

Instead a baby arrived at our own house. In April of 1953, my mother gave birth to her fifth child, Bok Sook. I knew my father had been boasting to his friends that this child would be a son, but this baby was also a girl.

"Ai-go," Mother sighed, "another daughter!"

"Whatever the Lord sends to us, we should accept as His will," Father consoled her. He brought home a set of pure gold rings for Mother. He also bought a lot of the most expensive grade of ginseng roots and seaweed for her. However my parents felt, we girls were thrilled to have a baby in the family after so many years. Bok Sook never lacked for affection or attention.

Some time after Bok Sook was born, the United Nations Civil Assistance Command left the area and the 21st Station US Army Hospital moved in to the site. My parents were allowed to continue their tailor shop on the post.

Father had saved much of their earnings from the tailor shop and decided to pursue his dormant dream of becoming the king of poultry in Korea. He built a house off the compound, gradually spending more time on the home site than at the shop, leaving the tailoring to the rest of us.

When he had completed the house, my parents invited some of our relatives to live there, and we continued to live on the post. Grandmother moved into the house along with other relatives. It seemed to me as if all of our living kinfolk flocked to our home from near and far.

During the winter Father built the chicken coop and

went away to learn how to build an incubator for hatching eggs. When he returned, he constructed several incubators and even built a special ondol for the newly hatched chicks.

One day in the spring, Father took me out to the farm to watch the hatching eggs. He explained that he had kept vigil for the last three weeks, relieved by his farmhand only long enough to eat meals and take catnaps. Father simply did not take any chances with the three thousand eggs, which he had to keep at a certain temperature continuously. He had even installed an emergency generator in case of a power outage.

As we watched, the first egg cracked. A yellowish-orange beak pecked at the shell from within. It seemed to be such a struggle that I wanted to help it by cracking the eggshell in half for the chick, but my father stopped me. "That's what I wanted to do at first, too. But my instructor said we must allow the chicks to break out of the shell alone. If we help the chick during the initial period, it will not survive as well as if it struggles out on its own." Impatiently I held my hands back and watched. At short intervals the chicks began to stagger out of the shells. They sprawled on wobbly legs as if on a sheet of ice. Father told us to lift them carefully when their feathers dried and place them under the brooders, which looked like gigantic Chinese coolie hats. The chicks wobbled about and started pecking at their food. The stronger ones dominated the feeders, and I empathized with the weaker ones, for they were pushed away by the aggressive birds and tottered around the edges of the hood. Father gently lifted them up and placed them separately in a box until they became strong enough to mingle with the flock. It fascinated me to watch the chicks struggle for survival.

As the chicks grew, Father would move them into the coop. Whenever he approached the chicken coop he would tap the feed bucket with his scoop. Soon the chicks began to identify Father by mere sight. Father devoted so much of his time to his chicks that they flocked all around him. He dragged his feet on the ground when he entered the chicken yard so that he would not step on them. Under his care the chicks thrived. He was a picture of contentment when he stood surrounded by his feathery friends.

One Sunday, when the pullets were about four months old, the whole family left for church as usual. When we returned, Father went to the coop to feed them, but all he found was a blanket of white feathers strewn over the ground. While we were gone, someone had snuck into the coop and sprayed the entire area with a sterilizing chemical that was used only after the chickens were put away for the night. The intruder had sprayed the deadly chemical all over the food, water, and even on the flock. The feathers of the lifeless birds were saturated with it.

Four months of labor had been destroyed in just a few hours. Our grief-stricken father slumped down on top of the dead chickens. After a period of meditation, Father gathered his strength. He and the farmhand carried load after load of dead chickens on A-frames to the dump. He wasted no time moaning over his loss but set out to rebuild the flock. I marveled at his ability to carry on.

As far as I could remember, my father had never missed a single church gathering since we had returned to Korea. Through blizzard or rainstorm, he attended the dawn prayer services daily. None of us children were ambitious or devoted enough to arise at the unearthly hour of four o'clock in the morning to follow him to the church. When he returned at six, Father opened all the windows, even in winter, to circulate fresh air, as he sang in his booming voice, "This Is My Father's World" or "Hail to the Brightness of Zion's Glory."

"Children," he would call, "it's time to arise. Look at the brilliant sunrise!"

Even though Mother never quite seemed to match Father's zeal, she was giving and full of hospitality. She never failed to give to the poor and serve meals, or at least refreshments, to guests. Mother always told us, "Never let a guest leave our home without some nourishment." On Sundays she looked around after the service for lonely faces. No one walked away from church without being invited to our home. She always cooked plenty of food and served them generously. Even during our lean days shortly after the war, she made sure that we shared whatever we had to eat with our guests.

The most remarkable practice of my parents was to put aside at least ten percent and sometimes up to fifty percent of their income for God. No matter how badly they seemed to need the money, they tithed without fail. Those times when they had no jobs, my mother still put aside one tenth of our grain and took it to our church. They were not immune from tragedy or loss, but I never saw them receiving charity from other people.

A high point in Father's life was being elected to be an elder of the Presbyterian Church. He had spearheaded the building of the church near our home in Pusan, so it was a doubly joyous occasion. The installation ceremony for an elder was considered to be as sacred and important as an exchange of marriage vows, so Mother immediately began preparations for the feast that would be served afterwards.

I Want to Walk!

I was the only one in the family who had to work in the tailor shop instead of being sent to school. Mi Sook went to school and even had piano lessons. I hid my slighted feelings as a dutiful daughter of Korea, obedient to my parents, honoring my elders, controlling my emotions. Back talk only brought punishment. No matter how furious and bitter I felt, I kept a placid expression on my face. My mask was so good that our relatives said I was as good-natured as Buddha.

One night, in the fall of 1954, I threw myself on the bed and buried my face in the pillow, crying out to God in anguish.

"Heavenly Father, tonight I feel sadder than other nights. Why can't I walk and run and go to school like everyone else? Why God? Please answer me, Omnipotent Father. Why can't I be like others? Can you hear me, God?"

At last my muffled sobs trailed off into a hopeless sigh. The only audible sound was my father's soft snoring from his partitioned bedroom in the Quonset hut. I was almost asleep when a compelling thought urged me to write a letter to the Commander of the 21st Station Hospital. I stole out of bed quietly and fumbled for a piece of paper and a fountain pen. Praying for guidance, I labored over the letter in the dim light of my room.

The following morning, a corporal named George from the US Armed Forces Radio Station AFKN came by to have his uniform altered. Sheepishly I showed him my letter and asked what he thought of it. George read it and said, "Susie, it needs some corrections, but other than that it sounds fine." He went over the letter and told me to recopy it.

> Dear Colonel Jensen:
>
> My name is Hyun Sook Lee, nicknamed Susie, a seamstress at the tailor shop on your post. Tonight I am sadder than other nights because of my weak leg. I want to walk and run like others. I know Koreans are not treated at your hospital, but could you please help cure my leg?
>
> I am sorry to trouble you.
>
> Yours truly,
>
> "Susie" Hyun Sook Lee

As I read the corrected copy of my letter, George volunteered, "Susie, I'll come back after lunch and deliver your letter to the Commander."

"Thank you," I said hesitantly, "but you are, well, just a corporal." I looked at him with a puzzled expression. "How could you get my letter to the Commander?"

"Don't worry," George said, "I'm an announcer and have access to top ranking officers." He grinned from ear to ear and whisked his blond crew cut. "Just have it ready, all right?"

After George left with my letter, I ripped open the

seam of a uniform and re-sewed it at least five times. I just could not sew straight.

Finally, George returned, wearing a long face. He removed his army hat and clutched it over his heart. Fearing the worst, I picked up the fatigue jacket which I had been working on and lowered my head to sew.

"Aren't you going to ask me what happened?

"Well, I already know the answer." I tried to keep my voice steady, "Thank you for trying . . . ."

"Look at me, Susie," George said. "Have faith. What if I told you that Colonel Jensen said 'Yes?' " He teased, unable to hide that ear-to-ear grin any longer. "Your letter moved the Commander. They will contact you soon." I squealed so loudly at the incredible news that the GI in charge of laundry in the next Quonset raced to our shop to see what the commotion was all about.

The following day an army doctor came to the shop to have an insignia sewn on his uniform. Later I found out that he had approached my parents, introduced himself as Dr. Philip Zeitler and requested their permission to perform surgery on my leg. My parents consented and the following week I had an appointment to see Dr. Zeitler at the hospital.

I could not maintain my composure throughout the examination. My heart surged with expectations. Following the exam, Dr. Zeitler took X-rays. After studying them seriously, he told me that I would have to undergo a triple arthrodesis, followed by several tendon transfers. He set the date for me to return October 20, five days before my father's installation as an elder of the Presbyterian Church.

George must have talked about me to his fellow announcers at the AFKN Radio Station, for the staff seemed to frequent our shop after that. They extended their help in more ways than one. It was obvious that to be announcers they must speak proper English, so I turned to them for help with my English lessons. They never seemed too busy to answer my questions. A handsome Navy announcer, who called himself, Swabby, and his friend Les Cooley presented me with a brand new hard-covered Webster's Collegiate Dictionary. It was the thickest dictionary I had ever seen. I was so happy to have my very own English dictionary that I treated it like a precious friend.

Several days before my hospitalization, a GI named Peter, a hair stylist in civilian life, stopped by. He said he had heard about my upcoming surgery and that he wanted to give me a gift, a Toni permanent. Excitedly I looked at my mother for approval. She nodded and sighed, "Are you already at the age to be primped?" She stared at me, "Nineteen years old. How time flies!" She consented with a smile. After a few hours, Peter held a mirror in front of me. I did not even recognize my own face. He came back the day before my surgery to set my hair and comb it out stylishly.

Finally, the long-awaited morning arrived. An army attendant wheeled me into the operating room. When I woke up from surgery, I found my right leg in a long cast. I groaned with pain. A beautiful Army nurse stroked my hand. I felt confused at first, but before I could ask, nausea overwhelmed me. She shoved basin under my chin. When I was done, I dropped back into a slumber.

Mother came to visit me that evening. While she was still with me, Dr. Zeitler came to my bedside to tell us that the surgery had been successful. After that the pain was easier to bear.

Many of my American friends came to visit me. They showered me with countless gifts and scribbled their names on my cast. One of the American Red Cross workers stopped by one afternoon with her basket loaded with candies, stationary and toiletries. She said that she had heard about a Korean girl being hospitalized.

"Choose anything you want, Dearie," she chimed. "Do you need hand lotion, dusting powder or stationary? Would you like a pack of Lifesavers?" I hesitated, watching my manners, but at her urging I chose a box of Desert Flower dusting powder. I liked the fragrance. She pressed on, "Would you like to have a plush chenille bathrobe? A lady in Lansing, Michigan sent it." I hesitated again. Without waiting for my answer, she dashed out, "Wait, dear, I'll bring the robe and show it to you. I'm sure you'll like it. I'll be right back!"

Within minutes she returned with the most beautiful robe I had ever seen. She helped me put it on. It was my favorite color, aqua blue, and fit me perfectly. I was not about to say the well-mannered triple "No" and lose out on this gorgeous robe. Instead, I hurriedly said, "Thank you!" and wrapped my arms around it. I was so grateful that I asked her if I could send a thank you note to the lady. Thus began my correspondence with Mrs. Fred E. Vanderlip of Lansing, Michigan.

Dr. Zeitler gave me a pass from the hospital to go home for the Christmas holiday, but when I got there, Grandmother was not home. Mother explained to me that my grandmother had passed away just one day before Father's installation. They kept the news from me because of my surgery. I took the news of her death very hard. The bond we shared was the strongest I had in my family.

After the holidays, I returned to the hospital for my final surgery. Then, in early spring, Dr. Zeitler asked me to come to his office. He explained that all the necessary surgery was completed, and the results seemed to be satisfactory.

"Your cast will be removed in a couple of weeks. I'm leaving an order for a brace to be made for you. The brace will be designed to give you support instead of using a stick or your hand."

I recalled refusing to wear one as a toddler, but now

nothing could have made me happier. Dr. Zeitler stood up and folded his arms. Assuming that he wanted to dismiss me, I reached for my crutches and headed for the door when he said, "Er, Susie . . . ." I turned around to look at him, but he just shook his black wavy hair. His warm brown eyes had turned solemn, and he looked pained. "Nothing, Susie. Nothing important." I left his office feeling puzzled.

A few days later I learned that Dr. Zeitler had been transferred to Japan. A wave of panic washed over me.

"Dr. Zeitler left explicit orders for us to follow-up and look after you," a nurse reassured me. "He is a remarkably gifted and dedicated surgeon who performed excellent work on you. You were very fortunate to have had him." She took my hand and consoled me, "Susie, please don't get upset. Another doctor is assigned to you."

On a balmy spring day, when the mountains were competing with pink, lavender and white azalea blossoms, hospital staff escorted me to the UN Rehabilitation Center for my brace. One of the technicians attached the right shoe to my brace and made adjustments to it while I waited. Although I still had a slight limp, I could walk more easily with the brace. I wished that Dr. Zeitler and Sergeant Fleming could have been there to watch me walk.

Soon after I began to wear my brace, my parents bought a bicycle for me. To my amazement, I could ride it comfortably. I felt like a bird freed from its cage and could no longer stay inside the gloomy shop. I rode all around the hospital grounds. The haunting memories of war dissipated as I gained confidence. Although I could not go to school because of my age, I felt so happy to move freely that I found myself smiling and laughing a great deal.

One place I often visited was the AFKN Radio Station. Lieutenant Eagan, the officer in charge, along with the staff welcomed my visit and gave me a tour of the station. It intrigued me to see all the complicated equipment with switches, wires and earphones. Some of the announcers, who had been tutoring me in English, said I could use their typewriters to practice. That opened up a new channel of learning for me. I studied the typing manual diligently and practiced typing on the Underwood several hours each day.

Another place I visited almost as often as AFKN, was the post telephone exchange. The Korean telephone operators welcomed my visits and showed me how to operate the switchboard. After a month of watching in fascination, I gathered up the courage to ask if I could relieve one of the women during her coffee break. They liked the idea of getting away from the switchboard almost as much as I enjoyed operating it.

In the summer of 1955, the 21st Station Hospital relocated, and a Swedish Red Cross Hospital moved in. My disappointment had a few consolations. The telephone exchange, the radio station and our shop would continue operating on the base.

Shortly after the transition, the telephone exchange needed another operator, and they hired me. Dutifully I turned all my earnings over to my parents. Parting with the money did not bother me because I enjoyed my work, and it helped me to improve my English. During the long night shifts, I acquired many phone pals. The happy hours passed swiftly.

During their stay the Swedish hospital staff arranged for me to receive physical therapy. The Chief of Physical Therapy devoted much of her time to strengthening my weak leg muscles.

That fall, a letter from Mrs. Fleming brought the wonderful news that she and her husband were expecting a child in November. I wrote back immediately, telling her that we had been praying for a child in their home and that my family and I shared in their joy. We thanked God for the answered prayers.

I had never imagined that life could be so good and happy for me. By mail I introduced Mrs. Vanderlip to the Flemings, and they began to correspond, becoming good friends. I spent all my free time in the office behind the switchboard typing my letters to America. I considered the English language to be the most beautiful sound in the world. In a period of four years, I wore out two Korean-English dictionaries as well as an English one. The more words I learned, the more I loved it.

In 1957, the Swedish Red Cross Hospital closed down after winter. The premises, which had originally belonged to the Korean Fisheries College, were returned to that institution. Needless to say, this terminated my family's main source of income. My parents moved out of their quonset hut. Father went on with his poultry farming and Mother found a job in an officers' clothing store near home to supplement their income. By then my younger sister Mi Sook had graduated from high school and was living with Onni in Seoul in order to attend a women's university.

Losing my job, the scattering of the family and not even having the tailor shop to return to shook me. Even though the Civilian Personnel Officer gave each employee a letter of recommendation, we had no guarantee of another job. I wrote to the Flemings and the Vanderlips about our predicament and my job-hunting at other US Army posts in Pusan. Like everyone else, I filled out job applications and waited.

Challenges

One day a letter arrived from a Colonel Al Maxman, the Commander of US Army Pusan Area Command (USAPAC). He requested that I report to his office on April 14, 1957.

When I visited the headquarters, the Master Sergeant buzzed the intercom. Immediately a tall, dignified colonel came out to the spacious lobby to greet me. I was so startled by his extraordinary greeting that I stood at attention like a soldier.

"Relax, Susie, please." He called me by my nickname, although I had used my Korean name on the application form. He ushered me into his office, seated me and took his place behind the glistening mahogany desk. Colonel Maxman picked up a thick pile of papers and said, "I've received some letters. One is from a lady in Lansing, Michigan and another from a family in Alaska." With a quick glance, he said, "Now I see a smile on you face. Mr. and Mrs. Fleming and Mrs. Vanderlip have written many nice things about you. They told me of your termination from the Swedish Hospital." He looked up and asked, "Can you type?"

"Yes, sir, I have been practicing for the last few years," I replied confidently.

"Have you worked in an office?"

"No, sir. I worked only as a telephone operator." I became apprehensive, assuming that I should have office experience before I could be hired.

"How would you like to be trained for your new job and work right here in the headquarters?" he asked.

I was still in a daze when he picked up the phone, recommending me for placement in the US Military Personnel Office at the headquarters. The mere thought of working in the office scared me.

"Well, Susie, I know you will do a fine job," Colonel Maxman spoke reassuringly, as if he sensed my apprehension. "But let me know if you are not happy there." He stood up to escort me to the front entrance. "Susie, you are to report to the office on Monday."

I walked out of the office, hailed a taxi in front of the gate and was still in a state of amazement when the cab jerked to a stop in front of my home. My father met me at the gate. "How did the interview go?" he asked eagerly.

"Aboji, I was scared, but the commanding officer was extremely kind to me."

"The Lord is good," Father said, looking up at the cloudless spring skies. "He looks after us."

"Yes, Aboji, God is really good to us. Do you know why the colonel was so kind to me?"

"Because the word got around that you are a good worker." His eyes lit up with the proud-of-my-daughter expression I had seen whenever he was with Onni.

"No, Aboji, the Colonel didn't even ask to look at the recommendation letter I took with me. Mrs. Vanderlip and the Flemings wrote to him."

"Oh, what a blessed thing for them to do." Father nodded his head.

"But, Aboji, I am afraid. The job he has offered me is in

the US Army Military Personnel Office. I would be the only Korean in an all American office. I told him that I had never worked in an office, but he said that I would be trained for the job. What if I can't do the work well?"

"Why do you worry? You have proven that you can do anything you have set your mind to do. Besides," he said earnestly, "the Lord will help you. Remember the Scripture verse. 'I can do all things through Christ Jesus which strengtheneth me.'"[37]

Father took me down to see his new flock of leghorn chickens. He wasted no time after the great loss. His incubators came to the rescue. He said he only needed to hatch more eggs. This time he bought a pair of geese, a pair of turkeys and several pigs to raise in addition to his chickens. His undefeatable spirit impressed me so much that I said, "Father, I will continue to bring home my earnings."

I left him in the chicken coop and went into the house. My youngest sister was napping, and Wha Sook was still at school. Mother had not returned from work, so I went to the kitchen to help the maid start supper. The kitchen was immaculate. Mother had always kept servants, and I had no reason to do housecleaning or cooking. Nevertheless, I started the kitchen fire and rinsed the spinach while the maid washed the rice and scaled a fresh sea bream.

Mother seemed very content with supper. Father urged me to tell her about my interview. She stroked my hair and told me how proud she was of me. On Saturday, my mother took me to a dressmaker downtown to be fitted for new suits and dresses. It irked me that they were fussing over me now, only after I was gainfully employed. The very fact that I had to earn their approval by obtaining a position saddened me.

---

[37] Philippians 4:13

Anxiously I waited for Monday and stepped into the office fifteen minutes early. The sergeant in charge welcomed me warmly. He was about six feet tall and introduced himself as Sergeant Campbell from San Antonio, Texas. The GIs assigned to the office strolled in and turned their heads to look at me. Shortly after eight o'clock, Colonel Maxman walked in. Everyone stood at attention, and I followed their lead.

"At ease," he commanded. The soldiers settled to their work, while Colonel Maxman spoke with the sergeant. Later on he walked over to me and said, "Susie, you're in good hands. The men will help you learn your work." He smiled, shook my hand firmly and left the office.

The soldiers in the office let out a sigh of relief and looked at me again. I felt as if I was standing before a panel of curious judges. Sergeant Campbell, however, broke the ice by looking at me cross-eyed. I covered my mouth, not wanting to laugh at him rudely. He stroked his crew cut and drawled, "Nobody's gonna bite ya, Susie Q. Relax will ya?" Then he hopped around like an ape. Everybody burst out laughing. Sergeant Campbell walked me around the office introducing me to the others. They decided to use my nickname instead of Hyun Sook Lee, so I became known as 'Susie Lee' to Americans and Koreans alike.

Sergeant Campbell took my hand and led me to my desk. He pulled out the chair for me. The drawers were neat and well supplied with office stationery. They had even installed a telephone. While I was still looking around and getting used to the office, Sergeant Campbell pointed toward two olive green filing cabinets. "You will be taking care of these files."

My spirit drooped. Reading my thoughts, he said, "It's just a matter of learning the basics." He took a folder from one of the drawers and thumbed through to show me different typed of mimeographed papers: Special Orders, Travel Orders, Temporary Duty Orders, Transfer Orders, Reassignment Orders. Orders, orders, and more orders.

I was just trying to muster up enough courage to tell Sergeant Campbell that I could not possibly live up to their expectations, when he looked at his wristwatch and stretched himself and said, "What d'ya know! It's time for coffee break. Susie Q, that's all I'm gonna tell ya today. You got a busy schedule ahead." He grinned at me, "After the coffee break, somebody from the Motor Pool will pick you up." He pulled his field cap all the way down to his ears, "You're a VIP!" Starting for the door, he winked, "Tell the driver you're going to the Personnel Office. They're expecting ya."

The American Personnel Officer himself handled my application and told me that I would be given two weeks of office training at no cost. At the end of my second week, Sergeant Campbell greeted me in a friendlier fashion that usual. He walked over and sat down on the chair by my desk.

"Susie Q, your instructor said that you've completed your training with flying colors. And we say you're a super worker!" Looking around the office he said, "What d'ya say, fellas, if we all go down to the snack bar and celebrate!"

"Yeah, great! Hurray for Susie!" The office almost exploded with joyous commotion. Men from the adjoining office, the Legal Section, and the Information office rushed over to see what was happening. I marveled at them.

During my third week, Colonel Maxman summoned me to his office and asked if I like my job. I told him how kind the men had been to me. Through their help and the training, I felt confident and enjoyed my work.

"Well, Susie, I knew you would do fine here!" I stared at him, astonished. "I hear many nice things about you, Susie.

Keep it up." I bowed and thanked him, but he said, "This is the American way," and he extended his hand to shake mine.

Just as I stood up to leave, he called, "One more thing – how do you come to work? Do you live far away from here?" When I told him the distance and that I took both a taxi and a bus to commute, he picked up the phone immediately. While it rang, he motioned me to sit down. "I'm calling the billeting officer. There are some barracks for the Korean waitresses on the post. The quarters are just big open spaces with army cots, lockers, and oil heaters." He studied my facial expression and continued, "Would you like to live on the post?" My heart danced. Colonel Maxman told me that I could move in any time, and authorized a staff car for me to go home and pick up my belongings.

At home I briefly explained my moving onto the post and rushed around to gather my things. When I was almost ready to leave, Father sat me down to pray for me. He was not happy about my living away from home, but under the circumstances, he said he understood. He advised me to stay away from temptations and to attend church services regularly.

It was dark by the time the car stopped in front of the barracks. I felt uneasy, for I knew none of the women there, but they all smiled and helped me with my bed and made me feel welcome. As the days passed, I discovered that some of the women had lost their parents during the war. A few of them had no living relative. They found strength and comfort by helping and confiding in one another, calling the older women Onni.

Some of the waitresses were very pretty and a few had dates with the officers or servicemen for dinners and movies. Whenever an escort came for one of them, I felt a tinge of envy. I knew too well that I had many obstacles. No one would want to date a girl with a leg brace. Even if someone would date me, my parents would be mortified and might even disown me.

Socializing with foreigners, not to speak of marrying them, had been frowned upon by Korean society for centuries. For over 4,000 years, Korean traditions had guarded the purity of their race. Furthermore, women were rarely encouraged to pursue any profession. With the outbreak of the Korean War, however, traditions suddenly collapsed. Females, both married and single, were forced to find employment. Many women sought jobs with the US Armed Forces as typists, telephone operators, waitresses and maids. Although these women were doing honest work, they were not considered ideal candidates for marriage. No matter how professional a relationship might be between the woman and a foreigner, Korean society in those days automatically considered her an immoral woman. It was a subtle but pervasive stigma and terribly hard to erase.

Most families objected violently to their daughters dating American soldiers. In extreme cases, the daughter was ostracized, and even removed from the family register. Regardless, some women were so touched by the way American men catered to women, after years of being subservient to Korean males, that they fell in love and married them.

Pondering these issues, I rationalized that it would make no difference if I mingled with the American men and even dated one of them. My parents had made it quite clear that no matchmaker would seek me out. In fact, I would have dated an American out of spite, but none of them showed the slightest personal interest in me.

Aside from that, I thoroughly enjoyed living on the post. It was next to paradise to be shielded from the taunting, unfeeling children of the street. My disability had caused me to be pegged me with every conceivable name under the sun.

When I started working on the post, some even called me a crippled prostitute. Since I could find the means neither to reform them, nor to convey my anguish, I simply stayed on the post, even on weekends.

During a period of five months many servicemen left Korea. As new faces replaced the vacancies in my office, my supervisors began to rely heavily on me to maintain continuity by keeping the files and order numbers accurately, as well as issuing various types of orders. I tried to adapt to the American way of being positive, outgoing and caring. Mutual understanding and friendship developed with my fellow workers. Some of them would sit on my desk and share their joys and, at times, their problems with me.

Such moments occasionally followed the morning mail call – the most awaited period of a soldier's day. Letters from girlfriends and wives back home would make the GIs jump up into the air, kicking their boots together. Some of the men would kiss the envelope repeatedly and waltz to their desks as if holding a lady in their arms. When a package arrived with a "Fragile. Handle with Care!" label, all the GIs flocked around the recipient like pigeons to scattered breadcrumbs. Homemade cookies and chocolate fudge neatly wrapped in foil squares and stacked in tin containers usually disappeared within minutes.

Some men seldom received letters. Those few usually sat hunched behind their desks, looking lonely, gloomy, dejected or ill tempered. They seemed to have no reason to laugh or be happy.

Before long I realized that not every letter imparted happy news. Some turned out to be painful Dear John letters. When a GI received such a letter from his girl or wife, nothing seemed to pick him up. The power of love, I plainly saw, could strengthen a man to endure almost any situation, but the loss of love had appalling results.

Once I saw one of the most mild-mannered men completely lose control after his wife wrote him for a divorce. He seethed with rage and cursed the fact that he was in Korea

"For these stinking gooks, I lost my woman. I'm gettin' drunk tonight!" Vile words poured out of his mouth, cursing Korea and its people. Nobody dared curb him. His accusations infuriated me, and it was so unbearable that I broke out into tears. I wanted to tell him that my people and I had also lost much and suffered horribly in a war we did not understand.

A sergeant took me into an adjoining room and sent in one of the officers. Major Johnson walked in and waited until I dried my eyes before he spoke.

"Susie, the sergeant told me what happened in your office. I am sorry. It should never have happened. What the soldier said was insensitive, ignorant, and immature. You must never tolerate such rudeness from anyone. We appreciate your loyalty, but don't let anyone misguide you into believing that we are doing Korea an exorbitant favor by fighting the war and standing by now. In essence we are here to prevent further infiltration of the Communist forces into other parts of the world."

Nobody expounded the war in Korea the way he did. "Communism is like a cancer cell," he continued. "If left undetected, or if it is not removed, it eventually consumes the whole body and destroys the living organism." His gray eyes flickered, "True, no man in his right mind would want to leave the comfort to his home and family, but if he doesn't – the war you have experienced here in Korea might be fought in our backyard."

Several weeks later the Commanding Officer announced that on October 24th anyone who wished to attend the United Nations Day Memorial Service would be excused from work. We piled into staff cars and jeeps joining a long procession of army vehicles.

I had passed the main road below the hill countless times and had seen the fluttering foreign flags upon the hill, but I had never been inside. The grounds of the UN cemetery were already bustling with foreign dignitaries, UN honor guards, military personnel and civilians.

A wreath was placed at the base of the UN flag. When the bugler sounded taps, the honor guard simultaneously raised their flags to full mast. After the ceremony, we walked around with an assigned guide who told us that US Army and Korean employees maintained the twenty acres. Men and women from twenty-one nations who had fought in the Korean War were buried side by side. Eleven of the nations had removed their deceased for burial in their homeland, but the flags of all twenty-one countries remained there as a tribute to those soldiers whose lives were lost on Korean soil.

At the top of the steps I turned around and looked across the rows of men and women who had sacrificed their lives to preserve freedom. Since the Communist invasion, I had not for one second taken my own freedom for granted, but I did not know that so many nations had sent their sons and daughters to our rescue. The mingled blood of many races had restored our nation's freedom.

The Guest House

My convenient living arrangements did not last long. The end of 1957 brought Colonel Rossing, a new commander, to the Pusan Area Command. Rumors spread that one of the many orders he had received was to close down the living quarters of all Korean employees on the post. To accommodate those who had been living in the barracks, a building off the compound was provided, however, it was in an unsavory location. Although many of the women had no homes to go to, they chose not to move in there. We all went our separate ways, and I returned home.

A week after I resumed commuting, Colonel Rossing asked me if I were moving into the Korean women's quarters off the post. When I informed him of the conditions in that area, he looked startled. He asked how I came to work. Then he commented,

"Transportation expenses must take almost all of your paycheck." His silky white hair bobbed as he shook his head. "But don't worry. Something will work out. This evening my chauffeur will escort you to your home."

The following day, Colonel Rossing summoned me to his office again. "Susie, I have good news for you." His firm-set mouth relaxed into a heartwarming smile, "How would you like to be a greeter at the US Female Guest House on the post in exchange for a room there?"

"So you mean, sir, that I will be allowed to stay on the post again?"

"Yes, I told you not to worry, didn't I?" He grinned. "Susie, you have earned this privilege through your commendable work, friendliness and integrity." A benign expression spread across his aged face.

"Sir, I don't know what to say."

"You don't need to say anything. Just be yourself." He paused for a second, and then his steel gray eyes twinkled teasingly, "You're going to be the envy of us all." I stared at him, puzzled by that statement. "You're going to see all those gorgeous USO show gals and blond nurses from the States firsthand!" At that we both laughed.

That evening Colonel Rossing sent me home again in his staff car. Inside my home, I excitedly told my parents the good news. While I gathered my belongings, my father managed to squeeze in another pep talk.

"Hyun Sook-ga, always read the Bible and pray. Go to the Chapel faithfully. And stay away from the wrong kind of people." He looked at me hesitantly and said, "My daughter, I am praying for you three times a day." I thanked Father and reassured him that I would not stray from my faith. My mother said that she would have all my favorite food prepared for me whenever I visited home.

I moved into the female guesthouse that evening. The chauffeur helped me bring in my trunk and bicycle. I had never lived alone before and disliked empty houses, but in this instance I felt perfectly at home, as if a friend awaited my arrival. Before unpacking, I explored the rooms. The walls were sherbet green and each of the three bedrooms were furnished with a twin bed of varnished oak, a nightstand, a chest of drawers with a mirror, lamps and roomy closets. The bathroom contained a washstand with hot and cold running water, a shower stall, and a toilet. The spacious living room contained a large oil-burning heater and, to the left, a rattan frame sofa and chairs with matching coffee table were arranged in a semi-circle.

The billeting officer told me before I moved in that my bed would be placed in the kitchen so that when there were many guests I would not have to shuttle in and out of the regular bedroom. I pushed the swinging door and looked at my own nook. A twin bed rested below the tall kitchen window for me. The broom closet was converted for my clothes. A desk, footlocker, lamp and mirror were placed alongside my bed.

After stowing my few things, I put a towel over my shoulder and headed for the shower. The shower was the most wonderful part of the house. Even though I preferred soaking in a tubful of steamy water, I loved the privacy of the shower stall and the hot spray on my skin.

The thoughtful housekeeper had already made my bed before she went home. The clean, starched white sheets and goose-feather pillow looked so inviting that I gladly succumbed as soon as I had rolled up my hair. With visions of giving my nook a personal touch, I drifted off to sleep.

One day after work, I parked my bicycle on the front porch as usual and opened the door. A blend of perfumes filled the air, and I saw several gorgeous women sitting in the living room. Startled, I back out slowly and closed the door. Swiftly a golden-haired young woman poked her head out and gently pulled me inside, saying, "We know you are Susie. Please don't go away."

"The billeting office told us to expect you," another chimed in. "My name is Lorraine. We're with the USO show. Won't you sit down and visit with us?"

I did not know what to say. When they invited me to

go with them to the post theater and watch their
performance, my mouth dropped open. I regained my
composure and thanked them for the invitation. Then I
excused myself to get ready. Excitedly I dressed in my best –
a peacock blue faille dinner dress, which Mrs. Vanderlip had
sent me for Christmas. I added some jewelry, which I had
received from Mrs. Fleming.

After the men unloaded and carried the luggage
backstage, Lorraine led me through the side entrance and
into the already overfilled theater. She sat me in a reserved
front seat and told me to enjoy the show. GIs and officers
alike stared at me. Some of the fellows from my office called,
"Hey, Susie, how do you rate?" My face grew hot, and I
remembered Colonel Rossing's remark, "Susie, you're going
to be the envy of us all."

Amid clapping, cheering and whistling, the curtain
slowly rose. The women wore sequin-studded ballet
costumes, outlining hourglass figures and shapely legs. Each
one shared his or her talent – singing and dancing, juggling
and tumbling, telling jokes and playing instruments. The
performance I enjoyed the most, however, was by Lorraine
and her partner. She assumed the role of a mannequin while
her partner carried her to the center of the stage, going
through the motions of setting her up in the showcase, using
intriguing ballet movements and gestures.

After the splendid show, the USO group took me to
the reception dinner, which included shrimp cocktail
followed by thick T-bone steaks smothered with mushrooms.
The show people were just as lovely to be with as they were
to look at.

A few weeks after they left, another USO team
arrived. One of the performers with short brown hair and
enormous eyes named Sally befriended me immediately. She
came from Dearborn, Michigan, and specialized in baton

twirling. Sally made sure I went with her to the theater on the night of the performance. When her turn came, Sally glided onto the stage, blowing kisses at the howling and whistling soldiers. She whirled lightly about the stage, tossing and catching her glittering baton. With precision, she caught the baton behind her back and legs as she spun around. Her act was so fantastic that the GIs hushed when she sprang, twirled her body in mid-air, and caught the baton before her feet touched the floor.

After we had enjoyed another steak dinner at the reception, Sally excused herself from the table earlier than the rest and asked me to accompany her to the guesthouse. Back in the living room, she told me that her team would be leaving early the following morning and that she wanted to talk to me alone.

"Sally, you were fantastic!" I exclaimed as I curled up on the sofa.

"Thank you, Susie, but it didn't come naturally." She smiled, but her face grew solemn as she averted her eyes. "I had polio when I was a young girl."

"You?" I wasn't sure that I heard her right. She nodded. "How-how did you recover so completely?"

"It was a miracle. Our doctor told my mother that I would never walk normally again, but she didn't give up on me." Her eyes filled with tears, moistening her thick, long lashes. "My precious mother worked with a physical therapist who recommended physical therapy, massage and ballet exercise."

"How, but how did you learn to dance?" I asked breathlessly.

"It wasn't easy. Mother prayed, massaged my leg and encouraged me. Each time I accomplished a new stop or movement in ballet lessons, she praised me profusely. She stood by me day and night. Mother just plain didn't give up.

I thank God and my mother for what I can do today. That's the reason why when I get on that stage I become so overwhelmed with gratitude and inexpressible joy that I literally float." Her voice faltered as she continued, "Susie, please don't let your brace prevent you from reaching out. Lift your eyes up high. Life is limitless. Whatever you want to do can be done . . .if you persevere."

She left me sitting there speechless and went into her room. Her dynamic words of encouragement had rekindled my yearnings. Sally came out with an autographed copy of her portrait, which read:

> To my wonderful Susie.
> My prayers are with you always. I know we will always be friends. May God bless you and take care of you until we meet again. All my love is with you, my little sister.
> Sally.
> See you soon.

Her message of encouragement, her genuine love and her compassion touched me deeply. The following morning, Sally and her team left. As much as I enjoyed meeting these talented people, I always felt a deep sense of loss each time they left. Yet each new person I came across had a specific effect on me. Sally left me subtly but definitely changed within, ready to take another step forward.

One of the next occupants of the guesthouse was an American Red Cross director, who introduced herself as Doris Klover. She insisted that I call her by her first name and helped me to relax my deep-rooted cultural barrier of formality towards people in positions of authority. Doris somehow conveyed to me that we were equal, very much like Sally in the way she reached out to me in friendship. She did not act superior toward me, and urged me to feel free to be myself. Even after she moved into her own quarters, Doris encouraged me to visit her and even gave me lessons in shorthand. We soon became very good friends.

Two chaplains came and went during my tenure at the women's guesthouse. The chaplains and the staff always welcomed me at the post chapel. Some of the assistants were ordained ministers or theological students. They saw to it that I got acquainted with the new staff and took me along with them on their visits to the orphanages.

The third chaplain was Reverend Leslie Albus. Within a month of his arrival, he organized a group called, 'Protestant Men of the Chapel.' These men visited local churches and orphanages. Many of them had written to their families and friends and to their religious and social organizations, describing the desperate needs in the orphanages. Their contacts responded to these appeals promptly and generously.

Chaplain Albus once asked me to give a talk for the Thursday evening discussion group. The invitation both pleased me and scared me. He assured me that I would be among friends and that he would help me prepare if I chose the topic. After much prayer and searching, I chose Matthew 25:1-13, the story of the wise and foolish maidens and their lamps. It was my first experience behind the lectern. My mouth went dry, my white-gloved hands shook and my legs felt like two rubber tubes. Chaplain Albus flashed a reassuring smile at me. When I finished speaking, everyone came forward to thank me for the message. I could not recall what I had said except the ending where I stressed the need to be ready at all times, like the soldiers at the front line, for Christ's Second Coming.

"I'm very proud of you, Susie," Chaplain Albus said, shaking my hand vigorously.

"Susie," one of his assistants, a Methodist minister,

said, "Tonight we accolade you as an Honorary Protestant Man." We burst into laughter. "You are really one of us now. We want you to join us at the Idle Hour Service Club for some snacks."

I had heard about the service club, but had never been inside. It was a hospitality house for the armed forces personnel. Beautiful, smiling American hostesses tended to a crowd of servicemen. My friends introduced me to Miss Hazard, the director.

"Everybody calls me Georgie," the director told me. "I already know you through Doris, the Red Cross Director. Please stop by anytime you want." I liked her friendly attitude.

I looked around the spacious hall. Orange and tan lounge chairs and coffee tables were arranged in clusters. Some GIs sat comfortably reading, while others played chess, bridge or dominoes. A few men worked on the puzzles at desks. Georgie offered to show me around.

"That stage is a busy one. We have movies and live shows. We hire local bands, singers and dancers at times, but many nights our boys perform. You are welcome to attend any and all of these performances."

She led me through a hallway behind the refreshment counter where there were pool tables and hobby workbenches. "This place gives the boys away from home a little comfort and helps them fill their lonely hours. We try to make it as much like home as possible. Well, let's get back to the fellows."

Letters continued to arrive from the Flemings and the Vanderlips, stating that they had initiated the procedure to sponsor my family and me to live in the United States. I had cherished such a dream since reading about the Empire State Building seven years ago and now it was actually happening to us.

I went home that weekend to break the good news to my parents. They looked dazed as they listened. "Ah, Mikuk, the beautiful land which overflows with milk and honey," Father said dreamily, "and where money grows on trees!" We laughed at his joke. "As soon as we settle there, I shall start a poultry farm and develop it into a gigantic one. My dream is bound to come true." He looked far away and commented, "Mikuk is blessed because it is the only nation that is founded on trust in God."

The Flemings and Vanderlips advised us to apply for visas under the refugee immigration quota, and I quickly filled out our application. I simply could not keep such exciting plans to myself and I told the fellows in my office about the possibility. They were happy for me and each one told me various aspects of life in the United States.

"Everyone has cars; some own two or more. And all the women are gorgeous." One fellow whistled as he outlined a shapely lady with his hands. I believed him, for all the pictures the GIs carried in their wallets were of beautiful women, almost like the USO show performers.

Charlie, who joked a lot, now put on a straight face and said, "Susie, we all use push-button appliances. All that women have to do is to go around pushing buttons with their dainty little fingers, chitchat on the telephone and drink coffee while we men have to work like dogs!" He brought a magazine to my desk and flipped it open to a page, which showed an American woman in an immaculate, spacious kitchen with sparkling appliances.

"Look here, Susie, you put dirty dishes in that thing called a dishwasher, push a button and presto! Them things come out sparkling clean!" He turned to another page. "You toss dirty clothes in that what-cha-ma-call-it, and they come out cleaner than Korean Mama-san can make them by scrubbing away in the stream!"

I exclaimed in astonishment, which encouraged him all the more. "Them clothes come out washed, dried and even folded automatically. I'm tellin' you, Susie, them women got it made. Yep, we men gotta open the doors, pull the chairs out, light their cigarettes and everthin'. America is a woman's world!"

David, a corporal and one of the studious ones in the office, shook his head slightly and winked at me not to believe everything. During the coffee break everyone left for the snack bar, but David continued to work. When the office had emptied, he came and sat down beside my desk.

"Susie, I hope you didn't swallow all that junk. Sure our living standards might be higher than other places, but it's not all glamour. Not everybody owns cars, and not every woman is gorgeous. And women work very hard there. The clothes don't come out folded. That joker! Don't let him kid you into thinking it's all rosy."

"David, what I want to know is, well, I guess I'm too old to start school now . . . ." I said wistfully.

"No, Susie, there's no age limit in America. It's not unusual to see gray-haired men and women in caps and gowns marching alongside their sons and daughters. Whatever you set out to do, that is if you work hard at it, you can achieve your goals there. Of course you can go to school!"

"How much is the tuition?"

"There's no tuition up to high school and in some city colleges. The expense is paid by the state, which, of course, comes out of the tax-payers' pockets," he chuckled. "And there are student loans and other forms of financial aid."

I later thought of Korean parents and how they struggled to educate their children after the war. They sacrificed greatly. Some even limited their already meager meals to once a day in order to save enough money for their children's tuition. Many parents regarded higher education as the sole key to success. Children were drilled to reach the lofty goals set out for them by their parents. Many of them studied from dawn until deep into the night in hopes of entering elite schools.

"America must be paradise," I commented, but David looked at me gloomily and shrugged his shoulders.

"It might be better than most countries, but we have our share of the other side." He signed. "Most of us haven't suffered, and we tend to take things for granted. I had everything I needed, wanted or wished for. My parents gave me a wristwatch when I entered first grade and a camera for my eighth birthday. I was dating girls at ten and my old man gave me a brand new sports car when I graduated from high school. There was nothing I hadn't tried by the time I started college. I got so bored, I dropped out during the first semester." It was inconceivable to me that someone could be bored from having tried everything.

"Soon after that I got drafted and was ordered to go to Korea. Susie, don't get mad, but I thought they were shipping me to hell!" David stroked his broad forehead and stared at the floor. "I brooded for weeks. I hated Korea. I called your people dirty names as I drove through the streets. Wherever I looked I saw only ugliness, the reminder of war and poverty. The stench of the 'honey bucket' in the countryside almost made me pass out. The more I detested this place, the more I drank and cursed at your people."

"I'm sorry . . . ." In great humiliation, I began to apologize for my country. I wanted to explain to David how immaculate and exquisite Korea had been before the war and that my people have always been honorable and courteous. We were the victims of an ugly war. Before I could tell him, David cut me short.

"Please, Susie, just hear me out." He put up his palm. "Then one day some guys in the barracks asked me to go to the orphanage. I didn't want to be bothered about orphans, but they insisted." David leaned back and continued, "I began to open my eyes when I saw happy smiles on those tots who had nothing. I watched them fold their tiny hands in prayer over small bowls of rice and smelly kimchi." He shook his head, "My face burned with shame. I was ashamed of my rotten attitude toward these people who'd suffered greatly and yet tried to make it."

By then the rest of the fellows returned from coffee break. When Charlie saw us talking, he laughed heartily, slapped his thigh and said, "Aha! Susie found herself a boyfriend!" David lightly tapped my desk and went back to his own, looking disgusted.

All afternoon I thought about our conversation. The understanding I had gained from our frank discussion was priceless. I realized that I, too, had taken much for granted when I lived in my parents' elegant home in China. Just like David, I felt ashamed for some of the things I had said and done to those who had worked for my parents and to people I had considered beneath us – maids, coolies and beggars. I resolved to be more tolerant of abrasive soldiers and be understanding when they spewed insulting remarks at my people. Still, it was hard not to react emotionally to the rude ones, and I wished the East and the West could gain the insight I had gleaned through David's openness.

During this time, a Corporal named Dennis Blank became the new Assistant Editor to the Information Office, which published a bi-weekly US Army newspaper called The A-Frame News. Dennis looked like an all-American football player – tall, blond and muscular. One day I shared with him some of my hopes of bringing about mutual understanding between our people. After listening to me, he said, "Susie, understanding is just what you are fostering."

"No, Dennis, what I do isn't enough. It's only like a

drop of water in a bucket."

"Wait, wait! A drop of water, that gives me an idea! Susie, I want you to write an article based on the phrase, 'A Drop of Water.' " Dennis grabbed my hand, "Write it in the third person."

"Dennis, I . . .I've never written an article for a newspaper."

"Then, it's about time you did. An idea usually creates an emotional response. Just write whatever comes to your mind. I'll help you in any way I can. Now, let's see . . ." He paused for a minute, deep in thought, "We'll call your column, 'Susie Says.'" Thus I began writing articles on a bi-weekly basis. Dennis praised and encouraged me as we went over the rough drafts together.

From Pusan Area Command, The A-Frame News, Monday January 11, 1960

There once was a soldier who taught a conversational English course to the Koreans. After completing a hard days work, the soldier lost energy to make preparations for his nightly task of teaching, and the piercing winter weather seemed to dissolve his interest for the class. On the evenings he had to teach classes, he would murmur to himself, "I don't care about the class anymore! I'm sick and tired of travelling back and forth . . . I'll tell them that it will be my last night!" But when he entered the classroom he was greeted by warn welcoming smiles and all were hungry to learn English.

As each evening went by, the soldier begun to see something besides teaching them English. He found himself sharing their thoughts by discussing various subjects with the students, and by doing so he understood more fully the students, the country, and the problems. In fact, he admired their courageous disposition and strength. He actually wondered, "Could I, and my people be that courageous if we were going through similar struggles of war and poverty, people over here have undertaken . . .?" He then realized what the task of teaching was, the beginning of a bigger task.

Many of his friends held untold bitterness toward some Korean people, mostly because of material things. Material things could do both good and bad, but when one depends on material things he is apt to fail somewhere along the way. Material things could be destroyed, but as civilized human beings, their very nature requires them to progress, and will remain within them no matter what. I could offer these students something many others couldn't give, he thought. It's also an opportunity to improve relationship between our two nations.

A second thought entered into his mind, doubts overwhelmed him . . . How far can I possibly carry and practice this intension . . . with my efforts alone. What good will it do? The quantity of my efforts, if compared to a small puddle couldn't be any more than a drop of water in a lake . . .

But WAIT! . . . there soldier, have you ever thought of a drop of water and what it could do in the lake? Yes, a drop of water makes ripples in the lake which spread further and further to reach the other end of the shore . . . with those soft waves touching each and every edge of the lake . . . representing many human hearts.

Army Dependents' School

One day in October of 1959, Lieutenant Smith, my supervisor, came to me. He usually handed me work and went right back to his office. However, this time he sat down on the chair by my desk.

"Susie, may I speak with you for a minute, please?"

"Yes, sir."

"There is a vacancy as a Korean teacher at the US Army Dependents' School on the post. The Civilian Personnel Officer just called me to ask if I would be willing to release you for it. Would you be interested?"

I did not mean to be rude, but it sounded like a big joke to me, and I laughed. "I'm serious," the soft-spoken officer said. "Miss Goodwin, the school principal, is looking for a Korean who can speak the English language fluently and has the ability to teach Korean language, culture, history, art and so forth. But most important, the applicant must know how to get along with the army kids."

"Lieutenant Smith, you're asking the wrong person. Why don't they look for someone in the university? It's a position for a professor."

"Susie, they had two professors apply for the job, but their English pronunciation was so stiff that they couldn't communicate with the children."

"Sir, I've never taught in my life. Besides, I'm very content in this office."

"We'll hate to lose you," he said, "but you would be foolish to pass this up. You'll be promoted from GS-4 to GS-7. Your salary will jump from 31,000 to 43,000 won a month!" The fellows in the office gathered around my desk.

Steve, a private who had been recently assigned to the office, commented, "Susie, what have you got to lose?"

"If you don't give it a chance, we won't have anything to do with you. We won't even talk to you!" the rest of the fellows chimed in.

"I'll have plenty to lose if I don't make it. My face! It'll bring me disgrace!" I told them off and turned to my typewriter to type, but they still stood around me.

"All right, Susie," Lieutenant Smith said firmly, "I'll tell you what. I want you to go over to the school this afternoon, just for a visit. Nobody except us will have to know. Go. See it for yourself. If you like it, great, but if you don't, you know you'll always have a place here with us." He squeezed my shoulder and left. I felt bewildered and apprehensive. I loved my little cocoon and was afraid to venture into the unknown, but I had no choice. I had to go.

That afternoon, Lieutenant Smith came to tell me a staff car was waiting to take me to the school. My heart thumped, and my hands felt cold. Miss Goodwin received me cordially in her office. After briefing me on the school, she stood up.

"Now, I want you to meet the students." She led the way into a classroom. "Good afternoon, boys and girls. I would like you to meet Miss Susie Lee." She introduced me to a roomful of American children.

"Good afternoon, Miss Lee," the room resounded. Miss Goodwin told them to ask me questions. Silently I asked the Lord to give me the words. Calmness seemed to surround me as the children darted friendly questions at me: where did I live, what I did at my office, my age, how many brothers and sisters did I have? Some children asked if I could teach them arts and crafts. One boy asked if I could operate a chu-pahn,[38] an Oriental adding machine. Many of them asked me to say various words, phrases and sentences in Korean. Then one red-haired, freckle-faced boy raised his hand and asked politely, "Miss Lee, would you please tell us a Korean folktale?" It was an unexpected request, but I felt confident, for I knew most of them by heart. Suddenly a flash of panic struck me. I had never told Korean folktales in English before. I said a quick prayer and began. "Once upon a time, long, long ago . . . ."

When I finished the story, all the children applauded and so did the principal. Two little girls ran over to me and hugged and kissed me. I had not seen American children at close range until that day, and I was pleased to be hugged by them. As Miss Goodwin led me out of the classroom, one girl shouted, "Please don't leave us! Tell us another story."

The principal looked over her shoulder and said, "Miss Lee is here to stay."

Back in her office, I immediately explained, "Miss Goodwin, I hope you understand that I've never taught before. I only came her at the urging of my supervisor."

"I know," she nodded her head, smiling, "but you were being observed and have just fulfilled the requirements. I have discussed this position with my faculty, the Civilian Personnel Officer and your supervisor. We need someone like you who has a natural ability to communicate with children. As you can see, you've won the hearts of my pupils."

---

[38] an abacus

It sounded so unreal – only eight years ago I spoke less than ten words in English. Now I was about to be hired as a teacher in an American school.

When I went back to my office, the fellows hovered around me. They had already heard from the principal and seemed happier for me than I was for myself. I didn't want to leave my office, yet deep down I felt a sense of achievement.

That weekend I went home to tell my parents about the unexpected promotion. I had not visited home for many months and was shocked to see my father looking older and weary.

"I am glad you came out, Hyun Sook-ga," he greeted me warmly. "I was hoping you would. You look happy and well."

"Thank you, Father, but is something wrong? You don't look well."

"I suppose I'm under pressure. I have been staying up for many nights. The price of chicken feed is climbing, and I'm afraid that I won't be able to afford it much longer. Chicken prices are at their peak at the market, and it seems best that I sell now."

When I told my father about my unexpected promotion his tired face lit up. "That counteracts my dismal news. The Lord is good. He always knows when to extend His helping hand. I never thought that you would . . . ." Father's voice trailed off. He did not need to finish, for I understood. "It's truly a miracle to achieve such a position . . . ."

Mother returned from shopping. Her eyes glistened when she heard my good news. They made a big fuss over me and praised me. Once again I caught myself resenting the fact that I had to earn their affection, but I also sensed that my emotional reaction was much less intense than the last time. Now I felt a surge of sympathy for them because they had no son to take care of them in their old age and to carry on the family name. At least I could give them some comfort. As usual, I told them that I would continue to send home my paychecks.

The invisible barrier of resentment I had built against them during the war crumbled a little. I realized that if I had been sheltered all my life without any suffering, I might not have cried out to God as I did during the war. Without the keen awareness of my own inadequacy, I would not have sought His wisdom and tried to better myself. Without the agony of rejection, I might not have learned to love and be concerned for the misfortune of others.

I reported to the US Army Dependents' School on October 27, 1959. My deeply instilled fears of rejection and ridicule rushed back to me that morning. Oblivious to my inner turmoil, Miss Goodwin sat me down beside her desk. I had expected a Korean teacher's manual and ready-made lesson plans, but to my dismay she had nothing for me.

That afternoon I plunged into planning my lessons. I worked deep into the nights, gathering materials, sorting and translating them into English. After the children were dismissed, I mimeographed the prepared lessons. Without the slightest doubt, I recognized that my new ideas and creativity were coming from God. My pupils were eager to learn, and they retained what I taught them. They were cooperative, well behaved, and bright.

In December, Chaplain Albus asked me if I would be willing to teach the primary Sunday school class at the post chapel, which would include most of the children from my day school classes. I had read the Bible and through my father had understood a little about it, but I was not sure I could handle so great a responsibility.

"The best way to learn the Bible and to strengthen

your own faith is through teaching these little ones," Chaplain Albus encouraged. "My assistants and I will give you all the help you need." I was doubtful at first but with prayers, a lesson guide and help from the chapel staff, I soon discovered that I could manage the responsibility.

A few days before Christmas, Dennis Blank came to visit me. He wanted to interview my classes for an article in The A-Frame News and also for the Pacific Stars and Stripes. Dennis stayed with me for several hours, following me from class to class, taking snapshots and jotting down what he observed in his notes. I had no idea what he wrote down until I read his article later.

KN Teaches Dep Kids, A-Frame News
February 22, 1960

PUSAN IO --In a quaint, but modern school house here, dependent children, ages 6 to 13, sit attentively while a pretty young Korean woman tells them the story of the Korean New Years.

This is one of the many classes Miss Lee Hyun Sook teaches at the U.S. Army Dependent School at Hialeah. Of the millions of American youngsters attending elementary school every year, the thirty six students here are the only ones exposed to a regular curriculum of Korean customs, traditions and language.

Nicknamed Susie by her friends, she began teaching a few months ago, and has won the admiration and respect of both teachers and children in her job as educational assistant. As one small youngster put it, "She's real swell."

During the Christmas season for instance, Miss Lee explained the similarity between the Korean and American way of celebrating Xmas. To help them learn the writing of Korean characters, each child was presented with a small Kimchi pot. With professional skill, each youngster inscribed his name in Korean on the jar.

A favorite class with the boys is learning how to manipulate that "crazy oriental adding machine", called a chupan in Korean. The girls on the other hand, enjoy hearing about how other little Korean girls their age live and what they learn in school.

"Compared to Korean children at their age", Susie remarked. "They seem much more receptive and eager to learn. Their interest in learning seems truly typical for Americans."

At the present time Susie's greatest ambition is to travel to the United States. Having already applied for sponsorship, she hopes to be going to Alaska in the near future.

The young woman not only teaches at the Dependent school, but instructs a Sunday school class of younger boys and girls.

In her spare time, she writes a warm human interest column for the Pusan Area Command Newspaper, "The A-Frame News".

Eager to learn the American way of life and ideals, she began working as a telephone operator in 1956. In 1957 she advanced to the position of special orders clerk in the PAC personnel office.

The statement, "Susie's greatest ambition is to travel to the United States," acted as a bellow to fan the spark of my latent desire.

I Shall Become a Buddhist

Just before the Christmas holiday, a man from an immigration agency came to the school looking for me. The final approval for our immigration to the United States had come through, he said.

"You could be leaving Korea anywhere from two weeks to two months from now," he informed me.

Excitedly, I took the afternoon off and hailed a taxi for the branch office in downtown Pusan. The cab lurched and screeched through the crowded open market place and bustling streets, but I felt as though I was floating to America on a plush magic carpet.

A clerk at the office asked for my father's name and started fumbling through high stacks of forms and documents. An hour later he was still searching. I noticed his face flushing, and a look of exasperation began to replace the confident smile that had greeted me. Haltingly he explained that the paper, which he thought was ours, was actually for an entirely different family. I protested that it could not be and pleaded with him to look further for our application, but he only shook his head gravely.

"I have just double-checked and searched through all my files," he said irritably, "You'll just have to wait until you are notified again."

I staggered out of the office. The magic carpet had plunged me into a chasm of despair. A hard knot in my throat prevented me from calling a cab. In the chaos of rush hour traffic, the teeming mob inadvertently pushed me to and fro on the sidewalk. Helplessly, I leaned against a concrete wall for support until the crowds subsided.

Back at the school I kept myself busy teaching. Toward the end of June, I found a letter awaiting me in my quarters. It was from the immigration agency, the organization through which we had applied for admittance to the United States. I tore open the envelope with shaky hands. After three years of patient waiting, I was beside myself, but when I finally opened it, the bold print stabbed at me: NOTIFICATION OF REJECTION. The letter fell away unfinished. Heaving uncontrollable sobs, I threw myself on the bed. Three, ugly, cruel words crumbled my tower of expectation like a sandcastle swept away by brutal, careless waves. I fled.

My father was startled to see me. "You don't look happy, Hyun Sook-ga. Is something wrong?" Father prodded. I couldn't answer him and just shook my head silently. Instead of going into the house, we strolled in the garden. The huge, pink peony blossoms gently swayed in the lazy breeze of the summer evening. Father walked over and pulled some weeds from the flowerbed and rearranged the rocks he had gathered from the mountain.

"Come, let me draw some cool water," Father led the way to the well. He dipped a dried gourd into the brimming bucket and handed it to me.

When Mother returned from the store, she also was startled to see me. We went into the inner room for supper. After the maid cleared the table, Father asked me again what troubled me. At his insistence, I blurted it all out.

"Father, if you really must know, I'll tell you. Our application for immigration has been rejected!" My heart pounded with anger and fear of the consequences of my rude behavior toward my father. I watched his hand, which might flash across my face any second.

Instead Father stared at me stunned. He cleared his throat and said gently, "My dear daughter, listen to me. What is all the rush? It may not be God's time for us to go there yet."

"Father, it's all right for you to say that. You have a family, a house and security. What about me? Now what do I have? I'm an old maid with no future!" Rage mounted with each spewed word. "If God was real, He would have answered our prayers long ago!"

"Don't talk like that!" Father sharply rebuked me. "You know better than anyone else that God does answer prayers!" He tried to calm me down by reasoning with me rather than inflicting physical force.

"I can talk like that, and I will! It's been almost ten years since I started dreaming about going to America. I'm tired of waiting. I'm almost twenty-five and have nothing to show for it. I can't wait anymore!" I had never dared to argue with my parents in my whole life, even when I knew they were wrong. The fear of punishment and rejection had always curbed me from even frowning at them. Now I was acting like a rampaging tigress.

"Father, I've tried to be a good Christian, but what do I get? Who cares? God certainly doesn't seem to! From now on I'm going to live as I please!" Mother sat silently. Only her huge eyes grew darker as she twisted her toes in rapid succession. Father tried to reason with me, to appease me, but I was beyond reason.

"Father, I don't care if you disown me, but as of this night I am no longer a Christian." My voice rose as I glared at my father.

"Hyun Sook-ga, you know very well what the Lord has done for you. You cannot survive without belief in . . . ."

"Then I shall become a Buddhist!" I shouted.

"You are not serious, are you?" Father sat up rigidly.

"Oh, yes, I am serious! I have never been more serious!"

Blood drained from Father's face as tears rushed down his coarse cheeks. I had not seen him cry since the day he wept over the American flag, thanking God for delivering us from the Communists.

"All our efforts to raise you in the Lord God were in vain," he lamented. "I never dreamed that I would live to hear one of my own flesh choose Buddha over our Lord Jesus." Heaviness spread in the room.

Late that night Father sent word to Pastor Hwang to come to our home. He came immediately and tried to woo me back to God with both kindly advice and grave condemnation, but my mind was too bitter to be swayed. After almost an hour of alternating persuasion and intimidation, the pastor rose to leave. Father's face tightened. His eyes flickered with urgency, and he glanced at me half pleadingly, half threateningly. When I made no response, he turned to the pastor with sagging shoulders, "Moksanim, please accept my resignation as a church elder." Uneasy minutes ticked away, but I acted as if I did not care. Abruptly I got up. Without a word I returned to the post.

All night long I tossed and turned in my bed, beating the pillow in fury and frustration. Long before dawn I came to the conclusion that it would be best to end my meaningless existence. Recklessly I glanced around the kitchen until my eyes rested on the medicine box. A bottle of aspirin. I emptied the pills into my palm, poured a glass of water and swallowed them. Back in my bed I closed my eyes and waited for the spirit of death.

The dull, buzzing noise from the clock, which I had set automatically, awakened me. I felt nauseous and my head was like an echo chamber. My ears were muffled and dull to surrounding sounds. Panic seized me. I did not want to die. The thought of calling Chaplain Albus flashed in my mind. He had been very kind and understanding. I staggered to the telephone by the bathroom and dialed his number. When he answered, I paused for a confused minute, breathing heavily.

"Hello, hello," he repeated. "Who is this?"

"Chaplain Albus." At long last I gathered enough courage to speak. "This is Susie Lee. I -I have a question to ask you. What do you do when, uh, when someone has taken a handful of aspirin?"

"Who took the aspirin?" he asked urgently, but I bit my lower lip, unable to admit it.

"Susie," his kind pleading voice vibrated over the phone, "Did you take them? Susie, tell me, please. You can trust me," he prompted gently.

"Yes, I-I-I took them," I broke into a sob. "And I'm scared, Chaplain. Please tell me what I should do. I'm in pain!"

"For now I want you to drink lots of lukewarm water. It'll make you vomit, but that's what you need." He spoke very slowly, "And I'll be right over."

"No, Chaplain, please don't come. I'm not presentable. I'll be all right now. Thank you."

"Susie, we can't waste time," he said firmly, "Just get a robe on. I'll be right over!" He hung up abruptly.

Shaking with guilt, I wrapped my robe around me, my long black hair draped around my face and shoulders. Obediently I forced down several glasses of water. The acid fluid erupted from my stomach. In just a few minutes, the Chaplain walked in through the door. I expected a severe rebuke, but instead a pair of the most compassionate eyes looked deep into me. His firm hands held my shoulders and he asked, "May I call a doctor?"

"Please don't. If you do, he'll put me away in a mental institution!"

"Susie, trust me. I know an army doctor who will keep it absolutely confidential. He won't ask you any question. Besides, I'll vouch for you." With my reluctant consent he called the doctor. Then he went to get his car to take me to the clinic.

After the examination, the doctor gave me assurance that no harm was done. The dull numbness in my head and ringing noise in my ears would clear away in a week or so, he explained. The doctor gave me some capsules to offset the aspirin and advised me to drink plenty of water. When Chaplain Albus came for me, he said he had called Miss Goodwin on my behalf and that I was granted a week off.

During the week, Chaplain Albus either called me or came by every day. No one found out about the incident, not even my mother. He neither pried, nor gave advice. He showed no sign of condemnation, self-righteousness or impatience but stood by me as a comforting friend.

When I returned to work, Miss Goodwin asked no question. She only said how much they had missed me and how glad they were to have me back. Instead of work piled up on my desk, I found that Miss Yun, the school secretary, had taken care of it. Everything had continued as if nothing had happened.

As disturbing thoughts accumulated in my mind, I went to see Chaplain Albus. Although the doctor had told me no harm was done, I needed spiritual assurance.

"Chaplain Albus, what punishment will I receive for having attempted suicide?" Fearing the worst, I took a deep breath. "And what must I do after I have committed an unpardonable sin? In anger and frustration I told my father that I would become a Buddhist, but I know that is not what I want to be. I realize that I had put my ambition of going to America above everything else."

Chaplain Albus closed his eyes for a moment, and then slowly replied, "Susie, God is more loving and forgiving than we give Him credit for. All of us experience similar shades of emotions, which you have expressed to a greater or lesser degree. I suppose it would be safe to say that the only unpardonable sin is when we don't allow God to forgive us through His Son Jesus. We block His forgiving power. There is not one unpardonable sin when we ruefully seek His forgiveness."

He paused and moistened his lips, "To your second question, it seems to me that you declared to your father that you would become a Buddhist at a point of great distress and utter disappointment."

"Yes, Chaplain," I interrupted, "It was the night our request for immigration had been rejected."

He nodded his head understandingly. "I am sure you are familiar with Peter denying Jesus three times. Jesus did not point an accusing finger at him. Rather, He merely asked Peter, 'Do you love me?' When Peter responded, Jesus said, 'If so, feed my sheep.'" Chaplain Albus looked at me the way Jesus must have looked at Peter and said, "Susie, let us pray."

From that time on my contact with the Chaplain and his staff became more frequent. Many times I would go to the chapel, just to sit in the empty sanctuary and pray. Time and patience on the part of Chaplain Albus helped me through those difficult weeks. I knew that I would always be grateful to him for his unconditional regard and for the encouragement he had given me.

Dance and Sing

When the school year ended, all the American teachers left for their summer vacation. Only the school secretary, Miss Yun, two janitors and I continued working, for we were on Korean payroll. I used the uninterrupted time to plan ahead for the fall schedule. The school had ordered several teachers' manuals and other materials, but none of them were suitable for American children. Therefore, I etched maps and pictures on stencils and translated Korean history, geography, language and songs into English.

"Miss Lee, you are too studious," said Miss Yun, "You only know about work. You'll age too quickly that way." I just shrugged my shoulders at her comments. "You can't always work." Flashing her enormous, sparkling black eyes, she declared, "Tomorrow I'm going to bring my phonograph and records, and I'll teach you how to dance."

"You must be out of your mind, Miss Yun. How do you expect a woman wearing a brace to dance?" I mocked her.

Nevertheless the following morning, she lugged in her record player and a stack of records. During our coffee breaks and lunch hour she put on the records and ignoring my protests, she pulled me onto the floor. Patiently she taught me dance steps. At first I felt very awkward, but she was an excellent dancer, and I soon learned several steps.

Then one day she announced that she had arranged a dinner date for both of us. She had such an iron will that I finally gave in and agreed to meet the blind date. Two young, handsome second lieutenants escorted us to the Officer's Club. After dinner, Miss Yun and her date got up to dance. I did not know what arrangements were made, but my date got me out on the floor, gliding me all over the hall. Miss Yun gave me an approving wink as she watched us waltz. After that evening, I began losing some of my inhibitions, and she frequently arranged double dates.

One evening she and I were invited to a party at a US Army Detachment on the opposite side of the city. Laughter, music and cigarette smoke filled the huge room. Officers and women mingled freely. Some danced. Others ate and drank. I felt uncomfortable, and was beginning to regret having come at all, when the commander of the unit came over to my table and introduced himself as Ted. For the rest of the evening he never left my side. We talked, dined and danced. Ted was so handsome and captivating that before I knew it, I found myself infatuated. Late that night Ted personally escorted me back to my quarters and promised to get in touch with me soon. He did call me several times and invited me back to his unit for a similar party. Then abruptly he stopped calling me. Miss Yun sensed my disappointment and managed to drag me out to other places, but my heart was not in it.

After a few tormented nights, I laid aside my pride and called Ted. I just needed to know why he had not called. He sounded as wonderful as the first night I had met him. "I am so glad to hear from you. It's been quite hectic here, but you have been on my mind. How about a dinner date at a restaurant this Friday?" With the reassurance from Ted, my world returned to normal. I went into the office and hummed happy tunes, dreaming about the date.

"Patience, my dear, patience," Miss Yun teased me.

On Friday after work, I rushed to my quarters and took an early shower. I carefully applied my makeup and slipped on an emerald silk evening dress. My long black hair draped softly over my shoulders and down to my waist. Dabbing some perfume behind my ears, I looked at myself in the mirror and liked what I saw. When at last the doorbell rang, I rushed to the door. To my chagrin, Ted's assistant stood there in place of my idol.

"The Captain had to take care of some urgent business," he said uneasily, "But he didn't want to disappoint you, so he sent me to tell you about it over dinner."

I felt terribly let down and did not want to go with his assistant, but out of courtesy, I stepped into the car. He escorted me to a luxurious Korean resort restaurant. Over dinner he told me with much hesitation that Ted was a married man and that he found it difficult to tell me so. He did not want to get deeply involved with me and eventually hurt me.

"I didn't see a wedding band on his finger. Why didn't he tell me the truth on the first night?" I demanded to know, "I would not have even danced with him!"

"Some men remove the ring for various reasons. He has attended many parties and met numerous women at social functions. But he admitted to me that you affected him emotionally. He also sensed that you were attracted to him. In essence, he said you are a very decent lady, and he didn't want to . . . ."

"Is that it?" I cut him short, "I'm too decent and therefore no man would want to get serious with me? All right then, order a drink for me and light me a cigarette, please!"

For the first time in my life, against my strict upbringing, I sipped the forbidden alcoholic beverage. It tasted so bitter that I grimaced. Then I took one puff of the cigarette, but I felt so dizzy that I had to lean my head on the table.

That night, back in my room, I took stock of my behavior. I was disgusted and ashamed of my attitude.

I had missed many mid-week fellowship services, and I realized that my staying away from the chapel in order to cope with my disappointments and loneliness only deepened my void and depleted my spiritual strength. The following week I raced back to my old friends at the chapel. As always I found a sense of belonging and fortitude in their company, which I could not find elsewhere.

Before I knew it, the teachers and children returned from their long vacation and school bustled with life again. It felt so good to be with the children once more. However, to my great disappointment, Miss Goodwin did not return. I missed her deeply.

Just as I began to get back into the stride of school life, the news came that Chaplain Albus had been reassigned to the United States.

"Chaplain, I'm afraid I will not have a source of spiritual growth if you are not here for me to come to," I admitted.

"Susie, it is not me you must lean upon. It is Jesus Christ who has forgiven you. I am only His representative. Through the ages many teachers and preachers of the Gospel have come and gone, but the Word of God has continued in the hearts of people. Always remember to call upon the Lord instead of mere men."

On the day of his departure, a group of us from the Chapel went to see him off at the Pusan Railroad Station.

Chaplain Albus took me aside before he left, "Susie,

you haven't mentioned your ambition to go to America. I sense that you've given up. But don't give up hope. Just pray hard and some day – perhaps quite a while from now – a chance will come. Remember, though, pray that God's will, not your will, be done." As he walked up the steps of the train, he turned around and waved goodbye to us. Then, as the train chugged away, he called to his assistants, "Take care of Susie!"

Sorrow welled up, but I stood there, silently praying and asking God to bless this man of God who had helped me more than any other clergyman.

One day I received an unexpected call from Steve, the GI assigned to the military Personnel Office shortly before I was transferred.

"Susie," he said, "I have heard about the attempts to get you to the States. Are you still interested in going?"

At first I was too stunned to answer his question. Even when I realized what he meant, I hesitated. I had been disappointed so many times that I did not want to hope again.

"Thank you, Steve, but I really have no desire to try at this time. Things are going well for me."

"Susie," he went on as if he had not heard me, "I just helped a Korean woman get to the States. I discovered that if you have a willing sponsor in America, the procedure is rather simple. It wouldn't hurt to try. Besides, if you don't like it there, you·could always return to Korea."

At his urging I agreed to check with my friends in Alaska. That night I sat at my desk to write a letter to Mr. and Mrs. Fleming. It had been a while since I had written to any of my friends, and I hesitated. Finally I wrote and asked if they would still consider sponsoring me. They replied immediately. They would be happy and willing to be my sponsors. The Flemings began to correspond with Steve, and the process of applying for passport and visa got underway. This time I prepared myself emotionally. My subconscious would not allow me to garner any hope.

I was working later than usual one day when Miss Yun flashed her eyes at me, saying, "Miss Lee, you are too stuffy. You've gone back to your old serious self again. Are you going to rot away and be an old maid? You've got to circulate." Nonchalantly I tilted my head at her and shrugged my shoulders.

"Miss Lee, have you heard about the Korean Employees' Talent Show at the post theater on November 26th?"

"No, I haven't."

"Well, I want you to participate in it."

"You must be out of your mind." I glanced at her, annoyed. "What talent do I have?"

"Oh, come on. I've heard you singing. Give it a try. You won't be sorry." She insisted, "Besides, I have already submitted your name! Now, don't make me lose face!"

"It's utterly senseless the way you keep on urging me to do things," I muttered irritably. "I know you mean well, but this time you've gone too far!" Nevertheless since she had already submitted my name, I thought I had better save her face and be prepared to save mine. I sought the help of Mr. Woody, a Department of Army Civilian and a bandleader. He readily agreed to coach me and offered to have his band accompany me.

When the dreaded day arrived, I adorned myself in a Korean festival dress: a multi-colored striped jacket and floor-length skirt of green silk brocade. The army theater was filled to capacity with both Americans and Koreans. Many excellent singers, pianists and dancers confidently strode out to the stage. The longer I watched them perform, the more insecure I became. When the Master of Ceremonies called my name, my heart raced. Steadying my trembling hands, I walked onto the stage. I bit my tongue and bowed slowly to the audience, asking myself how I had gotten myself into this mess.

Under the dim lights, all the faces grew blurry as I turned my head nervously to signal Mr. Woody. He looked baffled as he whispered to me that his amplifier needed adjustment and that it would take a few minutes before he could play. For a fleeting second I got panicky.

"Oh, Jesus, help me!" I prayed. Regaining my composure, I faced the audience and heard myself saying, "While we are waiting for the band to get ready, I would like to tell you a story I once heard." My voice held no tremor.

> Once upon a time, a missionary went to the deepest part of the jungle in Africa. While he was strolling down the narrow path, a fierce lion confronted him. The missionary became terror-stricken. Since he could not outrun the beast, he dropped to his knees and began to pray. He prayed and prayed. When at long last he opened his eyes, it shocked the missionary to find the lion beside him with its eyes closed. Greatly relieved, he shouted, 'Oh, Brother, how glad I am to find you praying with me!' To that the lion opened just one eye, held one paw over his mouth, and said, 'Shhh! Don't interrupt. I'm saying grace!'

The audience roared. The theater echoed with their clapping and whistling. By this time the band was ready and began to play. I sang my song, "Pretend," by Nat King Cole and went backstage. Other participants continued to sing, play instruments and even perform magic. It was an impressive variety show.

While the judges called the names of the runners-up, I headed down the ramp and was ready to leave through the back stage door when a man came running after me, "Miss

Lee, they are looking for you. You are the winner!"

The man ushered me onto the stage. The chairman of the talent show presented me with a silver cup, an RCA portable radio and an envelope of cash as the top prize. The photographers took pictures, and the audience cheered. Miss Yun, beside herself with joy, rushed backstage to congratulate me. Her maneuvering me out of my shell had often annoyed me, but the persistent attempts at building my confidence brought about unexpected results.

A few days after the talent show, Mr. Woody called me to ask if I would sing for his band at the NCO club. I liked the attention I had received on the stage. I would enjoy it as long as my parents did not find out. I had hurt them enough, especially my father. He was such a strict man, and I knew my singing in the nightclub would infuriate him, but I wanted to give it a try anyway.

After several rehearsals, I stood on the platform of the dimly lit club. I clutched the microphone to steady my hands and nervously glanced around the smoke-filled hall. Men stared at me from behind flickering candlelight at the tables. Some of them who recognized me grew wide-eyed.

The band started playing and the spotlight focused on me. I sang some of my favorite songs of the early 50's; "Pretend," "April Love" and "Sand and the Sea." As the evening progressed I chose more cheerful tunes like "Que Sera Sera," and "How Much Is That Doggie In The Window." Mr. Woody was so pleased with the response from the audience that he asked me to solo indefinitely. His offer thrilled me. I felt certain that a singing career would bring the happiness and fulfillment I sought. I had come a long way.

That night, back in my quarters, I stood in front of my mirror. With a cigarette between my lips, I addressed my haughty reflection. "This is my life, and I will live as I please. Who's going to stop me from singing? Smoking? Cigarettes will give me an air of sophistication!" I watched myself squinting one eye and inhaling deeply. Without warning my head spun, and my stomach lurched violently. Coughing madly and nearly losing my balance, I veered toward the bathroom.

I never smoked another cigarette again.

His Timetable

I had no way of knowing that in His mercy God had already set the wheels in motion for me to leave Korea, lifting the roadblocks in His own timing. I Corinthians 10:13 reads:

> There hath no temptation taken you but such as is common to man: but God is faithful, who will not suffer you to be tempted above what ye are able; but will with the temptation also make a way to escape, that ye may be able to bear it.

I had often heard my father quote that verse. True to that promise, the desire to sing in the nightclub was quickly eclipsed. The day after my first performance, I received a notarized affidavit, documentary evidence of sponsorship from Mr. and Mrs. Fleming. Steve told me I could process my application at once.

Since the argument with my father, I had avoided going home for several months. I bought a huge custard cake with butter frosting, my father's favorite, as a peace offering. I intended to tell my parents the good news and to apologize for my previous rude behavior, but we got so carried away with the good news that I never did get around to the apology.

Everyone from the Pusan Area Command went out of their way to assist me once the initial step was taken. The military Personnel Officer told me a set of travel orders was ready for me, which would authorize me to travel on any US Army transportation within South Korea. The dispatchers at the motor pool continued to send a staff car whenever I needed to go somewhere. The principal of the school granted me several days off so that I could visit the American Embassy in Seoul. The Army investigator processed my clearance of character in one week instead of the normal two to six months.

A family friend had returned from America and was the head of the Passport Department in Seoul. He issued my passport on the same day I visited him in his office. I passed my physical examination at the Severance Hospital. My visa would be issued at the end of December. This meant I would be on my way to Alaska in less than one month. The irony of the whole thing was that when I least expected it, everything happened at jet speed.

Upon my return to Pusan, I requested a six months of leave of absence from the school. I did not want to lose my position in case I wanted to return home after all. The principal granted my request and got a substitute. Next I went to the Chaplain's Office and told one of the assistants, "Bob, I'm finally going to Alaska!"

"Why do you want to go there? Didn't you see the movie Ice Palace? Brrr! Susie, you'll travel on a sled pulled by a team of Alaskan huskies on an icy road, surrounded by glaciers and snow-capped mountains. You'll turn into an ice pillar from living in an igloo!"

"Please don't tease me, Bob." I was not in the mood for jokes, and I wanted him to be serious. "Let me get it out of my system. I really came here to ask your help in finding a replacement for my Sunday school class."

"Susie, you're deserting us." Still grinning impishly he went on, "Why should we help you find someone? That's your problem. Find your own."

On the following Thursday evening, after the service, I told the Protestant Men of the Chapel about my sudden plan to leave for Alaska and asked if someone would volunteer to take over my Sunday school class. Silence filled the room. Nobody moved to offer. I looked around. At last one serviceman who had recently joined the group raised his hand. His clean-shaven, handsome face blushed. He lowered his gentle, sky blue eyes and said, "I'll give it a try, if you'll show me what to do."

"How nice of you. Thank you! By the way, what is your name, please?"

"I'm Don Beidel." He flashed a boyish smile as he stroked his slightly wavy chestnut hair.

On the following Sunday, when I arrived at the class, I found Don waiting for me in his sharp army dress uniform. He looked tall, slim and muscular, and I could not take my eyes off of him. The pleasant scent of Old Spice wafted as he took my hand and shook it firmly. Enchanted I went through the motions of showing him the lesson manual, the craft guide and the supply closet. When I introduced Don to the children, explaining that I would be leaving for Alaska soon, some of the girls came up and hugged me. I looked about the room while most of the children sat in their chairs quietly staring at Don. Big beads of tears rolled down the face of one girl. A boy seated next to her decided to get up and show off by clambering onto a table. As reserved as he seemed, Don had a way with children. All during the class, while I taught, Don moved about gently but firmly maintaining order. He knew when to be humorous and when to be stern with the little ones. The children took to him by the end of the morning.

After the class, Don casually asked me to have lunch with him. Over hamburgers and milkshakes, he told me that he was born and raised in the scenic state of Pennsylvania by a German father and an English mother. He had two older sisters and four younger brothers. He told me about one of his friends, a youth leader named Dean Young from a Presbyterian church.

"Dean asked me to join him on a weekend camp retreat. We had a great time. On the last evening, the pastor gave an invitation to open our hearts to Jesus. I responded to the call."

Don spent his off-duty hours at local orphanages. After we finished the lunch, he asked me if I would accompany him to an orphanage and interpret for him. Don was so amiable and polite in his approach that I readily agreed to go with him on the following Saturday. He came for me in a three-quarter-ton army vehicle with several other GIs. Cameras swayed around their necks as they loaded the truck with boxes of food and packages for the orphans.

As we pulled into the playground, the orphans stopped playing and ran to gather around us. Some of the children immediately grabbed Don's arms and practically carried him away from the rest of us. They climbed on his shoulders, swung on his muscular arms and clung to his long, sturdy legs. One girl leapt up and snatched Don's hat. While she ran away playfully, another girl pinned a hug red ribbon in his hair. He seemed completely at home with them. Whatever game they wanted to play, Don joined in, his ribbon still attached: hopscotch, hide-and-seek, racing, drop-the-handkerchief, basketball and even jump rope. The rest of us stood laughing until we almost doubled over. He completely captivated the little ones.

The director of the orphanage watched them for a while and then called the children into the reception hall.

Don told us that it was time for them to perform for the guests. The staff led us into the hall. The orphans sang and danced splendidly. Don recorded the program on tape and took movies of it. I felt so moved by Don that I willingly accompanied him to other orphanages.

Once he took me to a small orphanage, which only cared for infants and toddlers. The doorway was so low that Don had to stoop. Room after room was crammed with babies lying on army blankets on the floor. The infants were so undernourished that they looked like skeletons with parchment paper stretched over them, their puffed up stomachs protruding over diapers. In another room, two-year-old toddlers all sat up in an orderly manner, staring out through sunken eyes, instead of being full of energy, squealing and romping about. The sight made me cringe. The director explained to me that many babies were brought to her doorstep and left there. She faced severe hardship due to lack of funds and staff to care for the increasing number of infants.

After we started going to these orphanages, Don seemed to cross my path whenever I headed for my quarters after school, even though this was not the route for servicemen. He would just wave at me, say a few words of greeting and move on. He never made a nuisance of himself in any way.

Before Christmas I decided to move most of my belongings to my parents' home. Don came with the vehicle and hauled my things out. I introduced Don to my parents, hastily adding that he had replaced me as Sunday school teacher before they became suspicious. Their politeness warmed when they heard that Don was a Presbyterian.

For Christmas Don gave me a set of pearl earrings, a necklace and a ring. Politely, I refused the ring. Don's face turned red, and he stared at me for a second or two, but he took the ring back reluctantly.

A few days after Christmas, I had to pick up my visa in Seoul. Although I could have had a car through the motor pool, I accepted Don's offer to take me to the train station. He asked me when I would return, and I told him I planned to be back on New Year's Eve.

My elder sister and Mi Sook met me at the Seoul Station. After I picked up the visa and made my reservations with the airlines, Onni showed me around the city. As the driver sped through the familiar parts of the city, my thoughts raced back to the winter of 1951. Though I could not see any visible scars of the war on the surface of the reconstructed city, I vividly recalled the horror I had experienced ten years before. Now magnificent buildings sprang up as far as my eyes could see. Neon signs flashed in the windows of towering department stores, theaters, cabarets, tearooms and restaurants. Onni stopped the cab in front of a Chinese restaurant. After a feast we strolled along the sidewalk where vendors were selling roasted chestnuts, dried persimmons and rice taffy. Laughter, vitality and music sprang up where cries of agony, terror and bomb explosions echoed in my memory.

Onni hailed a taxi, and we headed for her home. Instead of the house where I had lived for a week during the second invasion, she led me through a huge gate, passing the courtyard and into a traditional Korean house. The rooms were furnished in elaborate black lacquer, embedded with mother-of-pearl. Ancient scrolls adorned the walls. She owned a phone, a hi-fi and even a TV console. After chatting for a while we both agreed that it had been a long day and decided to get ready for bed.

Just as I settled into my bed, Onni came in, "Mother told me that you have been helping the family financially all these years and that you don't have any savings of your own." She stroked my head as if I were a little girl. "I'll pay for your plane fare to Alaska as my gift to you." Her generous offer stunned me. Until then I had not stopped to think that I had no money for my ticket.

I stayed a day longer than I had planned, but I had no way to contact my parents who were to meet me at the station. Arriving toward evening on New Year's Day with the visa, passport and plane ticket in my possession, I headed toward the street to take a taxi but heard someone call me. Turning around, I found Don standing right behind me. He told me that he had waited there with my parents the night before until the last train from Seoul emptied.

Bob grinned and rolled his eyes when he saw me at the army chapel the following Sunday. After the service he hurried over to tease me.

"Just listen to this, Susie. Don Beidel gave up the USO show on New Year's Eve to wait for a friend at the train station. A GI never misses a USO show, unless he's on duty. Hey, Susie, what's going on? Something's cooking!" I brushed his teasing aside for I could not explain to him that I had not misled Don and had no intention of getting serious with him. Bob continued to tease me no matter what, so I kept my distance as best as I could.

I was scheduled to leave Pusan on January 18, 1961. My relatives and friends must have thought there would be no Korean food in Alaska as they invited me to dinners and parties almost every night before I left. The time that preceded my departure was a flurry of activities.

On the evening before I was to leave Pusan, Don asked me out to dinner. All the way to the NCO Club he acted jovial, joking and making me laugh with his Donald Duck impersonation to tell me how much he would miss me, but once he seated me and ordered our steaks, he quieted. Don looked at me over the flickering candlelight. Oblivious to the people around us, he reached across the red tablecloth and touched my hand. The soft glow of the candles made his eyes misty and luminous. Overpowered by his emotion, I lowered my eyes. I felt breathless.

"When will I see you again, Susie?"

"I really don't know. I may return to Korea within six months if I find it hard to adjust in Alaska. But I might stay on and get a job and see the country or go to college there. I've been waiting for this day, but somehow I'm almost afraid to leave."

The waitress brought metal platters with our sizzling T-bone steaks and left. In spite of the tantalizing aroma, I found myself toying with the meat. After dinner Don clasped my hands in his and said, "Susie, I was shocked when you told us that night that you were going to Alaska. I felt as if I had my head in a noose . . . ."

"But, why?" I asked him, puzzled. "I hadn't met you before the night you volunteered to take over my Sunday school class."

"I first saw you at the Idle Hour Service Club and then at the post chapel. Your bodyguards, the Protestant Men of the Chapel, always surrounded you. I didn't know how to get to you, so I joined the Protestant Men, but still I was afraid to ask you for a date, thinking that you would refuse or avoid me." Don's eyes reflected anguish as he went on. "A couple months ago, I requested an extension for another term in Korea," he sighed. I stared at him in disbelief. GIs very seldom wanted to stay even a day longer overseas.

"I know what you're thinking, but I fell in love with you the minute I first saw you. I didn't dare ask you for a date. Besides, it might sound odd, but I heard a missionary named Miss Alyward speak in November at the chapel. She's a famous missionary to China and her work was made into a film called Inn of the Sixth Happiness. She spoke of her response to God's calling and I felt a tug, as if she were speaking to me. It might be my calling to work with the Korean orphans here. I have had a great hope of marrying you and working together as a team for the orphans. But now . . . ."

I stared at Don incredulously. Except in jest no one had ever proposed to me. Had I met someone like Don even half a year ago I would have jumped at the opportunity, but now my head was so cluttered with all the wonderful things I felt I might accomplish in America that my heart did not even respond to his proposal.

I remembered a woman who came to put her half-Korean daughter into the dependents' school. The child was not readily accepted at Korean schools since the foreigner whom she had married was not socially prominent. Don was an enlisted man. I would face cold shoulders from both sides.

"Don," I said slowly, "When I marry I want it to last forever. There are too many barriers in an interracial marriage. It may be all right for the two who decide to marry, but what about the in-laws? What if your parents would not accept me? If we should have children, how would they survive? Would they have a place in society, either here or in America?" I was so full of doubts and apprehensions I talked for a long time. Don listened patiently.

"Besides, my cultural values and traditions are so different from yours. People who marry within their own race have enough adjustment problems, let alone those from East and West. I've heard of many Korean women who were promised marriage before their soldiers returned to America. Between parental objections from both sides, and competition from American women, most of them just gave up. The few women who did marry GIs and went to the States often returned to Korea because they didn't feel accepted by their husband's family and friends or were simply lonely."

"Susie," Don spoke calmly as usual, "I feel our marriage would be strengthened because we both believe in God. This is the most important element in a marriage to sustain the couple during their adjustment period, through difficulties, and in crises. Secondly, you speak English fluently, and we can communicate very well. As far as in-laws are concerned, I think your parents like me. I intend to visit them after you leave and get better acquainted with them. And I'm sure once my family meets you, they'll love you."

He had as many answers as I had objections. "As far as competition is concerned, my girlfriend back home broke up with me before I left for the service in '59." Don took a deep breath and said emphatically, "Susie, I love you, and I want to spend the rest of my life with you."

The band played Johnny Mathis' song, "Until the Twelfth of Never." The lyrics depicted the very passion Don expressed, yet I found it difficult to respond to him. I needed time – a long time – to ponder. From the recesses of my mind I dug up the notions that were pounded into me as a young girl: A disabled person should not marry.

"Don, what if I can't have children when you love them so much? I don't have a perfect body. Won't you be embarrassed to have your family meet me? No, it just wouldn't work. I can't marry you!" I shook my head. For a fleeting second, Don's eyes darkened but then softened again.

"Susie, your leg brace doesn't affect my respect and admiration for you. I love what's in you that radiates through your eyes, your words, your actions. You are such a big part of my life. Can't you see that? If you are worried about not being able to have children, we can adopt orphans." He looked frustrated. His broad, genuine spirit moved me, yet I could not give him the answer he wanted.

The band played their last piece, "Now Is the Time When We Must Say Good-bye." My eyes filled up as I sat shackled by external circumstances and cultural prohibitions. We got up slowly. Don helped me with my coat and escorted me out to his truck. Not many vehicles were on the road, just an occasional cab. Silently Don drove on. We were both engrossed in our own thoughts, trying to control our emotions. Near my home Don slowed to a stop under a pine tree. Without a word, he pulled me to him and held me tightly, his feverish lips searching and touching mine.

"Oh, Susie, I love you. I want to marry you. I wish you weren't leaving. I can't let you go," he whispered. I wanted to yield, but I could not. Don started the motor again and drove on. We did not speak until Don turned into my parents' driveway.

"Don, I don't mean to hurt your feelings, but please don't come to the train station tomorrow morning. There will be many Koreans who won't understand. We'll just say good-bye here." I glanced up at him sheepishly.

"I guess I have no choice," he said. "Write me as soon as you get to Alaska."

Forgive Me

"Children, it's daylight! Time to get up." Father had returned from dawn prayer service. I sleepily rubbed my eyes and looked at him. His nose and cheeks were red, so I guessed that the weather must be nippy. I felt almost like a child again, being awakened by Father as in the old days. Still yawning, I stretched myself and tried to sit up, but I did not want to move away from the warm spot on the ondol.

The maid peeked in from the kitchen and told me that she had a basin, full of warm water ready for me to wash my face. I washed, brushed my hair, put on my makeup with care and began to dress. Just to be on the safe side in Alaska, I pulled on a pair of heavyweight underwear, a charcoal gray pantsuit and a tangerine sweater. Then, I got out my camel's hair overcoat to wear later.

Mother and the maid brought in the breakfast trays and set the food on a round table so that we could sit together and eat. My parents and sisters ate a Korean breakfast, but as a surprise Mother prepared an American breakfast for me of an omelet, buttered bread and coffee.

"Mother made a special trip downtown to buy a loaf of bread and the coffee," Bok Sook told me. I was so touched that I almost cried. Mother was blinking her eyes, too, but tears trickled down her face before she could turn her head away.

Father said grace. I watched my parents eat in silence. Both tried to hold smiles on their aging faces, but they only succeeded in looking heavy-hearted. It would have been exciting if all of us were going to America. Wha Sook and Bok Sook smiled up at me shyly between mouthfuls of rice, broiled bass, and kimchi, wrapped in roasted sheets of seaweed. During my years living on the post, I hardly had a chance to know my younger sisters. I felt more like a distant relative to them than a member of their family.

After the maid cleared away the table, Father led us in family devotions. He read the Bible and began to say a long prayer, asking the Lord to go before me and prepare the way, to watch over me and grant my wishes according to His will. My eyes felt misty. Father closed the huge, tattered Bible he had used for as long as I could remember. We all stood up and headed for the foyer.

Father picked up my largest suitcase, and my sisters gathered the matching gray overnight case and followed him out. Mother held my hand tightly as she led me out to the gate where Father stood, hailing a taxi. A green cab screeched to a stop. We all piled in. The maid stood at the gate and waved as we sped up the slope. The taxi sped through the residential area, then swerved in and out of the open marketplaces where people swarmed, bargaining, selling and buying.

A crowd of relatives and friends were waiting for us at the Pusan train station. Even though gray skies hung over us, I felt sunny inside. The mere sound of train whistles made my heart soar with excitement and anticipation. We hurried toward my train. My widowed aunt was there with her three children, all of them taller than my own 4'11". I saw Pastor Hwang and some of the parishioners from my parents' church. Korean employees from the Pusan Area Command had also come to bid me farewell, including Miss Yun, the school secretary.

My father paced the station platform while others gathered around and talked to me. As the noise of the train rose, Father pulled me away from the others. My mother and sisters stayed with the group. Father took me into the waiting hall, which bustled with travelers. We sat down on a paint-chipped bench. I felt a little nervous as I glanced up at the huge clock. I didn't want to miss the train.

"When will I see you again, Hyun Sook-ga?"

"I don't know, Aboji."

"Do not let luxurious America pull you away from . . . ." Father cleared his throat anxiously before he went on to give his last minute advice. I was too excited to absorb any advice in the noisy waiting hall. It annoyed me that he still treated me like a little girl, unable to take care of herself. I glanced up at the clock impatiently. All around the immense hall people bought tickets, magazines and newspapers. Some shouted and darted through the crush. Several beggars huddled near the exit, holding out their grubby hands toward well-dressed men and women. Mothers, with infants on their backs, rushed past me. Some women pulled their crying toddlers away from the gate after seeing their husbands off.

Smoke bellowed from the train and swirled into the stuffy hall, stinging my eyes and nostrils. The train whistle blared, resounding deafeningly from the high ceiling. Pigeons fluttered across the floor, unafraid. I glanced at the clock. 8:35 AM. My heart danced. Soon I would be on my way.

People began to run toward the train with suitcases and bundles in a mad confusion to get better seats by the windows. Many bowed and some shook hands. I saw one couple in high school uniforms, holding hands, as the girl wept pitifully. The peddlers yelled above the noise and chaos. "Box lunch! Savory sushi! Cida![39] Roasted chestnuts! Persimmons! Chocolate! Lucky Strikes!"

Amid the noise, Father and I stepped out of the waiting hall. Suddenly my father clasped me in his arms, something he had never done before. His broad shoulders began to tremble as he sobbed pathetically.

"My daughter, Hyun Sook-ga, forgive me. Forgive me! Why did I leave you behind during the war? Why? My soul must have gone out of me! How can I undo all the wrong I have done to you? O, God, I have no peace in my heart. Forgive me, merciful Father, for my sin against my crippled daughter!" Father released me and covered his flushed face with his coarse hands. I stood there astonished. My father had never, never admitted his actions had been wrong. I wanted to tell him how I hated him for deserting me to suffer the horrors of the war; how many nights I wanted to scream at him for not even letting me study; how their praises turned my stomach when I began to make something of myself. Instead, I started to say what he wanted to hear, as I had always done.

I fumbled for my handkerchief and reached up to his hands and whispered, "Please don't cry, Aboji."

He stared at me with deep remorse. I gazed into his tear-drenched eyes. My own eyes welled up, regretting that this incident had to take ten years.

"Aboji, whatever happened was done in a moment of desperation. Please, let us forget about the past. I want you to know that I thank you for the time you have taken in teaching me about God. The faith you have implanted in me as a child has sustained me through all these years."

---

[39] A clear, carbonated soft drink.

Mysteriously, as I spoke these words, I became aware of a softening in my pent-up resentment toward my parents. I recalled the countless times Father had carried me on his back; the delightful folktales he told; and all those evenings that he faithfully taught us about God. I also remembered the many times I grieved him. For the first time in my life, I saw my father as an ordinary human being, not as an infallible superhuman who could do no wrong. In the recesses of my soul, I felt a wall of bitterness crumble. Just what it was I could not define, but a spirit of love and healing pierced through my bone marrow. A glow that had not been there before lit like a match in a dark, frightening, desolate room.

A voice on the loudspeaker announced, "Seoul bound passengers! All aboard! All aboard! Seoul bound passengers! All aboard!"

Father took my bag and held my arm tightly as we hurried on. While we hastened toward the train, I realized one matter still stood between me and Father. I stopped abruptly and clutched his arms.

"Aboji, w-w-would you please forgive me for all the hurt I have caused you? And I-I really didn't want to become a Buddhist. Aboji, I will never again denounce my faith nor depart from the Lord God. I promise!"

Suddenly I saw peace spread across his grief-stricken face, the likes of which I had not seen before. Father lifted his eyes toward Heaven and whispered, "Omnipotent God, thank you for answering my prayers."

The friends and relatives, waiting patiently, rushed toward me to shake hands. They bowed repeatedly and some shyly hugged me and wished me success. I thanked Miss Yun for her friendship and encouragement. I threw my arms around my mother and tried to tell her that my heart was at peace with her, Father and God, but I was so choked up that I could not speak.

Pastor Hwang began to say a parting prayer. One by one the people around me bowed their heads as the pastor asked God's protection and guidance upon me. He then began to sing the hymn "God Be With You Till We Meet Again" in Korean.

In the midst of all these farewell gestures, the conductor urged me to board the train and take my seat in the American compartment. I swept both of my younger sisters into my arms and said, "Be obedient to Aboji and Omoni. Study hard and be good to each other." Then I clambered up the steps and settled into my seat. I pulled up the window and stuck out my head to say good-bye to a new group of friends who had just arrived.

Then out of nowhere, I saw him. Don, in his dress uniform, raced toward the train. My heart pumped wildly. "Why?" I gasped. "I told him not to come to the station!" Oblivious of the people, this man, whom I credited to be so reserved, leaped up the steps and strode toward me, grinning boyishly.

"I know I'm not supposed to be out here," Don said, raising both hands, "but my First Sergeant asked me if I would volunteer to drive our unit commander to the station!" Flashing his eyes, Don swiftly removed his school ring from his finger and handed it to me. Before I could say a word or return it to him, he dashed out of the train.

I looked at the ring. I knew the significance of accepting a ring from a man. With the ring still in my hand, I poked my head out once again. Standing behind the rest of the crowd, Don winked at me knowingly. He towered a head above the rest of them and looked outstandingly handsome. It seemed ironic. Usually it was the woman who stayed behind and waved good-bye to the soldier.

The train lurched forward, sputtering smoke. The whistle blocked our voices as the crowd shouted farewell.

My parents waved their hands, tears cascading down their faces. Suddenly they raced down the platform alongside the moving train, waving their handkerchiefs, calling my name repeatedly and trying to touch my outstretched hand. As the train rounded a bend and the platform became remote and almost out of sight, I saw Don standing by my parents, waving his hat.

At last, I was on my way to Mikuk.

Mikuk

The little two-engine Grunman Goose I boarded in Juneau bounced through the air so turbulently that I became ill. There was a drastic difference between the plush Northwest airliner I had flown across the Pacific and this tiny aircraft. The pilot announced that we would be landing in ten minutes. I peered out through the window and saw little emerald mounds dotting the ocean below. As I reached for the sick-bag, again, the plane suddenly sputtered and seemed to nose-dive into the ocean. With my eyes tightly closed, I muttered my last prayer and, as I awaited an imminent crash, wished I had accepted Don's proposal to marry him in Korea. Now I would never see him again. When I opened my eyes, I found the Goose intact and taxiing toward the ramp. No one had told me that the plane would be amphibious.

Through the hazy window, I saw people waving. Before I knew it, Mr. and Mrs. Fleming rushed to welcome me with their daughters, five-year old Susan and two-year old Debbie clutching a bald-headed doll and a tattered security blanket.

Excitedly we greeted each other. Mr. Fleming had not changed much since he left Korea nine years earlier. With her beautiful red hair, Mrs. Fleming appeared much younger than her husband. Susan looked like her father with her curly brown hair and warm brown eyes and Debbie claimed her mother's baby blue eyes.

We boarded a shore boat to cross the channel from Sitka to Mount Edgecumbe. Although I expected cold weather in Alaska, the Flemings told me that Sitka's climate was mild because of the warm currents from Japan that surround the island. Snow-capped Mount Edgecumbe even resembled Mt. Fuji.

We unloaded my luggage at their neat government quarters. Mr. Fleming asked that I address him as Dad instead of being so formal. However, Mrs. Fleming preferred to be called Doris because she was only 12 years older than I. It felt awkward and rude to address her by her first name, but I obliged. I gave a toy piano to Susan and a doll to Debbie, but she continued to clutch Baldy tightly. By sunset, we were a threesome, reading books, and playing with their countless toys, dolls and games.

While I played with the girls, Doris prepared a ham dinner, with candied yams, a Jell-O salad with walnuts and cranberries, relish, biscuits and an apple pie. Doris set the dining table with her gold-rimmed china and matching crystal goblets. It amazed me that she prepared such an elaborate dinner and kept an immaculate house without a maid. Contrary to what that joker Charlie had said, American women worked very hard.

During the next few days, I followed Doris around the house. Intrigued, I watched her bake a carrot cake and then sat in front of the oven as the batter rose to a golden mound. The aroma of cinnamon filled the kitchen. When she used the washer and dryer, I chuckled as I remembered Charlie's claim that these appliances not only washed and dried clothes, but also folded them.

Although they attended a different church, the Flemings took me to visit a Presbyterian church on my first Sunday in Sitka. After the worship service, we met the pastor of First Presbyterian Church, Rev. William Gavin and his wife. They introduced us to Mr. & Mrs. Chester Latta, campus staff at Sheldon Jackson College, and Mrs. Holic, an English professor. They made me feel so welcomed that I returned the following Sunday. At the end of the service, the Gavins invited me to their home for dinner. As they served huge slices of roast beef, baked potatoes, and salad, they asked me about Korea. The Gavins took particular interest in my father's work with the Presbyterian Church and my involvement with the Sunday school there. Before I left, Mrs. Gavin asked me to teach in a Sunday school class. The next Sunday, Mrs. Latta invited me to join the choir. Within a month, I became a member of the church.

Through the intervention of the Flemings, the President of Sheldon Jackson College, Dr. Roland Armstrong, accepted me into the college based on my life experience despite my lack of formal schooling past the fourth grade. He offered me a full scholarship and arranged for me to work as an assistant dormitory supervisor to cover my room and board. I thought about all those times I felt humiliated whenever people asked me about my educational credentials. Now my mind raced ahead to all the wonderful things I might achieve and how it would feel to be confident. Before I returned to Korea, I was determined to succeed.

A week after my arrival, Doris handed me a letter from Don. He had written it right after he saw me off at the Pusan Train Station. From then on, I received at least one letter a day from him. He wrote in part, "I visited your family. I taught your father to play chess. After several games, your father beat me." In another letter he wrote about the dinner my mother prepared for him and his friends. My mouth watered as Don described the huge deep-fried prawns as big as a child's hand. He told me about his first experience of eating red-hot kimchi and the gallons of water he drank afterwards. Hearing about the dinners my mother prepared for him made me homesick. Don always ended his letters with his love for me.

In the middle of February, Don wrote to tell me that the Army Personnel Office had denied his request for extension in Korea. He would be reassigned to Florida. He wanted to visit me en route to the Sunshine State. I wanted to see him, but I immediately replied that he could not visit me here since I was a guest at the Flemings.

The following day, Doris handed me another letter from Don and winked at me, "Hyun Sook, he must be a very special friend to be writing to you every day!"

My face flushed as I answered, "He is a soldier whom I met before I left Korea, and he wants to visit me on his way to Florida."

"I don't mean to be inquisitive, but do you mind if I read a letter or two from him? I can size him up." While she read the latest letter, I brought out a shopping bag full of letters from Don.

"Well, Hyun Sook, if you don't want this fellow, I am going to invite him. I have some nieces who would love to meet him."

Without another word, Doris went to her desk and wrote two letters, one to Don and another one to his friend Bob, the Chaplain's Assistant. A week later I received a telegram from Don, informing me of his arrival in Sitka. Doris clapped her hands excitedly over the news. She was worried that her letter might not have reached him before he left Korea.

The Flemings and I met Don at the Sitka airstrip. After hugs and kisses, we piled into a cab. On the shore boat, Don told us that he had received the letter from Doris on the morning of his departure.

That evening before a candlelight dinner, Don whispered to me, "When I received the letter from Doris, I took it for granted that the invitation was your consent to marry me. I rushed over to the PX and bought this diamond ring before shipping out of the post." Don slipped a beautiful diamond ring onto my left hand. Although his expression of love touched me, I felt unsure. I had always assumed that I would never marry. Except for Don, no one had seriously proposed to me. We celebrated our engagement with the Flemings.

Time sped by. We went sightseeing, took pictures and talked endlessly. One afternoon as we walked past the totem poles in the park, Don asked me if we could marry before he left Alaska. He wanted me to meet his family in Carlisle, Pennsylvania and go on with him to Florida. It sounded like an easy way out of my uncertain future, but I told him that I wanted to go to college. After two weeks, Don left for his home in Carlisle. He looked forlorn as he boarded the Goose, and I felt a sudden sense of emptiness as the plane took off.

That same day I moved into Stevenson Hall, a women's dormitory on campus and began my work as an assistant to the dormitory supervisor. I had a beautifully furnished private room. I looked forward to each evening as the students gathered in the lounge for time of devotion where we sang hymns, read from the Bible, shared from the heart and prayed for one another. In time the students felt free to confide in us and shared their problems. Between my duties, I attended classes, feeling grateful for the opportunity.

Sometime after I moved onto the campus, the president of a local elementary school's PTA asked me to speak at one of their meetings. I briefly touched upon my war experience and on Korean life in general. Before I finished, I expressed my gratitude to the Flemings, their friends and the people in the community for accepting me.

Later a PTA member Mrs. Philip Moore approached me. "I enjoyed your talk very much. We have a lot to thank God for here." She paused for a moment and then continued, "My husband is an orthopedic surgeon. I think he might be able to help you with your leg." My face flushed. Reading my expression, Mrs. Moore apologized, "I didn't mean to make you feel uncomfortable. I meant if you wished, I could make an appointment for my husband to see you. How about a week from now?" I thanked her.

Not knowing what to expect, I walked into the office a week later. Mrs. Moore, in nurse's uniform, greeted me warmly and escorted me into her husband's office. After a physical examination, Dr. Moore advised either a four-inch lift to my shoe on the brace or an amputation above the right knee. He explained that I would be fitted with a prosthesis resembling my healthy leg. I could feel my eyes widen. The self-conscious little girl inside me stirred eagerly.

"Would I be able to walk in high heels?" I asked impulsively.

"Yes, indeed! With physical therapy, you can walk in heels, dance, drive a car, even climb a mountain, if you wish." Dr. Moore replied.

"Really?" I exclaimed breathlessly. I felt like Shim Bong Sa, desperate to restore his sight with 50 sacks of rice, but then I remembered that I had no money.

When I told him hesitantly that I could not pay, Dr. Moore chuckled, "Do you think we are concerned about money? We've taken care of that. The Sitka Community Hospital has offered your hospital stay free of charge. The State of Alaska Department of Rehabilitation will cover the price of the prosthesis and physical therapy. The Bank of Alaska will purchase your round trip ticket to Seattle. One of our dear friends in Seattle will take care of you while you are there. And I, of course, will perform the surgery. We want to help make your life easier."

"I don't know what to say. Thank you, thank you very much." I stammered.

The goodness of these American people overwhelmed me, but the thought of walking down the street in a beautiful pair of heels was thrilling. No one would stare at my leg brace or call me names again. I wanted to look normal, and I did not want any objections. Without consulting the Flemings or Don or even my parents, we set a date for the surgery.

Shortly after the Flemings left for a vacation, I entered the hospital. That night I hummed as I took a shower. Engrossed in dreams of my new look, I failed to watch my step. As I turned to leave the shower, I banged my big toe against the sill.

The following morning, two nurses came to wheel me into the operating room. Waiting on the chilly operating table, I doubted my decision, but just as I turned to question the nurses, the anesthetist injected me. The nurses instructed me to count backwards from ten to one, and by the time Dr. Moore entered the room, I was already dozing off.

When I opened my eyes, I found myself in a private room with a nurse by my side. Floral arrangements and cards from friends and strangers fill the room. Sensing a sharp pain in the toe I stubbed the night before, I reached down to rub it, but to my horror, my whole right leg was missing. For a fleeting second, I thought I had lost my mind. No one had explained phantom pain to me. Eventually the ache passed, but a wave of guilt swept into its place. I had not requested my parents' permission to have the amputation.

When Mrs. Latta came to visit, I shared my remorse with her and she listened compassionately.

"How will I explain to my parents the reason behind my decision? What will I say to the Flemings and to Don?"

"Susie, I can't imagine how traumatic it must be for you to have a major surgery in a foreign land. You are brave." Mrs. Latta dabbed her eyes with a lavender handkerchief. "I will contact a missionary friend in Korea near your parents' home. I am sure he will visit your parents and relay the message to them." As she stood to leave, Mrs. Latta invited, "Call me Mother Latta. I have 'adopted' many young people who are far from home, and they all do."

As I recuperated, I began to wonder how I would break the news to Don. Years of socialization replayed in my mind. I could not marry him because of my amputation. Besieged by guilt and confusion, I decided to write to him for the last time. Ending the letter, I wrote, "I don't want you to marry me out of pity. Please feel free to date other women. My engagement ring will be returned to you as soon as I'm discharged from the hospital."

Don telegraphed immediately asking me not to return the ring. He said that the surgery made no difference to him. This he followed with flowers, numerous cards and letters to reassure me of his love, but I did not respond. He sent a beautiful floral arrangement to my dorm to welcome me back, but nothing moved my heart. I took off his engagement ring and placed it in my jewelry box. More than ever before, I determined, I would devote myself to my studies and to remain single.

Before long the Flemings returned from vacation and came to visit. Shock and disappointment registered in their eyes when they realized my leg was missing. Feeling guilty for my impulsive decision, I acted aloof and polite. To make matters worse, I received a long letter from my father after his visit with Mrs. Latta's missionary friend. I dreaded opening it. Father wrote, "I understand your desire to look normal, but you have no right to severe a part of the body which God has given you." His lecture angered me. Familiar childhood resentments knotted in my stomach.

As soon as the swelling went down enough to be fitted with the prosthesis, Dr. and Mrs. Moore contacted a friend in Seattle. Mrs. Sophie Krause, a slim, elderly lady with an aristocratic manner of speaking, met me at the airport. She hugged me as if she had known me all her life and asked me to call her Sophie because it made her feel young. Once again, I pulled against my upbringing and called an elder by her first name.

My eyes widened when Sophie drove her navy blue Mercedes through an ornate iron gate onto a lengthy, park-like drive. Her gardener, maid and cook greeted us at the front entrance. The foyer presented a cathedral ceiling, and a staircase with a hand-carved banister swept away to the right. Straight ahead a magnificent crystal chandelier adorned the formal dining room. The drawing room, the guestroom and even the kitchen captured a breath-taking view of Lake Washington. Her spacious, manicured lawn surrounded prize-winning roses whose intoxicating scent permeated the air all the way down to the blue lakeshore.

Financially endowed, Sophie had traveled all over the world. Although a graduate of Smith College, she continued to attend classes to enrich her mind. Each morning as we ate our breakfast, Sophie spoke fondly of her deceased husband. Her only regret in life was not having a child, but she indicated that young friends like me made her feel fulfilled and youthful.

While we waited for an appointment with the prosthetist, we went sightseeing, dined out, and swam in the lake. She said the Moores had told her about my "obsession" with high heels, and she took me to the largest shoe store in Seattle. I felt like a little girl at a toy fair. After inspecting numerous shoes, I selected a pair of black pumps with three-inch heels. With my new shoes in hand, we entered the prosthetic studio for a fitting.

The prosthetist left the cubicle with my leg measurements. I waited ecstatically, but to my chagrin, he returned with a block of wood. Tears rushed to my eyes. I had expected a beautiful, ready-made slip-on leg. He explained that this would shape the "thigh," but it took numerous adjustments before the crude form began to resemble my left leg.

Finally the day arrived for my last fitting. The prosthesis did look very much like my real leg, and when I slipped on my stockings, I could hardly tell them apart. At first I wobbled like a toddler, but after several weeks of rigorous physical therapy, I walked out of the clinic without even a cane. Sophie shook her head and wiped her eyes.

As much as I enjoyed being in Seattle with my wonderful hostess, I needed to return to Alaska. The night before my departure, Sophie gave me an elaborate send-off dinner party.I had met many lovely, talented friends and I would miss them.

I visited the Moores as soon as I landed in Sitka. Like proud parents over their child's first steps, they snapped pictures of me with my new leg. From there I went to visit the Flemings. They were very happy for me, and the tension between us eased.

However, when I returned to the dorm, loneliness engulfed me. When the spring semester started, I could not muster any of my former zeal for study. All the instant coffee I made with hot tap water failed to keep me awake, and my concentration declined.

One day in late February, Doris called to tell me that Don would be in Sitka in a week. She said, "Don told me that you have not responded to his letters but he still wants to come. You know the only reason for his trip here is to be with you." Displeasure sounded in her voice. "We've lined up a job for him with the Alaska Lumber & Pulp Company. I expect you to be at the airstrip."

On March 5, 1962, I went with the Flemings to greet Don. When he arrived, he told us that he had driven straight from Jacksonville, Florida, through to Seattle in three days. He shipped off his station wagon on the barge and climbed onto a plane himself. Doris teased,

"Three days from Jacksonville? You couldn't get here fast enough!"

We spent the whole day at the Flemings. They invited Don to stay with them until he found an apartment. Before returning to the campus, I nudged Don and quietly asked,

"Don't you see my new leg?"

"Yes, I noticed it. It's beautiful. But, Susie, it doesn't matter how you look. I love you." His tired eyes misted as he squeezed my left hand. His engagement ring was still in my jewelry box.

I returned to my dormitory that night. Whenever Don called me, I did not respond. Even on weekends, I studied deep into the night, determined to make something of myself.

A month after Don came to Sitka, I saw him in town. He walked with his hands in his pockets. His downcast expression tugged at my heart. I knew that he moved to Alaska because he loved me. Remorse overwhelmed me for having shut him out. I called his name. Don looked startled and rushed over to me. Sheepishly, I apologized to him for my unkind behavior. "If you still want me," I whispered, "I will marry you." Without a word, Don pulled me to his trembling body and kissed me right on the sidewalk, oblivious to passersby.

When we broke the news to the Flemings that

afternoon, Doris wept and hugged us. Since Sitka had no bridal shop, she brought out a catalog and asked me to choose any dress I wanted. I selected a white floor length gown, overlaid in lace, with a scalloped neck and full sleeves. A fingertip veil with rhinestone and a pearl tiara also caught my eye. Finally, I picked out a pair of white satin shoes with three-inch spike heels.

That evening I labored over a letter to my parents, worrying about their reaction to the interracial marriage. Furthermore, I hadn't even asked for their permission. Ten days later, I received a letter from Father.

My beloved daughter Hyun Sook-ga:

Your news about your plans to marry Don Beidel came as a total surprise to us. But your mother and I are glad that we had a chance to meet the fine young man. Don visited us often after you left for Alaska and played with your younger sisters. Your mother prepared many dinners for him and his friends from the post. He ate everything, even tried kimchi once. He drank jug after jug of water. One day he brought me a set of chess and taught me how to play. I even got to beat him in the game once before he left Korea! And now he is taking our daughter away.

Don seems like a faithful Christian and we like him very much. Your mother and I give you both our blessings for a happy life together. I urge you never to depart from the faith.

Consult with your pastor there regarding the following scripture I selected to be included in your wedding homily:

I Timothy 6:9-10–But they that will be rich fall into temptation and a snare, and into many foolish and hurtful lusts, which drown men in destruction and perdition. For the

love of money is the root of all evil: which while some coveted
after. They have erred from the faith, and pierced themselves
through with money sorrows.

How I wish I had wings to fly across the ocean to
be at your wedding!

His letter of approval touched my heart and relieved
my anxiety.

Don and I visited Dr. and Mrs. Moore and invited
them to our wedding. I told them about the spike heels I
planned to wear. Narrowing his eyes, Dr. Moore warned me
to be careful when I walked down the aisle. "I'll be perspiring
and holding my breath the whole time!" He then turned to
Don and advised him to take a good care of me.

I felt free to go ahead with our plans. We set the date
for May 19th, the day after the end of my spring semester. As
soon as we announced the wedding, the whole church,
campus, even people I hardly knew, buzzed with excitement.
It became a community affair.

Mother Latta beamed as she hugged me. "Oh, Susie
dear, I am so happy for you! Don seems like such a
wonderful Christian man." Her gentle eyes sparkled as she
clasped my hands in hers, "I'll coordinate the wedding
reception."

The following Sunday, Mrs. Holic, my English
professor, announced that she would make a five-tier
wedding cake for me. Some of the Japanese executives' wives
from the Alaska Lumber & Pulp Company heard about it and
offered to help with the floral arrangements.

Meanwhile, Don saw an advertisement for a two-
bedroom trailer for rent with the option to buy. When some
of the Sheldon Jackson staff heard about it, they offered to let
us house the trailer on an acre of property that they co-
owned. Immediately, Father Latta and Don started to clear

the area on James Town Bay about three miles from the college. They even built a deck that ran the length of the trailer.

I asked Doris to be my matron of honor and Dad Fleming to give me away. Mother Latta, dressed in lavender lace, acted as my proxy mother. Father Latter stood as Don's best man and one of my professors served as an usher. Thus the people of Sitka and Mt. Edgecumbe graciously filled the place of our families.

At last May 19th arrived. Organ music filled the sanctuary of the First Presbyterian Church. Doris looked radiant in her aqua silk dress and a matching hat. She gave me a last minute touch-up and hugged me before she slid into the vestibule. My friends filled the seats. Elegant floral arrangements and pew after pew of white and aqua blue satin ribbons adorned the sanctuary. I saw Don waiting by the altar looking very handsome in the English worsted suit my parents had sent him. The music of the wedding march made my heart quicken. Everyone stood up as I started down the isle, escorted by Dad Fleming. Dr. and Mrs. Moore beamed as they eyed my heels. Doris wiped her eyes, as Dad gave me away.

Rev. Gavin recited, ". . . For richer and for poorer, in health and in sickness, till death do us part . . ." As I repeated the wedding vows I wanted ours to be for life.

After the feasting, as we started to leave the church, all the guests threw rice at us. Don carried me through the front door of our trailer. For a long time he cradled me in his arms as if I were a precious jewel. Kissing me tenderly, he whispered, "At last you are my wife, Mrs. Beidel."

The next morning I slipped out of bed and started breakfast. The toaster and other gifts were still loaded in the station wagon, so I placed slices of bread in the broiler. While I stirred the porridge, the bread caught fire and filled the kitchen with smoke. Don rushed into the kitchen flinging open the windows. Meanwhile the oatmeal clumped up. I was terribly embarrassed.

Don just hugged me, "Don't worry about it, Susie. Usually, I just have a cup of tea and some toast." He cleaned up the mess and scrambled some eggs for us. His gentle spirit eased my mind. Nevertheless, I purposed to buy some cookbooks and learn how to cook.

Sometime after the wedding, I started feeling nauseous. At first I thought I had the flu, but when it persisted, Don took me to a doctor. After an exam, the physician told us that I might be pregnant. When the test confirmed it, anxiety gripped my stomach. I knew nothing about caring for a baby, and I would have to postpone my college education.

That night when I broke the news to Don, his face lit up. He held me gently in his arms. When I told him of my fears, Don assured me that he would help care for our baby. Praying daily for God's wisdom for us to be good parents, we studied the Bible together. As a surprise, Don bought a Baldwin console piano for me. Excitedly I called Mother Latta for piano lessons.

One month after Christmas while Don was on a midnight shift, I tossed and turned in the bed. Not finding a comfortable position, I decided to get up and make some pies. As I pushed and strained with the rolling pin, my water broke. Frantically I telephoned Don. Within minutes he came and we sped toward the hospital.

"If it's a girl," Don decided as he drove, "Let's name her Sophia, after your Korean name, Hyun, wisdom." In the rush we agreed to the middle name LeeAnn – Lee after my maiden name and Ann to add a feminine touch.

"If it's a boy, I would like to name him David Lee," I said. "It means my beloved. My father would be happy to hear that although he didn't have a son, his grandson's middle name would be Lee."

As soon as we pulled into the Emergency Room, the nurses wheeled me into the maternity ward. No one had prepared me for the agony of childbirth. The pain felt so intense I screamed like a wild woman as I thrashed my body. My eyes bulged from pushing and straining, while Don looked on helplessly. I thought my chest would burst from hyperventilating. After a few hours of agony, I heard a cry, and my body went limp. One of the nurses handed me a tiny, five-pound baby wrapped in a white blanket. It overwhelmed me to hold my own beautiful daughter. As Don lifted our tiny girl to his chest, his eyes glistened.

After ten days in the hospital, we brought our baby home. As he drove Don commented,

"Sophia sounds too sophisticated for a baby. Let's call her by her middle name." LeeAnn was so small that she could fit into Don's shoebox. I was afraid to pick her up, because I feared I might hurt her frail body. Just to be on the safe side, I sterilized everything and doused my hands with rubbing alcohol before I touched her. At first, as I tried to change her little diapers, my hands shook terribly. Don, on the other hand, would calmly finish them. He claimed no training, but it seemed so natural for him.

The days progressed, but no matter how long I nursed her, LeeAnn kept sucking. She cried day and night. After two weeks of struggling at home, I collapsed. Don rushed me to the hospital. The doctor admitted me for a week and told us that I was exhausted, dehydrated, and not able to produce enough milk to satisfy the baby. During this second stay in the hospital, the Flemings cared for the baby. Even Susan and Debbie took turns feeding LeeAnn from a bottle. Once we started her on formula, LeeAnn slept through the nights. Without my asking, Don took over preparing the bottles and folding the laundry before he left for work. Gradually our lives returned to normal.

In her sixth week, we had LeeAnn baptized at our church. Don and I took our vows to nurture her in the love and knowledge of God very seriously. Since I knew so little about raising a child, I begged God to help me be wise and loving mother. I started by purchasing a set of children's encyclopedias as well as the World Book Encyclopedia. Each night I read the Bible and nursery rhymes to her. After I finished practicing my lessons, I played children's songs on the piano for LeeAnn.

At the invitation of a friend, I joined a mothers' club. We developed close bonds with each another as we prayed and shared our concerns. Some of the Japanese women also invited me to attend their weekly luncheons. We exchanged recipes and took turns preparing lunches. One of the women invited me to her silk flower and doll-making classes. Another taught me how to arrange flowers and the art of the tea ceremony. I looked forward to these gatherings each week.

Just as I began to feel confident about mothering and to enjoy LeeAnn, I discovered I was pregnant again. Don was thrilled. He decided that we needed a larger house, so we drove from one end of the island of Sitka to the other. After passing a particular cozy ranch with a white picket fence several times, we decided to knock. To our surprise the owner of the house said that they had outgrown it and were thinking of selling. Through the pulp mill credit union, Don took a loan, and within a few months, we had the deed to our first home.

Excitement filled our two-bedroom home. We hummed and whistled happy tunes while we painted and hung curtains. When we needed fresh air, we tended the flower garden along the fence. Finally, we unpacked our boxes and arranged furniture.

Life seemed so blissful. I had a wonderful husband, a beautiful daughter and a second child on the way. Now, we owned our own home to complete the happiness. One of my secret childhood dreams had become a reality.

Three days after our second wedding anniversary, Don rushed me to the hospital for the birth of our second child. I felt more relaxed and knew what to expect. In the early hours, I heard the cry of a newborn.

"We have a baby boy!" I exclaimed, "My father will be happy that he has a grandson!" Later, Don grinned as he told me that he had heard me all the way in the waiting room.

The Shattered Vase

Several months before the birth of our son, Mi Sook wrote to me from Korea.

"Dear Onni, I am graduating from a women's University with a major in music. There is no future for me in Korea. Could you please sponsor me to America?"

I consulted Don. He felt we should help her, and the application for her visa went through smoothly. We purchased new furniture and carpet for the living room, as well as a bunk bed. Don rearranged the children's room to accommodate her. In order to cover the extra expenses, Don took a second job as a church custodian.

In order to cover extra expenses, Don took a second job as a custodian of our church besides his fulltime work at the Alaska Lumber & Pulp Company. Thereafter, he spent very little time at home. When I complained to Don about devoting more time than he should to the church, he sat quietly for a while and then said, "It may not make any sense to you, Susie, but I work as if I am doing it for the Lord."

As soon as Mi Sook spotted me at the airstrip, she dropped her luggage and raced toward me. I did not realize how much I had missed her until I saw her. She shook Don's hand and then carried LeeAnn and David as we headed for our car.

I took it for granted that Mi Sook would have learned English while in college, but to my dismay, she spoke very little. When I shared my concerns with Mrs. Holic, she offered to tutor Mi Sook.

Don and I threw a welcome party for Mi Sook, and she sang many songs for our friends. They were impressed by her remarkable voice. Gradually we introduced her to the people we knew in the community. Mother Latta invited Mi Sook to sing at her recital. The Soroptimist Club arranged for her to give a concert at the auditorium of Sheldon Jackson College. The audience, enraptured by her dramatic soprano rendition, spontaneously rose to their feet.

As proud as I was of her, I felt a twinge of envy. Beneath all my smiles, the resentment I felt toward my parents for not having allowed me to go to school rose again. My childhood disappointment and anger toward God and my parents rekindled in my heart. I felt threatened by Mi Sook's ability to command the adoration of others. Shocked and ashamed of my reaction, I suppressed my jealousy and put on a pleasant facade.

The following year, Mother Latta and Mrs. Holic arranged for Mi Sook to enter University of Washington. Mi Sook kept us abreast of her new life in Seattle. The following summer, however, she called to convey a tragic message from our mother. Father had passed away from carbon monoxide poisoning. The news devastated me and once again I regretted the years that bitterness had stolen from us.

In one of her letters, Mi Sook mentioned that she was selected to compete in the regional competition for the Metropolitan Opera. I was so proud of her that I made her an evening gown to wear on the stage. On the night of Mi Sook's competition, Don left for the evening shift. I bathed the children and read them some books. After tucking them into their beds, I went to kitchen to do the dishes. LeeAnn got out of her crib and came to me dragging a soiled diaper behind her. To my horror, she had smeared the feces all across the new carpet. I bathed her again, changed her sheets, and put her back to bed. Tears streamed down my face as I got on my hands and knees to clean the rug. No matter how hard and how long I scrubbed, the awful odor and stain remained. Exhausted, I decided to quit.

Just as I prepared to soak in the hot bathtub, the telephone rang.

"Onni, I won!" Mi Sook exclaimed over the wire. "I won the regional competition for the Met. They will fly me to New York City to compete at the Metropolitan Opera House!"

I congratulated her profusely, but after we hung up I sobbed miserably. I felt overwhelmed by the endless diapers, bottles, cleaning, singing and reading to the children a dozen times a day. Bitterly I recalled the advertisement in Charlie's magazine of a beautifully groomed blonde woman smiling at her children in her spotless kitchen. Mi Sook's victory only served to mock my bruised spirit.

Days later, while I still nursed my jealousy, Mi Sook phoned from New York.

"Onni, the judges at the Met selected me as a semi-finalist. I want to stay here and attend the Julliard School of Music." Mi Sook sounded very self-assured and ready to tackle life in the Big City.

"Oh, I'm thrilled for you. I wish you the best, Mi Sook!" I tried to convince myself as I congratulated her.

The next winter Mother wrote to say that her life in Korea had become increasingly difficult since Father's death. She asked us to sponsor her and my two younger sisters, Wha Sook and Bok Sook. Don readily agreed to help, but although we petitioned to bring all of them to Alaska, only my mother was given an early entry.

Tears streamed down my cheeks when I saw Mother getting off the little plane. She looked much older than when I left her at the Pusan Train Station. Her lustrous dark brown eyes had dulled with grief. As we embraced each other, I prayed silently that I would be able to comfort my mother and be a good daughter to her.

Mother had brought gifts for each of us. She gave me an exquisite jade-shade porcelain vase and a Korean gown - peacocks embroidered with gold and silver thread on white silk satin. We talked, wept and laughed as we reminisced until our voices grew hoarse.

Our first few weeks together whizzed by. She attended parties given in her honor by my friends, met many people and practiced on my kitchen appliances. She spent a great deal of time with LeeAnn and David. Although she became frustrated by her inability to communicate with her grandchildren, she compensated by letting them do anything they wanted. When the children started to take advantage of their permissive Harmoni, Don and I asked Mother to stop them when they misbehaved, but she would not listen.

One day I found my mother lying on her bed weeping. Startled I asked her why.

"They get into my things constantly." She complained. "I'd rather go out and work than to be around these children."

Daily, Mother urged me to bring Wha Sook and Bok Sook from Korea, even though I repeatedly told her that I had no control over the delay. Finally I exploded.

"You always loved the other sisters more than me!" I yelled. "You left me behind during the war. Don't you see that I am doing everything I can for them?"

Mother started to cry. Feeling remorseful, I asked her

to forgive me for my rude behavior and the ill feelings I had harbored toward her. She rebuked me.

"You shouldn't dwell on past events! I can't live with you anymore."

Tension mounted. Mother managed to mail a letter off to Mi Sook, telling her of our rift. A few weeks after the argument, despite my apologies, she abruptly left for New York City.

After Mother took off, I felt as if I had been abandoned once again. I grew increasingly irritable with Don and the children over minor things. Don began to spend more time at work, returning home only to eat and sleep. I stopped attending the Mothers' Club. My daily routine became a vicious cycle. Oblivious to my turmoil, the children snuggled up to me as I read the Bible and other books to them. Like a robot I played nursery songs on the piano or listened to Walt Disney records with them. The only place we went as a family was to church on Sundays.

Even my limb started to bother me. When I consulted Dr. Moore, he told me that a bone spur had grown on the tip of my stump, and I needed to have it removed surgically. He said that it would take a while to heal the incision and that I would need a new prosthesis.

After the surgery, I isolated myself from everyone. Abruptly, I stopped going out, even to the church and the hobby class. I refused to be seen without my prosthesis. I barely made it through the day, just caring for my two toddlers. Mindlessly I read one story after another. Dirty dishes and soiled clothes piled up. No matter how messy the house became, Don never complained. He tried to help me as much as he could in-between jobs, but seldom spoke with me. I stopped putting on a fresh dress and make-up before he got home.

As soon my sutures healed and the swelling went

down, I went to Seattle with the children for another prosthesis. At last the prosthesis was completed. This time, I changed my heel height to two inches. It would be more practical to have lower heels with two children. That evening when Don made his nightly call, I told him, "I love you. We'll be leaving in a few days." In my heart, I resolved to be a better wife and mother.

In spite of my best intentions, once I returned to my daily routine, my dismal spirit also returned. I resumed the basic tasks of housekeeping, but did not interact with others. One afternoon, the shrill ring of the telephone broke the coveted silence of naptime.

"Hi, Susie, this is Grace. I haven't seen you for a few months, and I wanted to know how you are." A woman I befriended at the mothers' club spoke cheerfully over the wire.

"I'm fine. Everything is fine." I tried to sound casual, but my voice betrayed me.

Grace let seconds tick away. "I don't mean to pry, but I have the feeling that everything is not all right. Would you care to talk about it?"

Her kind words unleashed my pent-up feelings, and words tumbled out.

"Grace, I can't explain what's happening to me. Lately I don't feel like going places or seeing people. You'll think I am a terrible mother. I get irritable over the slightest things and I yell at the children. My eyes well up easily and Don and I haven't been talking to each other for a while. When I am alone in the tub or in my car, I feel like I'll explode if I don't scream." I sighed and continued, "It might be best that I go away before I wreck my family."

"I think I know what you might be going through." Grace commented. "I haven't shared this with anyone else, but I also had my set of problems until I went to see a marriage counselor. His empathy, insight and humor helped me deal with my turmoil."

"It's hard to believe that someone like you could have problems. You always smile and seem happy," I remarked.

"Oh, that's just a facade. I couldn't deal with my life, but someone told me about Father Stratman, a priest at the St. Peter's by the Sea Episcopal Church. Susie, please give him a chance to help you before you decide to go away."

"How could I in this small town? Everybody would know I'm having marital problems. I can't promise, Grace, but I'll think about it. Thanks for caring." After I hung up the receiver, I shook my head and muttered, "No, I can't! No one can know about this."

The following morning, I dressed LeeAnn and David for Sunday school. After their father drove them to the church, I decided to dress for the morning worship service. Don returned in a few minutes and poured himself another cup of tea while he waited for me. Suddenly something unexpected took hold of me. I stormed into our bedroom and slammed the door. Don followed, bewildered.

"What is wrong, Susie?"

"Nothing's wrong! I just don't feel like going to the church. I am tired of having to smile like a hypocrite!"

"You don't have to smile."

"But, everybody smiles!"

"Susie, something has been bothering you for quite a while."

"Nothing's bothering me. Will you leave me alone? I am sick of everybody. We should never have gotten married. The East and the West just don't mix. I want to go away and make something of my life!"

"You can't go away."

"Oh, Yeah? Then, let's get a divorce!"

"You don't mean it. You can't leave us."

"Just watch me. If you don't divorce me, I'll make myself look like a mad woman, and they'll take me away! Then I won't have to put up with these dirty dishes, scrub the floor and the rest, like a maid!" I disheveled my hip-length hair and tore off my dress. When Don tried to restrain me, I screamed and flung my arms at him. Grabbing Mother's porcelain gift vase from the nightstand, I flung it against our bedroom door. It shattered all over the floor. Like an activated volcano, rage exploded and insults spewed out of my mouth. I even spat at Don to free myself from his grip.

"I was raped during the Korean War!" I seethed desperately. "Now, you have reason to leave me." No matter what I said, Don did not retaliate. Nothing would make him turn away from me.

After what felt like an eternity in hell, I sighed as my body went limp. I had never sworn at anyone before. Since our wedding Don and I had not even disagreed. Our friends often commented that our marriage was made in heaven. Don was a devoted Christian husband and father, who neither drank, nor looked at another woman. He loved our delightful children. I sewed most of their clothes and dressed them impeccably. We owned our own home. Whatever I wanted, Don bought for me, even a new car every two years. Often we hosted elaborate Asian dinners for our friends. We served as deacons, sang in the church choir and active in our community. Yet I felt like the shattered vase, waiting to be swept away. Sheepishly I looked up at Don. His eyes turned dark and his ruddy complexion pale.

"Don, I don't understand what came over me. You're the last one I would ever want to hurt. Could you forgive me?"

"There's nothing to forgive." Don hugged me tightly, "But if it'll make you feel better, you're forgiven. Susie, I love you more than you realize. I want to make you happy. Let's work it out, somehow. And please don't think about leaving."

I realized that I had to deal with my unresolved anger and I needed help. Later that afternoon, I told Don I wanted to see a marriage counselor. He readily agreed to go with me. I dialed the number. When Father Stratman answered the telephone, I hesitantly said,

"I, I do not attend your church, but I need help."

"You don't have to be a parishioner to use our services. Of course, you are welcome to come. Let's see - how about tomorrow at one o'clock? See you then."

The soothing tone in his voice calmed my distraught spirit. Yet by Monday I felt very edgy and found myself hollering at the children to put away their toys and books. I rushed the kids over to Grace's house, since she had offered to watch them. Although it was dismally gray day, I donned sunglasses and drove apprehensively into the parking lot of St. Peter's. With the motor still running, I stared at the scarlet door with its upside down cross. I knew the symbol. The Apostle Peter had supposedly asked to be crucified in this manner, since he felt unworthy to die on the cross in the same manner as His Lord Jesus.

Glancing around to make sure that no one saw me, I slipped through the red door, passed a stained glass window and hurried up the winding staircase. The vestry and living quarters on the second floor gave a settled look with tan plastered walls and dark carved wood trimmings. To my dismay, all the doors, even the ones to the bedrooms, were opened.

A slim man with brown hair stood up and greeted me with a firm handshake. As I sat on the edge of the seat across from his paper-cluttered desk, I had nothing to say. I felt miserably boxed in with this stranger. Unchecked tears trickled down my cheeks as a wave of helplessness swept over me. Quietly, Father Stratman handed me a box of

Kleenex. He lit a worn pipe and leaned back in the black swivel chair, waiting.

I glanced at the ceiling-high bookcase behind him and scanned the titles. Wondering where to start and what to say, I twisted my wedding ring. How could I explain my discontent to this total stranger? The rage I have toward my mother? My secret vow never to set foot on Korean soil until I became successful, and the remoteness of my goal now that I had two little ones to care for and a house to keep? Surely this holy man would reprimand me for my ingratitude toward the Lord and His blessings. Inadvertently, I pulled the ring off my finger and dropped it on the beige Persian rug.

"I am sorry," I apologized as I bent down to pick it up. "I just don't know what to say. My thoughts are scattered and I feel like a shattered vase. Is there any hope for someone like me?"

"With time and prayers, yes," he nodded his head reassuringly.

"Where do I begin? Lately I have been crying a lot and feeling like something is going to explode inside me if I don't scream. And I dread going places or seeing anyone. I yell at my children. And last Sunday, I said awful things to my husband and . . . ." I lowered my head in shame.

"You are not alone. Many women suffer with similar symptoms. Feel free to say anything that comes to your mind." His perceptive light brown eyes must have observed many others like me.

When our time came to a close, Father Stratman straightened his clerical collar and said, "For our next session, I would like to see both you and your husband. Meanwhile, please answer this questionnaire. This temperament analysis profile is a useful instrument in targeting a client's problem areas. It would help a great deal in the counseling process if you and your husband could complete and return them to me before our next session."

After shaking my hand, Father Stratman stood up and opened the door onto his deck. He scattered some stale bread to seagulls. The birds seemed to recognize the feeder and they fluttered around him to feast on the morsels. It intrigued me. I left Father Stratman's office with a glimmer of hope.

The following Monday, Don and I sat nervously while Father Stratman interpreted the temperament analysis profile. He glanced over his bifocals at us. Turning to Don, the priest said,

"Mr. Beidel, I am quite impressed by your profile. According to the analysis, you are very calm; pretty optimistic; sympathetic; quite objective; and extremely tolerant. Because of the degree of your tolerance, I feel very hopeful for both of you. I have never met anyone who scored so high in this area. Some qualities that you need to focus on are being more communicative, assertive, and active socially. He paused to observe Don's reaction. Then he turned to me.

"Hmm, Mrs. Beidel, your profile indicates that you are extremely nervous, terribly depressive, self-absorbed, quite hostile, withdrawn, pitifully submissive, and rather impulsive. Out of nine areas, only two are in the acceptable range: your sympathetic and expressive-responsive traits. Father Stratman removed his bifocals and leaned back in his chair.

"Normally I would refer clients with this profile to a psychotherapist. But considering both of your faith and Don's tolerance, I feel hopeful. That is, if you both follow my recommendations seriously." He lit his pipe and continued.

"For now, I would recommend that you start to do something together, like bowling or swimming. You need to communicate with each other. I suggest, Mrs. Beidel, that you don't repress your feelings. Do some gardening to relieve your tension and frustrations. Saints of old tended flower gardens."

Immediately we signed up for swimming at the college. During the day, I vigorously worked in our flower garden. Even on rainy days, I weeded. Don changed his work schedule to be home in the evenings. After we put the children to bed, we sat at the table trying to express our feelings.

Several joint sessions later, Father Stratman advised that I start coming in for an individual counseling. As time went on, I began to feel more comfortable confiding in him. Although he made it safe for me to express myself, he encouraged me to release my anger in constructive ways. Instead of repressing it, he advised me to verbalize it calmly. Gradually he helped me visualize the consequences of holding a grudge as being similar to that of ingesting poison.

One day I shared my feelings of inadequacy. "If only I could have a college degree," I said wistfully.

"Why not take a course this summer? According to the Chinese proverb, a thousand-mile journey starts with the first step. But when you get your Bachelor's Degree, there will be others around you with a Master's Degree. After a Master's Degree, you would feel inadequate around those with a Ph.D. What would you do, then?" His usually gentle brown eyes stared at me sternly. He handed me a copy of *Good News For Modern Men* and *The Power of Positive Thinking* by Dr. Norman Vincent Peale. "Read these from cover to cover. They will change your life."

Almost five months after the start of our marital counseling, Father Stratman suggested we repeat the questionnaire. To my surprise, I scored within excellent and acceptable range. To celebrate the occasion, I prepared an elaborate dinner. We invited Father & Mrs. Stratman, Grace & her husband, the Lattas, and the new president of SJC, Dr.

Stratton and his wife.

A few days after the dinner, Dr. Stratton called to say that he was impressed by my culinary skills and asked me to teach an Asian cooking course at the college. Confidently I accepted the challenge. I learned much about teaching cooking by doing research for the lesson plans, testing the recipes, and typing them on stencils. Ten students registered for the course. They worked hard and learned rapidly.

A few weeks before the last session approached, the students voted to prepare a banquet. They formed pairs and selected recipes, planned the menu, shopped and prepared each dish. We invited one guest per student to the banquet and I extended an invitation to Dr. and Mrs. Stratton, and, of course my husband. The students arranged an elegant table with candles and floral arrangements, calligraphy name cards and lace-bordered menus for each couple. They even hired high school students, dressed in white shirts and black pants, to serve the guests. My students displayed such impressive culinary skills that Dr. Stratton asked me to offer the course indefinitely.

As the summer approached, I asked Don how he would feel if I took a psychology course. He encouraged me and took time off from work to care for our children. He even converted the garage into a spacious kitchen and sewing room.

Having been away from classroom for six years, I found it extremely difficult to keep up with all the reading and writing. I thought about dropping out, but the Asian concept of losing face deterred me from quitting. Somehow I muddled through the class with a B.

That weekend Don, the children, and I drove up the side of Harbor Mountain. After our picnic lunch, I joked to Don, "I want to climb up to the mountain top."

"Let's do it." Don took me seriously and refused to let

me back out. By the time we stopped to rest, the path leading upward seemed like a cliff. Our car below looked like a little toy. It took us three hours to reach the top, but the view of Sitka and Mt. Edgecumbe rewarded us richly. I felt exuberant. Just in case no one would believe me, I carved my name on a log. When I told Father Stratman about the mountain, he interpreted,

"The climb is symbolic of your need to overcome obstacles." The priest leaned back and continued, "The shattered pieces of your life are coming back together through divine intervention. They are forming a different picture than before, like a unique stained glass window."

Empire State

Don and I continue to work on rebuilding our relationship. Although we had skipped last year's Alaska Day[40] celebration, we decided to attend the Baranof Ball this year. Don grew a bright auburn beard, as men were fined $2 in jest if they did not have a beard. Although Don did not have brown hair, his beard turned out to be auburn. I made a top hat for him to wear with his tuxedo and bought a pattern for a period ball gown and peacock feather hat for myself. On a whim, my hairdresser fitted me with a platinum blonde wig. I looked like a different woman. When Don saw me, he started and stared. After he got over the shock, he exclaimed, "You look gorgeous!"

At the ball, we danced all evening and giggled when our friends approached. As soon as they saw Don dancing with a blonde woman, they gave him dirty looks and waltzed away. When the lights came up and our friends recognized me, they howled at us for deceiving them with my wig. Don won a prize for his fabulous beard, and I won one for my gown and headpiece.

---

[40] celebrating the transfer of Alaska from Russia to the U.S. on October 18, 1867

Not long after the ball, I received a letter from my mother. In part she wrote,

"Your younger sisters have joined me in New York City. I am at peace, but Bok Sook seems to have difficulty in school. A small place like Sitka might be better for her. I am sending her there. Help her with English and adjustment in school."

Just when I thought I was making headway with my life again, I felt fresh anger and resentment toward Mother. I did not want to take on another responsibility. But, despite my turmoil, I could not disobey. Like a dutiful daughter, I agreed.

When Bok Sook arrived, I went through the motions of welcoming her. The little girl had grown beyond recognition. Don and I rearranged my sewing room into a bedroom for her and enrolled her at Sitka High School. The first few weeks flew by for her as she met new friends, but after the novelty wore off, she struggled to keep up with her school demands. Often at night she wept with homesickness for Mother.

The pressure of juggling my responsibilities started to take a toll. While my heart festered, a friend from the church came to visit me. I envied Martha. Her face glowed with peace and she always had appropriate Bible verses at the tip of her tongue.

"Susie, I have a prophetic message for you from a Spirit-filled woman," she said.

"What does that mean?" I wondered suspiciously.

"I can't explain it in words. You have to experience it," Martha replied solemnly. "Susie, you have to come and meet her in person." She flipped through her worn Bible. "But for now, this is what she asked me to relay to you.

I John 4:20-21 If a man say I love God, and hateth his

brother, he is a liar: for he that loveth not his brother
whom he hath seen, how can he love God who he hath
not seen? And this commandment have we from him,
that he who loveth God love his brother also.

I felt as if a thunderbolt struck me. How did she
know? No one beside Don, Father Stratman, Grace and the
Lattas knew my problems. My heart fluttered like a captured
sparrow. It petrified me to learn that a stranger had pierced
my thoughts without even knowing me.

"Please, Martha, take me to this woman. I must meet
her."

After Agnes, the mysterious woman, heard my tearful
confession of hatred for Mother, she placed her hot hands on
my head. Then she began to pray with strange sounding
words, the likes of which I had not heard before. As her
hands shook violently, my body felt as if an electric current
coursed through it. The same sensation whirled over my
head. At long last Agnes removed her hands from my head.
From then on, whenever her group met, I attended.

Meanwhile, I began to sincerely care for Bok Sook and
our relationship improved. However, after six months had
passed, she missed Mother so much that she returned to
New York City.

Several months later, Agnes called on us while Don
was home. She said she had a message from the Lord.

"You are to move to New York City to be reconciled
with your mother," she told us. "You are to start writing a
book. You are to attend Marble Collegiate Church. And you
are to minister to wounded veterans at the VA hospital in
New York City. You will go through a long, dark tunnel, but
Jesus stands at the other end."

Shortly after our visit from Agnes, Mi Sook
telephoned from New York. "Onni, I'm engaged to be

married to a company president. Come. Work for my fiancé. Besides, it would be nice for us to live close to each other." We hesitated, but she urged us to come for a visit.

Don and I discussed the invitation with the Lattas. They thought a visit to New York would be wise and offered to take care of the children while we were gone. LeeAnn and David packed their overnight bags with glee.

My family met us at Kennedy Airport. Mi Sook looked sophisticated in her dark mink jacket and matching hat. Mother and my two younger sisters seemed very happy and well adjusted in New York City. Mi Sook's fiancé invited us to a Chinese restaurant for a feast.

The following day, we toured the Empire State Building. My thoughts raced back to 1951 when I had wistfully read the tale of this building in Dixon's English Conversational Book for the first time. The shadow of an emotionally battered 15-year old girl flickered before me. I stood on the observatory tower and stretched out my hands to touch a passing cloud.

Mi Sook and her fiancé escorted us all around New York City, sightseeing, attending concerts and operas, and dining at the finest restaurants. A week slid by swiftly. As exciting as it was to be in a glittering city, I felt it would not be the best place to raise our children. When we returned, I called to thank Mi Sook and her fiancé, but told them that we would not be moving to New York.

I ignored my own inner discomfort, but after a year of grappling with our decision, Don came home to tell me that he had submitted his resignation to the personnel office.

In shock I asked him, "Why didn't you even discuss this with me beforehand?"

He shrugged his shoulders. "It's better to obey the Lord than to argue with Him. He will take care of us."

Within a week we found a potential buyer to purchase

our home. We telephoned Mi Sook and informed her of our plans to move to New York within the month. Frantically she attempted to dissuade us.

"My fiancée's company went bankrupt," she explained. "You'll be on your own if you move here."

Don and I stared at each other in confusion, but he felt strongly that we should obey the Lord's inner guidance. Friends came to help us pack and clean our home. We pulled LeeAnn and David out of their second and first grade classes. On October 30, 1970, we tearfully said good-bye to our friends and flew to New York.

When we arrived, we checked into a hotel feeling bewildered and desolate. Although I felt uneasy calling Mi Sook, I dialed the number anyway. I needed to reconcile with my mother. As soon as she heard my voice, she wanted to come and take us to her apartment.

That night when we were alone I asked my mother to forgive me for my resentment against her.

"Hyun Sook-ga, it's hard for me to tell you this, but In Sook and her husband promised to get us to Pusan on a ship before the second invasion if your father and I agreed to leave you behind with Grandmother and the maid to watch their house and their belongings." Mother sighed and continued. "After all the suffering we endured during the first invasion, we could not bear to face another torture. But there was no way we could have escaped to Pusan. I can't tell you how I grieved and regretted the decision we made to leave you behind."

It shocked me to learn that my own sister and her husband had used me as a bargaining chip. My stomach turned over to think that my parents had accepted the offer knowing the second invasion was inevitable. The events of the past could not be undone. We wept and reconciled.

The following day, we set out to look for an

apartment. We called a realtor from a public telephone. We told him that we wanted to rent a house near a good school and close to public transportation.

The man's voice sounded smooth, "I'll treat you like my own brother and sister! Stay where you are. I'll pick you up."

He took us to a high ranch in a wooded area. After a quick tour, he told us,

"You can't find a better place than this one. The best school area and the bus stops right in front of this house. You won't get a better deal than that. Now you need to pay one month's rent plus the same amount for the security deposit. Both of you sign this lease for one year. That's it. Good luck."

After the rental agent left the key to the house, we looked around again. We found no furniture, not even a refrigerator. The bus, we discovered, only stopped once in the morning and once in the evening.

We registered LeeAnn and David at the school, but it was not really within walking distance. The next morning Don and the children left early to begin the hike. Soon he returned.

"A woman in a station wagon with two children stopped and offered to take the kids to school," he explained.

"How could you let a stranger take them? What if . . . ."

"She looked like a trustworthy person."

Just then the doorbell rang. " My name is Inga. I live around the block from here. It's too far for the kids to walk to the school. That's why I offered to take them. But I thought you might be worried. I stopped by to reassure you."

Looking around the bare kitchen, she added, "I have a kitchen set that we don't use. You are welcome to borrow it."

By the time we bought a car, bedroom sets, a refrigerator, and living room furniture, we were getting low on funds. Don searched for a job as a safety inspector but there were none to be found. Eventually in desperation, he took the only job available at a supermarket. The salary barely covered our rent and basic needs.

In the beginning of December, we heard from our realtor that the buyers in Sitka had not qualified to purchase our home and were canceling the contract. Now we carried our mortgage payments as well as the rent. By the middle of December, we had no extra money to buy the children toys for Christmas. We folded paper birds and flowers, and strung popcorn to decorate our windows.

The night before Christmas Eve, as huge flakes of snow covered the ground, the doorbell rang. The assistant minister of a local church we were attending stood outside with his wife, their arms loaded with gift-wrapped boxes. A crate of groceries, including ham and turkey with all the trimmings, rested next to them. I felt so touched and humbled by their generosity that tears streamed down my cheeks.

Shortly after Christmas, Don and I put the children to bed and returned to the kitchen for some tea. I complained quietly, "Don, why can't we return to Sitka? Our home is available now. You can return to your old job."

"Susie, if we return to Alaska, I will not be going back to the church."

"Why not?" I demanded to know.

Don's face turned solemn. "Well, if we do return to Sitka, we will be telling our friends that God cannot take care of us."

A few days later I dreamed that we were back in Sitka, but Don was drinking bottle after bottle of beer. I was so devastated that I started to sob. Don shook me awake. "I'll stay, Don," I promised. "Whatever happens, we'll get through this together."

Nevertheless, no matter how we tried to cut corners,

there was not enough money to buy clothes for the children. A few days after Christmas, I saw an ad for a position in a hospital and applied for the job. After the interview, the personnel officer asked me to start work the following Monday. That night when I told Don about the job, he looked perturbed. "Susie, I appreciate your desire to help out, but we are not starving. It's important for one of us to stay at home with the children."

Disregarding his objections, I got myself and the children dressed on Monday morning. We were on the way out the door, and had just stepped into the foyer when David suddenly vomited. Don glanced at me sidelong. "Do you think the Lord is trying to tell you something?"

"All right. You both win. I get the message."

"Susie, I appreciate your effort. We may not have a mansion to live in or own an impressive car to drive around. But we will not lose sleep over our children if we nurture them in the Lord while they are young. They won't remember all the fancy clothes and toys we may give them, but they will remember the warmth of our love and the time we spend with them." He wrapped his arms around me protectively.

That January, Don reminded me that one of the messages Agnes conveyed had instructed us to attend Marble Collegiate Church. So the next Sunday, we bundled up the kids and headed into Manhattan. When we walked through the main entrance on 5th Avenue, a friendly usher in a gray suit greeted us and led us down the center aisle to a pew. Although it was the second service, the sanctuary and balcony were already filled with people from a wide range of ages and ethnicity. I felt vibrant energy coursing through the worship hall. Majestic pipe organ music resounded throughout the lofty sanctuary. The maroon walls were decorated with golden fleur-de-lis. At precisely 11:15 a.m.,

Dr. Norman Vincent Peale entered, escorted by his associate ministers, and took his seat at the center of the dais.

Although the church was in the financial center of the world, Dr. Peale preached with the enthusiasm of an old fashioned evangelist. As he challenged his parishoners to develop positive faith in Jesus Christ. He spoke with a depth and simplicity that even the children could understand. At one point he pulled out a letter from a parishioner and read it. His black-robed arms swung back and forth as he emphasized his point. I felt so energized by his message that I wanted to stand up and cheer, but I sat still expectantly as the order of service progressed. Except for the responsive readings and Lord's Prayer, no one spoke out during the service, and during the hymns, the congregation sang joyously from outstretched hymnbooks.

I noticed various programs in the bulletin, especially the Action Table for volunteers. At the close of the service, the associate ministers stood at each doorway to shake hands. Everyone seemed so friendly. As we we made our way to the Action Table, Joanie Collyer, a charming lady with a British accent welcomed us. When we expressed our wish to volunteer at the Veterans' Administration Hospital, she offered to recruit other volunteers to join us.

LeeAnn and David bounced up and wanted us to follow in the direction of a delicious aroma down in the basement cafeteria. As soon as they finished their chicken soup and sandwiches, they offered to help at the food counter.

On Monday I spoke with the Director of Volunteers at the VA Hospital in Manhattan. He assigned me to the rehabilitation ward to do bedside visitation. Every Sunday after services, our family prayed together before separating for our various tasks. Since the children were not allowed in the ward, they helped out in the Senior Coffee House with

Don and then explored the Museum of Natural History or Central Park and its zoo. This became our family's Sunday routine.

A few months after I started my volunteer work, the Chief of Occupational Therapy invited me to visit her floor during the week. After a tour of the department, she mentioned the need for a mechanical apparatus. To raise funds for the equipment, I decided to offer Asian cooking lessons. One of my friends contacted five other women. We enjoyed the weekly cooking sessions, but I still did not quite gather enough money to purchase the item. Joanie arranged for me to present the patient needs to the Young Adults group. Afterwards they took up an offering.

Two weeks after the equipment arrived, the Chief of OT invited one of the associate ministers, Joanie and a member of the Young Adults group to attend the unveiling of the Help Arm. One of the patients who could not use his arms demonstrated on the apparatus. He told us that after exercising on the Help Arm for a few weeks, he was able to lift a cup of coffee to his lips. The Young Adult member watched carefully, and returning to her group, encouraged them to provide Easter entertainment at the Veterans' Hospital. The veterans, especially those who seldom had visitors, enjoyed it as much as the young people.

Eventually Don did find a job at a lumber company in Great Kills. The owner offered us an apartment to rent, and we moved there during the summer of 1972. Once a week I attended a women's Bible study class at a nearby church. The following summer, the women asked me to give Oriental Cooking lessons and to participate in the mothers' Bible study while our children attended vacation Bible school.

One of the women in the cooking class invited our family to attend a weeknight Bible study class at Calvary Temple, a church in Oakwood that wasn't too far from us.

There we met the pastor, Daniel Mercaldo and his wife, Evangeline. They were a lovely young couple. At the end of the evening, LeeAnn and David rushed over to us and told us that they loved the class and had made many new friends. These children lived close enough that they could visit them during the week. We learned a great deal from the pastor and developed close friendship with many of the members.

After a few years, Pastor Mercaldo sat down with us.

"You and your children have been attending our weekday Bible study for two years. Your children need to have roots in one church. You need to choose one or the other."

Later that evening, Don and I discussed the pastor's comment. As much as we loved worshiping and volunteering at Marble Collegiate Church, we agreed that Pastor Mercaldo was right. We lived too far away for the children to maintain any friendships with classmates they only saw once a week.

We found it very difficult to terminate our association with the ministers, staff, and friends at Marble. However, they understood our situation and reminded us that we would always be a family of the church. The VA Hospital staff and patients thanked us for volunteering and asked us to visit whenever we could.

The following week, I met with the social worker, at the public Health Hospital on Staten Island that would supervise me. Peter Mazzella assigned me to the rehabilitation ward. He particularly wanted me to talk with men and women who needed or had received amputations.

One of the patients on my list had a severe case of gangrene in her left foot. I sat by her bed and listened as she raged. She knew the dangers of untreated gangrene, but did not want to sever her foot from her body. I showed her my prosthesis and explained that with exercise she would be able to walk again, but she screamed at me.

"Get out of my room!" she ordered. "I would rather die than have the doctors mutilate me!" Disheartened, I visited Peter and reported what had happened,

"If I were a counselor, I could have helped her. I wish I could return to college," I lamented.

"Susie, that patient has already rejected the advice of her surgeon. She won't listen to anyone. Don't be discouraged. You cannot help someone who refuses help," he consoled me. "But if you want to go to college, what's stopping you? Your children are in school. You can work your schedule around their time at home. I'll get you an application from the College of Staten Island if you want."

When I mentioned my desire to return to college to Don, he immediately offered to help. "Susie, that sounds great! I'll clean the house, cook, and watch the children after I get home from work." Even the children cheered me on.

With my application form in hand, I went to see one of the professors. As I faced him insecurities poured out of my mouth. "I am forty years old. I don't know if I'll fit in with young students."

"You are the kind of student we want, motivated by a clear goal," he answered. "You have taken a giant step today."

I passed the placement test that September and the college accepted the 36 credits I had earned at Sheldon Jackson College. I arranged my schedule so that I would be home before the children arrived. In the evenings when we sat down to do our homework together, I recalled the positive sermons I had heard from Dr. Peale, and applied them frequently.

In January, 1978, I completed my course requirements. My transcript read: Bachelor of Arts Degree, Major in Psychology, Grade Point Average: 3.89. Once my undergraduate coursework was complete, I enrolled immediately at St. John's University Graduate Center to major in Rehabilitation Counseling.

June's commencement approached, and I invited my family to celebrate with us. Donned in caps and gowns, graduating students filed into the quadrangle for the ceremony. From the dais, the first notes of "Pomp and Circumstance" summoned us forward. I marched steadily down the aisle. Don, LeeAnn, and David smiled and waved. Tears streamed down my mother's face.

I knew that I could not have come to this point without the help of my husband and the cooperation of our children. So many people came along side to give me the help I needed - professors, librarians, staff and fellow students. Most of all I thanked God for wisdom and strength. Peter Mazzella gave me the push. Dr. Peale, Joanie Collyer and the whole staff of Marble Collegiate Church prayed for me and taught me to overcome difficulties in life through a positive faith in Jesus Christ. Soon after I started graduate work, I wrote them a letter.

Dear Dr. and Mrs. Peale,

I simply cannot let another day slip by without sharing some wonderful news with you -- as the result of one of your sermons, which had a profound effect on my life.

You preached on "Why Positive Thinkers Get Positive Results. " You said, "They are not controlled by the three L's -- lack, loss, and limitation. They react positively to life, instead of fretting and mourning over what they don't have or what they've lost. You cannot expect right thoughts without pumping out wrong thoughts. Put your cherished dream in your mind, offer it to God, and keep thinking and working toward it. Praying, thinking, and working equal undefeatable results! "I can do ALL things through Christ Jesus who strengtheneth me! "

That sermon awakened me from my gloomy, stale, angry thoughts and regrets over the lack of opportunities in my life. Instead of shifting blame on others and circumstances, I followed your advice.

I enrolled in the College of Staten Island. Initially I was quite shaken, for my educational background was not solid - I had never stepped into a high school. I earned a GED High School Diploma and one year of college before the children came along. At any event, I put your sermon to work. Believe me, it was not an easy task at the age of 40 with a family and social obligations.

However, through the help of God, my family, and the faculty and staff of the college, I completed the term and was awarded the 'parchment,' B.A. in Psychology, summa cum laude. I can do ALL things through Christ Jesus which strengtheneth me!

I am deeply grateful to the Lord, to both of you, and the ministerial staff, for having instilled Positive Thinking into me.

Sincerely yours in Jesus,
"Susie" Hyun Sook Beidel

P.S. Currently I am working on my Master's degree in rehabilitation counseling at the St. John's University.[41]

---

[41] *The Positive Power of Jesus Christ* by Norman Vincent Peale, 1980, with permission by Tyndale House Publishers, Inc.

Epilogue
Unilateral Forgiveness

Mi Sook received an invitation to perform in Korea. While there, she located our older sister who was living in a pitiful situation. Mi Sook did not elaborate, but some months later, she called. "Susie, Onni called from Seoul this morning!" Mi Sook's excited voice vibrated over the telephone. "She will arrive at LaGuardia on March 13th."

My elder sister whom I had not seen in fifteen years would actually be here in New York City. Desperately I tried to say something, but only a croaking sound came out.

"Sister," Mi Sook paused for a second and then slowly told me, "Let's bury the past and start anew. Onni has suffered a lot. She's lost all her belongings. Her husband divorced her and wouldn't let her see their children. Please, she's our flesh and blood."

I said a quick prayer. I could sense Mi Sook's disappointment as the seconds ticked into minutes. She had expected me to feel as joyous as she -- joy towards a sister from whom I had emotionally alienated myself ever since Mother's comment. I had neither loved, nor hated, her. In fact, I very seldom thought of her at all.

As Mi Sook silently awaited my response, my thoughts raced back in time. In desperation, I breathed out another prayer. I knew deep in my heart that Onni needed all the love and care we could muster. Now the tables had been turned, and she was at the receiving end. Instead of the compassion I should have had for her, untimely nightmarish scenes flickered though the cracks of my suppressed memories -- desertion by my parents, interrogations by the Communists, escape from the enemies, incessant explosions, freezing weather, hunger, and even rape. I simply could not stand to recall all those scenes of terrifying war and beastly men.

I groaned. I wished my mother had not told me that it was Onni who urged her and Father to leave me behind, just to have someone to guard her property. I prayed again. God of love and mercy, somehow, someway help me to let go of the past and feel affection for this woman who needs us now.

Mi Sook spoke, "Onni has returned to the Lord. She is a changed person. Mother has been praying for her all these years."

"Yes, of course," my hoarse voice at last forced itself out. "You are right. She needs us. We must help her."

"Sister, I understand it's not easy for you, but all I ask of you is just to love her."

All I ask of you is just to love her. I repeated her statement inaudibly. What was I expected to be? A saint? I could have easily given material things to help her out, but I simply could not feign love for someone when I do not feel it within me. It would take time, a long time, to develop our relationship.

Oblivious to my thoughts, Mi Sook continued, "The plane will land at 6:30 AM. Let's all greet her there to show her our support."

I stared at the receiver long after Mi Sook hung up the

phone. In two days I would have to face Onni. In Sook, the firstborn of the Lee family, on whom my parents had poured their love and whom they had prized like a jade vase. She always wore beautiful clothes. She had never had to move a finger. Servants hovered over her throughout her life. She lived in a mansion, had a limousine at her disposal, basked in her husband's prestige and power, and bore handsome children.

Alone in the living room of my home, I did not like the memories which stirred within me behind the cobwebs. I could usually handle almost any situation, but this time I needed a tangible way in which to free myself from the ensnaring thoughts.

Listlessly I sat at my desk and scanned my books. I noticed *The Renewed Mind* by Rev. Larry Christenson, which my pastor's wife, Evangeline, had recommended. I glanced through the table of contents and proceeded to scan the chapter on Unilateral Forgiveness. My eyes followed the lines and then stopped abruptly. It read:

> Have you ever thought that you were beginning to make some real progress in your Christian life, when suddenly a situation comes up which evokes hostilities in you that you didn't even know you had?[42]

Hostility? No, I don't have hostility. It couldn't be hostility. It's just that I can't adjust my emotions like a faucet. My affection for another person can't be coerced. It has to well up from the depths of my heart. I don't have any strong feelings toward Onni. That's all. I muttered to myself and put the book down. But then, what is it that I am feeling now?

---

[42] The Renewed Mind by Rev. Larry Christenson, 1974, with permission by Bethany House Publishers

Why is the tension building up within me? My heart is throbbing. My voice is sharp. I'm reluctant to face her. What am I afraid of?

After supper that night, I poured out my mixed feelings to my husband. Don, as usual, listened silently and attentively. I had always felt a deep sense of relief after talking and praying with him. He intuitively understood me even though he had never suffered as I had.

"Don, I really don't know why, but I would do anything right now if I didn't have to face her. I simply can't see her. I wish I didn't have to go!"

"Susie," Don spoke as he looked deep into me with his loving, blue eyes, "I understand how you feel, but it's not healthy for you to remain this way. The only way to find out how you'll react to your sister is to face her. It may not be as hard as you imagine it to be. We must go over to Manhattan whether you feel like it or not."

His gentle face turned stern for a moment. I had not seen that expression since my near-fatal car accident in Alaska seven years ago when, disregarding my protests, he had insisted that I drive the next day. I had to drive then. Now, once again, I had to make the trip.

I almost resented Don. It's so heartless of him to be this way. Why doesn't he understand my situation?

On Saturday morning, I awoke with a start to find I had overslept. My sister would just be landing. I felt a tinge of shame. Mi Sook would surely think that I purposely did not show up. It would be a justified accusation if she did. I had never overslept on days when I had classes. Hastily I called the airport and paged Mi Sook.

Gloomily I pulled myself up. The gray sky seemed to dampen my already dismal spirit. Everything looked drab. I needed to find a way to fill the long remaining hours before I faced Onni that night. On the spur of the moment, I decided to have my hair restyled. I might feel better. It took longer than usual for my hairdresser to finish. When I looked at my watch, I realized that I did not have much time.

With mounting tension, I rushed home and ordered my children to get dressed. Just before locking the door, I grabbed *The Renewed Mind*, and got into the car. As Don drove I read slowly to let the message permeate my thoughts. Mysteriously the inspired words of the author began to make sense to me.

> It is not natural to forgive people who are in the wrong, to forgive them unilaterally. The natural human response is to demand justice. Oh, if they would come to us and repent, we would forgive them. But to forgive unilaterally, the way Jesus did, when they don't even think they need to be forgiven -- that rubs us the wrong way....
>
> If we do not unilaterally forgive those against whom we have anything at all, God's hands are tied. He can't forgive us. Don't think about whether he or she deserves to be forgiven. Just think of yourself as a projector of forgiveness, a reflector beaming out the power of forgiveness . . . .[43]

I read and reread the pages. Could it be that I needed to forgive her unilaterally? Was my reluctance to see her controlled by a subconscious bitterness against her?

"Lord of mercy," I prayed, "I do want to unilaterally forgive her. Now, You must do the part which I cannot do."

We stood at the door of my mother's apartment where Onni would stay temporarily. My fingers tightened as I hesitantly reached up to press the bell. At the sight of my sister, my heartbeat quickened. Our eyes met as we stood

---

[43] Ibid.

there for a long second. Then spontaneously our arms reached out and locked in a wordless embrace.

Just what was taking place, I could not quite describe, but slowly and unmistakably my heart began to swell with an unfathomable love for my sister, which had not been there behind the cobwebs of the ugly memories. The unconditional love of Jesus flooded my spirit. That Agape love overflowed into the heart of a desolate woman who needed that love.

Glossary

A-frame: wooden backpack in the shape of a letter A

Aboji: father

Ai-go: An expression of gladness, sorrow, surprise, such as Oh, dear! Dear me! Oh! Ah!

Ajoshi: uncle

Ajumoni: aunt

an-nyung hah shim ni-ka?: How are you?

bahn chahn: side dishes; usually seasoned vegetables

bi-bim-bahb: a bowl of cooked rice topped with savory beef strips, shredded vegetables, hot pepper paste and a fried egg

Bok Sook: the fifth daughter of the Lee family

bo ri cha: roasted barley tea

bur-go-gi: charcoal grilled, marinated beef tenderloin strips

chahp sahr tuk: glutenous rice cake

chi-mah: a long, full skirts worn by Korean women

chomahk: a straw-thatched farmhouse

chupan: an abacus, an Asian adding machine

cida: clear, carbonated soft drink

coolie: Chinese laborer

DAC: Department of Army Civilian

ga: a suffix added to show endearment; similar to adding "y", such as John to Johnny

Gak-sa: dying while on a journey

Han River: the river which flows between Seoul and Yong Dong Po

Hangul: Korean alphabet

Harmoni: grandmother

honey buckets: containers for carrying excrement on the farm

Hyung Bu: Brother-in-law

Hyun Sook: the second daughter of the Lee family

Inchon: a port city on the west coast below the 38th Parallel

In Sook: the oldest daughter of the Lee family

ji-ge: a large backpack used by farmers to carry huge loads

jin-rik-i-sha: a two-wheeled carriage, pulled by a man

jo-gori: a long-sleeved short jacket worn by Korean women

kahm-sah hahm ni dah: Thank you

Mr. Kang: the bookkeeper for the Lee family in China

kim chee: sliced, pickled Chinese cabbage spiced with hot pepper, green onion, garlic, salted shrimp, and salt
kim jang kim chee: kim chee for the winter

ko-jang-i: big nose, nickname for Americans
kong na mur: bean sprouts

mak-kur-le: cloudy and coarse residue of rice wine

Mansei: Hurrah!

Mi Kuk: America, the Beautiful Land

Mi Sook: the third daughter of the Lee family

mok-sah-nim: a pastor, a minister, a clergyman

MP: military police

Nam Dong Village: a village in Song Do

NCO: Non-Commissioned Officer

Omoni: mother
ondol: a floor usually warmed through the kitchen furnace

Onni: elder sister

Origami: the art of paper folding

PX: Post Exchange, a general store on a military post

Pusan: a port city in the south-eastern tip of Korean

Pyongtack: a town on the lower west, one of the thoroughfares to Pusan

Pyong Yang: capital of North Korea

Quonset hut: a pre-fab, half cylinder shaped, metal shelter

R.O.K.: Republic of Korea (South Korea)

Rev. Tae-Up Kim: The pastor of the Lee family in China

Seoul: The capital city of the Republic of Korea

shoji: Japanese rice-paper sliding door or window shade

Soon Ja: The oldest daughter's maid

sushi: a Japanese dish of seasoned cooked rice topped with raw fish or filled with vegetables rolled in pressed seaweed

Taegu: a city located in the lower southeast of Korea

Tah-shi mon-nahr te kah-ji: Till we meet again

tatami: A thick Japanese floor mat made of rice straw

Tientsin: a seaport city in northeast China

Tok kook: rice cake soup topped with meat, egg, vegetables

UNCAC: the United Nations Civil Assistance Command

Wha Sook: the fourth daughter of the Lee family

yo-bo: a familiar term used by couples -- similar to dear

Yo-bo se-yo: Hello

Yong Dong Po: a city across Seoul

yut: A Korean New Year's game

Wormido: an island near Inchon

About the Author

Susie Lee was born in Tientsin, China, and raised in Korea. In 1961, she immigrated to America, where she enrolled in college; her life-long dream. A year later, she married Don Beidel, a soldier she had met before leaving Korea. Soon, they had two children, Sophia and David.

In 1970, the Beidel family moved to Staten Island, NY where Susie returned to college and earned her B.A. in psychology as well as an M.S. in rehabilitation counseling.

Susie is an honorary member of the Corporal Allan F. Kivlehan Chapter, Koreans War Veterans Association of Staten Island. She was appointed by Borough President Guy V. Molinari as his representative to the Korean community, to the Anti-bias Taskforce, and has served as Vice President of the Korean-American Association of Staten Island.

A frequent speaker at churches, schools, veterans and civic organizations, Susie shares her message of encouragement and hope with young and old alike. She now resides in Franklin, Tennessee with her daughter and family.

If you need more information or would like Susie to address your organization, you can contact her at:

Susie Lee
P.O. Box 256
Franklin, TN 37064

-or via email at: susie@SusieLee.org

If you would like to help support the work of Susie Lee, please make your tax-deductible donation to:

The Center Ministry
PO Box 158933
Nashville, TN 37215
(615) 646-0991